☆

☆

SIMON & SCHUSTER

New York

London

Toronto

Sydney

Tokyo

Singapore

PILOTS

The Romance of the Air:

Pilots Speak About the

Triumphs and Tragedies,

Fears and Joys of Flying

WILLIAM NEELY

Simon & Schuster
Simon & Schuster Building
Rockefeller Center
1230 Avenue of the Americas
New York, New York 10020

Designed by Liney Li
Manufactured in the United States of America

1 3 5 7 9 10 8 6 4 2

Library of Congress Cataloging-in-Publication Data

Neely, William.
Pilots: the romance of the air: pilots speak about the triumphs
and tragedies, fears and joys of flying / William Neely.
p.   cm.
Includes index.
1. Aeronautics—Miscellanea. 2. Air pilots—Biography.
I. Title.
TL553.N44   1991
629.13—dc20   91–15092
                                                    CIP

ISBN 0-671-70257-2

☆

ACKNOWLEDGMENTS

*I wish to thank the following for their help in making this
book possible, and for their insight, sometimes the thrill of
flights and a seemingly endless supply of stories:*

*General James Doolittle, General Chuck Yeager,
Colonel Charles Brown, Colonel Jack Moore, The
Goodyear Tire & Rubber Company, Jon McBride, Tom
Kaufman, Jack Albrecht, Dusty McTavish, Micky Rupp,
Jack Yount, Dave Turner, Lowell Gentzlinger, Deke
Holgate, Dorothy Stenzel, Sam Moses, Johnny Rutherford,
Cale Yarborough, The Federal Aviation Administration,
The Smithsonian Institution, Ralph Albertazzie, Betty
Skelton, Bob Wilbur, Embry-Riddle Aeronautical
University, Edna Gardner White, General Robin Olds, Al
Haynes, United Air Lines, the United States Navy, the
United States Air Force, Eastern Airlines, and the Air
Lines Pilots Association. Not to mention the brothers
Montgolfier and the brothers Wright. And particularly my
agent, Peter Sawyer, who gave me encouragement, a
shoulder upon which to lean, and, more importantly, the
idea for* Pilots *in the first place. And to Whitney, bless
her, for her faith and love.*

☆

To the greatest

influence upon my life—my father.

I can't imagine what life would

have been without him.

CONTENTS

Introduction

We were sitting in the family room of the California ranch-style house, nestled in a canyon near Carmel, the place where nearly all who have been there would like to spend the rest of their lives. Across the room, sitting straight as a ramrod in a wing chair, was James Harold Doolittle, the man who perhaps epitomizes the pilot more than any other. There's nothing he hasn't done: He's the only man who even *survived* air races in the heinous Gee Bee plane; he was the first to bomb the Japanese mainland in World War II, leading a squadron of land-based B-25 Billy Mitchell bombers from the deck of the aircraft carrier *Hornet*—that's right, *bombers* from a carrier deck (it's the last time it was done, by the way); he's received commendations and medals from nearly every country in the free world—and a few that *aren't* so friendly anymore.

Jimmy Doolittle is ninety-four years old now and remarkable— not for his age, for *any* age. But once in a great while his thoughts wander, as he seemingly peruses the reaches of his intellect for stories to tell. He stares straight into the past. And what a past it is.

Aware that he has been silent for a while, he shakes his head gently to clear his thoughts and returns from his personal trip to the daring exploits of yesterday; he looks at me. There's a bit of a squint in the spirited blue eyes, as if the sun has risen out of the South Pacific and is partially obstructing his view of things. For a moment there, I could almost hear the battle commands. But this time it wasn't a command; it was an admission.

"I'm sorry," he said. Softly. "My mind wanders from time to time." There is a brief petulance in the sparkling eyes, as if he dreads thinking of the past, because of all the aggravation it creates; you know, just keeping things in place. Jimmy Doolittle is and always has been a perfectionist. Things must be in order.

"General," I said, "You don't have to apologize to *anybody* for *anything. Ever!* The twinkle returns to the blue eyes because even the unpretentious Doolittle seems reluctantly to admit that he *is* one of the true heroes of flight.

But Jimmy Doolittle wasn't the beginning, just a brilliant star along the way. We must go way beyond his time, past Orville and Wilbur Wright, the first to fly successfully, but surely not the first men who wanted to fly. I'd be willing to bet that had man been around in the Mesozoic era, he would have looked skyward as the huge pterosaur made erratic loops in the sky. And, not having the concept of flight quite together yet, some of them surely leapt off a cliff or two, flapping their arms wildly as they realized too late that this was an impossible task for landlocked creatures.

I doubt, in fact, that there's a single one of us—if we were perfectly candid—who hasn't on more than one occasion watched a bird catch the wind currents and soar, and didn't wonder what it would be like. It would be either man's first or second greatest pleasure, the order depending, of course, on how well one *flew*.

What was it like for Orville Wright to crawl into—or *onto*—that first airplane? There was absolutely nothing for either of the brothers to draw on in terms of experience, except the fact that all previous attempts at flight had ended up in disaster, to one degree or another. They didn't even have any benchmarks when they were building the plane, but they knew full well that they somehow had to learn how to control it before they tried to fly it. They worked out what they thought was every detail. They built in what they called "wing warping." Wing warping indeed. Where did they get their ideas? From the flight of a bird, of course. It's the only model they had.

Courage such as the Wright brothers had has never been properly defined. It is one thing for Chuck Yeager to get into the X-1 and blast through the sound barrier; even though it never had been done, there was design and aerodynamic principle and, well, *experience* to draw upon. But these brothers from Dayton, Ohio—these bicycle makers—didn't even know if their curious creation *could* fly, let alone *would*. On December 17, 1903, a twelve-second, forty-yard flight changed the lives of every person in the civilized world.

When the flight was over, Orville characterized their matter-of-fact attitude about one of the world's great accomplishments by saying simply, "Isn't it astonishing that all these secrets have been preserved for so many years just so we could discover them." A bit dogmatic, perhaps, but he did make a good point.

Now, of course, we realize that the ultimate adventure is flight. It is one of a handful of experiences in a lifetime that offers limitless freedom. Charles Augustus Lindbergh avowed: "Flying encompasses science, adventure, and freedom; who could ask for more?" Who indeed.

The sky is not man's element, so those who frolic through the clouds belong to an elite band of adventurers. And there probably isn't a vocation—or avocation, for that matter—that is as appealing to people as flying. Kids learn to fly before they can—or are *allowed* to—drive a car. Octogenarians pursue it. Men. Women. Children. It may be the suppressed desire of more people on earth than any other form of recreation.

As retired General Robin Olds said of combat pilots, from his home on the ski slopes of Steamboat Springs, Colorado, "There are pilots and there are pilots; with the good ones, it is inborn. You can't teach it. If you're a fighter pilot, you have to be willing to take risks."

As it turns out, there's more to the romance of flying than valor. It's a way of life to the millions who fly, either as a career or as a way to unwind, as they dart through the clouds and leave behind their earthly adversities. But for every military or stunt or commercial pilot, there are a thousand who fly for the sheer relaxation of it. For every aerial dogfight there are a hundred thousand mundane excursions from East St. Louis to Cicero or from Bakersfield to Fresno or between myriad point A's and point B's.

Not all flying is exhilarating, although you would never get the average pilot to admit he's bored during a cross-country flight, even if he has resorted to cloud imagery. And certainly you would never get a combat pilot to concede there's *ever* a tedious moment. Almost never do they admit to anything but "the thrill of flying." There is a common bond between aviators, even though it's described in various ways: Chuck Yeager says it's the "right stuff." In the movie *Iron Eagle*, it's "the touch."

There is a magic, however, that every pilot experiences, one they all feel in their fingertips and in their psyches. As Yeager says, "The really good pilots are filled to the brim with drive and determination; it doesn't make a damn if they're in a fighter plane or a Piper Cub."

Race driver and pilot Cale Yarborough said much the same thing: "If you're a pilot, you're born with it, and maybe the best way to teach someone to fly a 747 is to just put them *in* a 747 and forget the Piper Cub."

Without doubt, pilots *are* free spirits. "Flying," said Dusty McTavish, an old-time crop duster, "is a lot like playing a musical instrument; you're doing so many things and thinking of so many other things, all at the same time. It becomes a *spiritual* experience. Something wonderful happens in the pit of your stomach."

Pilots is a cross-sectional view of lofty virtuosos. A profile, if you please, of *the* pilot. We strip away the outer layers, much as one would peel an onion, to reveal the inner workings of the pilot. Before I started, I was sure there was a common thread that ran between them. They all have highly similar traits. Nearly all are individualists; highly confident, if not *over*-confident; aggressive, and fun-loving; they will talk at the drop of a flight chart about their skills. They are not an unassuming group. In fact, they are a little on the cocky side, if you want the truth. It was not surprising to find that they are a lot like race drivers.

I talked with combat pilots, bush pilots, crop dusters, the NOAA guys who fly into the eyes of hurricanes, and DEA pilots who make forays into the jungles of Colombia in search of drugs. I talked with carrier pilots and stunt pilots; with commercial pilots who have miraculously brought huge airliners into fields and onto runways in fiery half-crashes, and half-landings, and saved hundreds of lives with their skill and bravery. And I talked with kids who are just beginning, and with old-timers who are flying desks after, say, six decades of piloting the real things.

Along the way I got to fly in a P-51 Mustang and was euphoric as we blazed along at four hundred or so miles an hour at a mere fifty feet off the deck along the beaches of Florida. I made an aircraft-carrier landing and subsequent takeoff. I did aerobatics and came as close as one can get to the jumping-off-the-barn-roof-school of flying as I tried hang gliding over Utah. All in all, it has been a highly worthwhile experience.

I talked with pilots who have done daring things and, in some cases, who have done things that were *verboten*, if you must know. There are a lot of pilots in this book who will either remain nameless or who have been given new names—otherwise they wouldn't have opened up to me. Some have told of airline practices that would, if we were on a 747, for example, make us cock our heads and look disdainfully at what's happening up there on the flight deck. Others blast the military and the FAA and a lot of so-called accepted practices. A lot of myths are shattered.

General Olds perhaps said it as well as any of the hundred or so pilots I talked with: "There's a lot of Hollywood bullshit about flying. I mean, look at the movies about test pilots or fighter pilots who face imminent death. The controls are jammed or something really important has fallen off the plane, and these guys are talking like magpies; their lives are flashing past their eyes, and they're flailing around in the cockpit. It just doesn't happen. You don't have time to talk. You're too damn busy trying to get out of the problem you're in to talk or ricochet around the cockpit. Or think about what happened the night after your senior prom."

I have always considered my friend the late Art Scholl to be the best stunt pilot in the business. His demise while doing a gag for the movie *Top Gun* underscored General Olds's philosophy. As he dove his Pitts aerobatic biplane toward the Pacific Ocean to film footage that could be used later as dogfight sequences, he was his usual sanguine self. He had just executed an upright flat spin and had climbed to five thousand feet to begin an inverted flat spin. As he started the dive everything seemed fine. But at three thousand feet he said simply on the radio: "I've got a problem." At fifteen hundred feet he uttered his last words: "I *really* have a problem." There was no time for talk. By the time the observer plane got there, all they spotted was an oil slick and a few pieces of debris.

This book is about the Art Scholls and the Robin Oldses and Jimmy Doolittles and the hurricane spotters. It also is about people who do their own things, in a variety of aircraft and circumstances, from the pilot who flies drugs out of Colombia to the guy down the street who flies his Cessna 172 on weekends. It is about Edna Gardner White, who at eighty-eight is still flying and instructing from a tiny Texas airstrip. It is about them and all the other pilots in between.

Pilots is not just about life-threatening situations; it describes the mundane as well, with the terrible boredom of flying, the fatigue, drinking of coffee, and taking of uppers merely to stay awake. Most pilots have never *been* in a life-threatening situation. To them, flying is pure recreation; it is as much fun as they possibly can have, legally and morally.

Some of them say they never have been "afraid" of anything; others say they *are* afraid but still face up to the problems that arise. And they handle them as well as they do the ordinary happenings. Assuredly they have a high regard for danger, and even though they might approach it in different ways, they all confront it with an offhand respect that borders on the curious.

In short, pilots *are* slightly bigger than life.

Chapter One

We made the art of flying possible,
and all the people in it have us to thank.

— WILBUR WRIGHT

T hey were pioneer days of flight—those languid, now some-what hazy days shortly after the turn of the century—when wobbly planes with gossamer wings took to the air and made lopsided circles in the skies, and then bounced down a grass strip in what approximated a landing. Those who flew them decidedly *were* "those magnificent men in their flying machines." It was the beginning of a romance between man and machine, the likes of which may never pass this way again. That illusion of darting in and out of the clouds is as fervent today as it was then; in fact, it has been an unwavering dream for almost a century now for an abounding segment of the world's population, particularly its youth.

While this love affair with flight was taking shape, instructors waited impatiently in the wings to teach the third or fourth pilot *how* to fly.

It comes as no surprise that the profession of flight instruction began within a few years after the Kitty Hawk experience. Most experts agree that it was the Avro 504, a British biplane built by pioneer designer A. V. Roe, that made it possible for one person to teach another. Aviation became a science with the plane's arrival.

The 504 was a superior aircraft; mistakes could quickly be detected and rectified, which was important because there was little or no pilot instruction at the time. At that point it was pretty much "by guess and by gosh." Needless to say, there were plenty of mistakes among early pilots. Often they were fatal. Most previous planes went into a spin and crashed. Simple. But with the Avro there was a margin for error.

The first 504 was built in 1912; it was designed for training and private flying. Unlike any airplane that had preceded it, the 504 would respond to what was asked of it. It was to become the first *real* airplane.

And, although the 504 was designed as a plane for private use, somewhere along the way, it became one of the world's first bombers. In an attack on German Zeppelin sheds in 1914, several 504s, each carrying four bombs, wreaked havoc at Friedrichshafen.

If the Avro was the first trainer, who was the first instructor? That's hard to say for sure, but probably it was a British World War I major, R. R. Smith-Berry. At least he became the first *serious* instructor. And the first successful one. Naturally he used the Avro 504. He felt new flyers actually could learn from it. Smith-Berry evolved a completely new system of flying instruction, based on demonstration and explanation. No longer was it every man for himself.

His squadron became so proficient that the School of Special Flying sprung up around it, with pupils encouraged to fly the 504s "to the limit of their capabilities."

Smith-Berry trained thousands of combat pilots. He felt most pilots weren't flying properly so he took as his goal the job of "correcting the problems." The principles he developed remain the basis of our present training.

The Royal Air Force later went on to equip the 504s for instrument and blind-flyer training use. The manual the major developed was decades ahead of anything at the time.

R. R. Smith-Berry and the 504 turned flying into an art.

Let's face it, most kids want to fly before they are old enough to ride bikes. Assuredly, many of them outgrow it, but few ever totally escape the dream. And a lot actually get started with their quest for the freedom of the skies at a very young age. The decades haven't changed things. For example, listen to this:

"You want to know when I started flying? When I was twelve; I used my brother's birth certificate and I had a part-time job to support my habit. My parents didn't know about any of it. You've heard about obsessions; flying was mine.

"Nobody ever wanted anything as bad. I had decided I was going to get a pilot's license, by hook or by crook. If I didn't, my life wasn't going to be worth a plug nickel.

"It all started when I went to an air show at the Dubuque Airport with a couple of buddies on a summer Sunday afternoon. A long time ago. A guy was giving rides for five bucks; I had saved some money and . . . you know the rest. I was hooked. I made up my mind in English class one day—as I recall, I should have been thinking about John Milton or somebody like that—I was going to do it. The rest was easy. I was big for my age and, what the hell, there was no time like the present to start my life's career. Besides, I *had* to start flying before all the other guys were driving cars. My whole life depended on it."

An aging Dale Riffee sat in the hangar of the Lantana, Florida, airport, straddling a cane-bottom chair backwards, his arms locked around its high back, and he talked of the days a few decades ago when flying an airplane first became a passion.

"You know," he said, "things haven't changed all that much. The only difference between then and when I became an instructor is that in the beginning, I was living for flying and later I was flying for a living. But I still loved it just as much as I did when I was a kid." A droll smile crept across his face as he remembered the days of his youth.

"Actually, it wasn't all that tough then, if you really wanted it. Getting a license was simple. Paying for the plane was tough. But I worked like hell so I could afford it, and then I took my buddies up and anybody who wanted to go. I was a hero in my school. It was three years before somebody ratted on me, and then I had to wait until I was sixteen and then go back and take lessons again so I could get a license. Hell, I could have *given* lessons."

Dale Riffee's story is not unusual. There probably were more fraudulent I.D.s used in the pursuit of a pilot's license than the Federal Aviation Administration would ever care to admit. The drive is that powerful and the romance that great.

"Kids lying about their age is not as bad today as it was in the early days. Oh, there's still room for improvement; but then maybe we're making too much of it. If a kid can fly an airplane, why shouldn't he have a license? It doesn't make any difference how old he is, does it—give or take a couple of years?" asks an FAA executive, who remains nameless because his agency's regulations say that one must be sixteen years of age—a rule he obviously isn't convinced is even *now* all that enforceable. Or prudent.

"It's predictable that kids will go to any length to get a pilot's license," he admits. "I mean, damn, it's the thing to do for more kids than you would imagine. Flying is so damn glamorous that any kid would be nuts if he didn't want to."

Riffee agrees: "The thing is, flying an airplane probably was easier for me than driving a car would have been, just because I wanted to do it so bad. At least, there were fewer things to run into, and if you paid attention to takeoffs and landings, you could stay out of trouble; you could spend as much time flying around as you wanted. Or could afford."

The unyielding desire to fly an airplane is, for all practical purposes, unparalleled in a large percentage of children's minds. Before aerial battles and aerobatics made the airplane the most glamorous vehicle in history, a lot of children dreamed of being cowboys or policemen or whatever. But, as time went on, there wasn't a kid in the country—and a good-sized group of adults, for that matter—who didn't watch wistfully as a small plane made lazy passes through the sky. It became the quixotic dream of millions.

The time frame was perfect, because the history of heavier-than-air, manned flight is a twentieth-century phenomenon. For all practical purposes, it has been contained within our century. Granted, there were lighter-than-air flights a hundred years before two brothers from Ohio flew, and even a few scattered attempts at powered flight were recorded prior to the 1900s, but these were cases of a machine "bouncing" into the air for a second or two rather than actually flying. Needless to say, all of them ended up in one form or another of disaster.

Perhaps when the brothers Montgolfier went into an alfalfa field in France in 1783 and ascended in a balloon, they unwittingly opened the curtains for one of man's greatest adventures. Still it was 1890 before another Frenchman, Clément Ader, ricocheted a steam-powered, bat-winged creation into the air for a second or two before plummeting back to earth. For the next thirteen years, would-be aviators—mostly French—tried unsuccessfully to emulate the hawk.

Whatever contribution the Montgolfiers and Clément Ader had made to flight, the Wright brothers, Orville and Wilbur, unmistakably outdid them when, on that magnificent December day in 1903, they successfully launched the Flyer across forty yards of sand dunes in North Carolina. Even though the flight was shorter than the length of a football field, it was decidedly one of a handful of monumental feats of mankind.

Without the benefit of previous knowledge, Orville and Wilbur solved the two aerodynamic dilemmas that had to be resolved before flight was possible—the problem of lateral control and that of stalling and spinning. The recognition of these mysteries alone was an incredible feat, unsurpassed only by their invention and development of the first adequate set of aerodynamic flight controls—a forward elevator for longitudinal control, wing warping for lateral control, and an aft rudder for directional stability.

Add to this new lexicon the moments of pitch, roll, and yaw, and the Wright brothers' flight becomes an incomprehensible accomplishment, ranking right up there with man's discovery of fire or the wheel, or Gutenberg's innovation of movable type.

The matter of wing warping, which simply stated means the flexing of the wingtips—à la birds—enabled the brothers to bank their flying machine and thereby control it. Nobody else had been able to do that, and it is surely why most other attempts at soaring ended up as a pile of wire and canvas.

The saga of the Wright brothers might have been more exciting had they not become embroiled in so many legal battles. Their time in court enabled the French and the rest of the world to fly right past them in terms of development. But it was a matter of principle. After all, they were sure they had created the science of flight, and damned if they weren't going to hold onto what they felt was their right to *own* the skies. Obviously it didn't work, but that did little to dampen their spirits. Wilbur stated stoically, "We made the art of flying possible, and all the people in it have us to thank."

He may have been a little on the uncharitable side, but, no matter, it certainly set the stage for pilots that were to follow. Most, it turns out, have had the same dogged determination and positive attitude.

• • •

Perhaps pilots are born with the desire to fly. Who knows? If not, it doesn't take long for them to acquire it. Dorothy Stenzel, who has held the world's inverted snap roll record for more than half a century, substantiates the theory: "When I was a little girl, I didn't play with dolls. That was for *kids*; I built and played with model airplanes. And there never was a question in my mind; I was going to be an aviator, and the world would just have to get out of my way—this *chauvinistic* world."

Test pilot extraordinaire Art Scholl drew pictures of airplanes when presumably he should have been learning to make perfect cursive *A*'s or *R*'s. "I got in a lot of trouble from designing airplanes when I should have been listening to the teacher," he told me several years ago at his Riverside, California, airport. "But I figured, what the hell does it matter if I can add or not, I'm going to be a pilot anyway. School was just *there*; I was cooling my heels until I could get out and fly."

A lot of kids didn't even bother with a pilot's license; they simply *learned how to fly*. They either taught themselves by watching others or by getting an older person to enlighten them. Formal flight training came later for some; for others, they were content with their *informal* license.

One such case of on-the-job-training was stock-car racing great Cale Yarborough, who learned to pilot a plane in the most rudimentary way. He was sixteen years old:

"My buddy Bobby Weatherly was a pilot—that is, if you consider having an hour and a half of instruction as being a 'pilot.' I did. After all, Freddie Huggins, who was a local crop duster, had traded him a couple of lessons for the use of Bobby's motorcycle.

"Bobby was the closest thing to a pilot I knew, so I took a copy of *Trade-a-Plane*, the classified-ad newspaper, over to Bobby and said, 'Let's buy an airplane.'

" 'Are you out of your mind?' he asked. "Or did you find gold back there in the swamps?'

" 'No, neither one,' I said. 'But here's a J-4 Piper Cub up in Van Wert, Ohio, for six hundred dollars.' I held up the paper.

" 'It must be a winner,' he said. 'Lemme see that ad.'

"It was going to be easy.

"He read the ad and said, 'I'll meet you over at Vince McDaniel's store tonight. We'll talk about it.' "

Vince McDaniel's was a typical old country store, over in Cartersville. Cale hung out there, and the guys always talked football and racing and coon hunting—the same things people talked about in all country stores in South Carolina. That night, Bobby, Pete Workman, and Cale decided to drive up and take a look at that plane:

"We left early Saturday morning—Bobby and Pete and I, and Olin Spears, who we talked into going with us. Olin could really fly a plane, so we figured he could help us get it home, if we bought it."

The trip to Ohio was a nightmare. For openers, they wouldn't even let Cale drive because they said he would get them arrested for driving too fast. They finally made him get in the backseat because he complained about the way Bobby and Pete were driving. "Get back there and go to sleep," they told him.

"I was fine until we got to the West Virginia mountains," Cale said. "The winding roads made me sick; that alone would have been bad enough, but I wasn't content just to be sick. I had to get up on my knees and rock back and forth and moan. It was an awful trip. For everyone.

"The airplane wasn't much to look at, but Olin said it would fly, so I, for one, had made up my mind that we should buy it. It was worth it to me not to have to ride back in the car. Everybody agreed. We offered the guy five hundred and fifty dollars."

The owner of the plane split the difference, and they bought the Cub for $575.

Cale announced that he was flying back with Olin. There was no argument. From anyone. The other guys didn't want him in the car any more than he wanted to be in it.

"The weather was so bad going back that Olin had to fly around it. We landed in Asheville, North Carolina, to wait out the storm, long enough that Bobby and Pete beat us back. Naturally I got sick in the plane too. All in all, it wasn't one of my better trips.

"The weather stayed bad for a couple of days so all we could do was sit in the country store and *talk* about flying. About the second day, Bobby's brother, Wib, got to telling me how good a pilot he was, and the more he bragged, the more I bragged. It wasn't long before each of us were the best pilots since the Flying Tigers.

" 'Why don't we just go over and fly your plane?' Wib said.

" 'Fine with me,' I said. 'I'll meet you over there about four o'clock tomorrow evening.' "

They kept the plane in a cow pasture on Bobby's farm. Cale was there on time; Wib was half an hour late, but when he got there, he was full of enthusiasm. As they walked toward the plane, Cale said to Wib, "You go ahead and get in the left seat. I'll ride on the right." Of course, the pilot always rides on the left and the copilot on the right. Cale *knew* that much.

"Naw, Cale," he said, "it's your plane, you go ahead and ride over there."

Swell, Cale thought.

The plane had two sticks, so he wasn't concerned. If he did have to fly it and he got in trouble, Wib would be there to get him out of it. As one might imagine, Cale was long on confidence. Besides, he had watched everything Olin did, so he didn't think there was much to the business of flying an airplane.

"I got it started, which sort of surprised me," he said, "and then I taxied it out to the middle of the pasture. And then I took off, all by myself. I took that rascal off, just like I knew what I was doing.

" 'That was real good, Cale,' Wib said. 'Real good.'

"If Wib thought it was good, I figured I had a knack for flying. So I flew all around, experimenting with this and that and making the plane go up and down and turn and do everything. Of course, Wib didn't know I was experimenting; he thought I really meant to do all those things. At one point I even considered trying a loop, but I thought I might be pressing my luck. But I was having a ball.

"I kept asking Wib to try it, and he kept saying, 'That's okay, Cale, you're doing jes fine. Jes fine.' How 'bout that?"

Cale buzzed everything and everybody he could think of buzzing, and after an hour or so, he decided it was time to go back. It was going to be dark soon, and the fuel was starting to get a little on the low side. Getting back was no problem, he just followed the highway. Landing was to be a different story. That much he *knew*.

" 'Uh, Wib,' I said, stammering, 'I'd like you to land it, just to see how you like the plane. I mean, you haven't flown it all day.'

" 'Naw, Cale,' he said. 'It's your plane. *You* land it." Cale was a little more insistent this time: "Wib, I'd like *you* to land it."

It went back and forth a couple more times, and finally Wib said, "Cale, uh, there's something I think I have to tell you."

Cale was sure he didn't want to hear it.

"The truth of the matter is," Wib said, "I've never flown a plane before."

There was a long silence.

Finally Cale said, in a very small voice, "Neither have I."

"Oh, shit," Wib said.

"There was nothing to do but land it," Cale said. "There shouldn't be much difference in landing than in taking off, I figured; all I had to do was reverse everything I had done before.

"It turned out that landing was a hell of a lot harder than taking off. For one thing, I couldn't get the damn plane all the way down. I could get it close, but it was like there was some force pushing it back up. It was like turning two magnets the wrong way, so they repelled each other.

"I tried time and time again."

Meanwhile, Wib didn't have much to say. He just sat there white-knuckled, staring into space.

" 'Wib,' " I said. He didn't answer. '*Wib*?'

" 'What, Cale?' he finally said. He still had a blank look on his face.

"We're gonna be out of gas after the next try. So hold on tight. I'm gonna get this thing in one way or another.

" 'One way or another,' he said. 'One way or another.' He kept repeating it.

"I brought it in over the strip and got as low as I could. And I did the only thing I knew: I cut off the engine. I thought that was called a dead-stick landing, but I wasn't sure. I don't know, I read it somewhere.

"I pushed the stick clear forward, and the plane sort of dropped to the ground. It hit hard and bounced back in the air. Wib let out a series of moans, followed by 'Oh, shit.' The next time it hit, it didn't bounce quite as far. The third time, it stayed on the ground and was rolling down the pasture. We had put up some posts to mark the landing area; I hit one of them with my right landing gear, breaking the gear off. The plane skidded to a stop.

" 'See, that wasn't so tough, was it?' " I said. "Wib just looked at me. He didn't say a word. He got out of the plane, went straight to his car, and left."

The next day Cale started repairing the plane. He went down to Huggins Airport in Timmonsville and got the landing gear off an old plane his father had crashed a few years before. He found some aluminum tubing and some bolts, and he went back and sawed and cut and bolted until he had the new gear spliced on.

"The right landing gear was several inches shorter than the left one, and from then on, the plane always went down the runway with the right wingtip about a foot closer to the ground than the left one. 'Gunsmoke' was popular on television then—you remember, with Dennis Weaver, who walked with a limp—so I called the plane *Chester* after that.

"I took the plane back up, and I taught myself to fly. I spent the entire day at it, but I mastered it.

"Bobby and I flew a lot after that, but Pete Workman, who was part-owner, wouldn't fly it himself or even fly with us. All he wanted to do was taxi it up and down the pasture. By himself."

Even that was to come to an end. One day he was taxiing with the stick all the way back and the elevator up, when a gust of wind picked up the plane and flipped it over on its back. It only broke the prop, but it was the end to Pete's flying career. Bobby and Cale bought out his interest for two hundred dollars.

If there's one thing pilots have in common, it's tall tales. It doesn't matter if they've only flown once or if they've been at it for a lifetime, there are stories to tell. Flying seems to be Murphy's Law in action. The fact that most beginners go through the proper channels enroute to their license doesn't seem to matter; it's still steeped in the unexpected. Obviously fewer things go haywire if beginners get the proper instruction—ground school, basic flight instruction, soloing, and then possibly advanced training, and right on through instrument and multi-engine ratings, and the sky's the limit.

Some of the best pilot stories come from flight instructors. They are the ones on the hot seat. For example:

Boo Stevens now flies a corporate jet in the Poconos of Pennsylvania, but he spent several years training greenhorn aviators. "Instructing had all the earmarks of being a hair-raising experience; I guess that's why it appealed to me. I was getting bored with just flying around. But, damn, as it turned out, it's the next thing to lion-taming. I *knew* that; it's just that I didn't expect it to happen on the first flight.

"Picture this: Harry Mays was in his fifties and he had his own Mooney. That's right, he *owned* it. Obviously he had a buck or two. He had gone through ground school and had been up a lot of times. It had been a couple of months or so since he had flown and the guy who had instructed him, right up to the point of soloing, had moved on to somewhere or something else. So they gave him to me. 'Check ol' Harry out,' the guy who owned the fixed-base operation said, 'and see what he needs before he's ready to solo.'

"I watched him preflight the plane and asked him all sorts of questions; everything seemed fine, so I said to him, 'You ready to go get 'em?'

" 'I guess,' he said, with a decided lack of enthusiasm. His indifference made me a little skeptical, so I asked, 'Whatta'ya mean, *I guess?*'

" 'It's okay,' he told me, 'I just got a little stomach problem. It's all right; probably just gas.'

"I told you, I was new on the job, so I shrugged my shoulders and let it go. Now I know better. 'Okay, take 'er up,' I said. He taxied right out to the east-west runway and made a good takeoff. Hell, he did everything right, so, after I had checked him out on everything, I told him to make a couple of approaches and then land the airplane. He didn't say anything but he lined the airplane up for a final, and then I heard him sort of moan. It was then that I realized that there were beads of sweat on his forehead. Nerves, I guessed.

"We were getting pretty close to the runway, so I said, as matter-of-factly as possible, so I wouldn't excite him anymore, 'You're doin' fine. But, uh, you're coming in just a little too fast. Just cut 'er back a little.' There was no response. I started to sweat a little. And then Harry slumped forward, pushing the wheel to the firewall.

"I didn't know what the hell had happened; all I knew was that we were too damn low and too damn fast. At the rate we were going, we would slam into the hill. You see, they had leveled off a couple of small hills and filled in the valley between to make the runway in the first place, so it was a little like landing on a carrier—a *big* carrier, I'll admit, but it wasn't exactly like landing in Kansas. I *had* to get the nose up.

"Harry was big and fat so I pulled like mad, but I couldn't get the wheel in front of me to budge. I cut the power, but the glide path was still much too steep; besides that, I wasn't scrubbing off much speed, even though I had full flaps.

"The bank at the end of the runway was coming up fast. It looked like the Matterhorn. I gave one big pull on the wheel. The adrenaline must have been pumping through me like mad because when the wheel came back, it came with such force that it rocked Harry back in his seat.

"It was too late to try to land it, so I slammed the throttle open and pulled back on the wheel. The Mooney lifted up enough to clear the end of the runway. I gained a little altitude, banked hard to the left, and came back in. I didn't waste any time with a 'pretty' landing; I just wanted to get it on the ground.

"As I taxied back to the little terminal, I shook my pupil. 'Harry,' I said. 'Harry, talk to me, goddamnit.' He didn't move.

"There were three guys waiting for us when I came to a stop on the tarmac; they had seen the aborted landing and knew something was wrong. One of them opened the right-side door the minute the plane stopped. He didn't have to ask what the problem was. Harry was still out.

"He put the fingers on his right hand to Harry's neck. 'How 'bout calling the emergency squad or an ambulance or something?' I said. His eyes were real wide-open when he looked up at me. 'There's no hurry,' he said. 'He's dead.'"

Stevens learned later that the man had died of a massive heart attack. His boss suggested Boo take a couple of days off, but in the time-honored tradition of flying, he "got back on the horse" the very next day. In fact, he started with three new students, taking each to their license.

After many years of giving private lessons from the Washington County (Pennsylvania) Airport, flight-instructor-turned-corporate-pilot Lou Scariot says, "The most difficult thing by far for most student pilots is landing. You have to control your descent and your airspeed, and that's tough for a lot of people. A steep descent isn't going to make for a desirable landing, and airspeed that's too high means you'll end up scooting down the runway too far before you bleed off. Some learn it right off, but then there's the guy who can't walk and chew bubble gum at the same time, and he has a tough time with landing an airplane.

"I try to teach a traffic pattern first," Scariot remarks. "There are reference speeds in the pattern; you're slowing the airplane down, maybe ten knots on the downwind leg and then five more knots on the base leg and then five more on final. It's hard for most people to get a feel for it at first. I mean, maintaining the speeds in descent is tough for *beginners*.

"Almost everybody feels that power controls the speed of the airplane, but when you're coming in for a landing, it's backwards; the speed is controlled by the elevator and the power controls the descent. It's hard for people to figure that out. If you want to go faster you just put the nose down and the airplane will go faster. Pull it back and it will slow up.

"It's all pretty simple, if you pay attention to what you're told and what you're doing. Unfortunately many pilots don't pay attention; they overlook small details and rush through their preflight. These are the ones who usually become statistics.

"A lot of students think that by turning the wheel and adding more power the airplane will fly, because that's the way you drive a car," he says. "It takes them a long time to realize that there are a lot more controls and a lot more coordination required in flying a plane than in driving a car."

What about aerobatics? Why do some instructors teach it to beginners, and why does the military teach it to their pilots, even if they're going to fly a bomber? Surely they don't expect them to loop a B-52, so why do they teach young flyers such things as stalls and spins and loops and some of the other maneuvers that one usually associates with an air show or a stunt pilot? "A lot of instructors have stopped teaching aerobatics, and I don't exactly know why," says Scariot. "I think they should instruct pilots in the art of spins and some of the other things. They've lost a lot by not giving pilots unusual flight attitudes. They know how everything looks in flat turns and easy turns and little stalls, but to get unusual attitudes like being upside down or going straight down or flipping over on your back, hell, it gives them confidence and an understanding of what the airplane is doing. The military won't train anybody without including aerobatics, and they have the best all-around training in the world.

"Too many pilots don't receive proper training and they couldn't any more handle an extreme situation if it arose than they could land on an aircraft carrier," exclaims Scariot. "There's a helluva lot of difference between the flying characteristics of various makes and models of airplanes. And there's just as much difference between certain configurations and flight conditions. Far too often, a pilot learns just enough to be dangerous.

"Many pilots have trained only in good weather, flown with one other person in the airplane, and have never experienced the demands of a spin or engine failure. They haven't been given the proper instructions on what to do in any of these situations. Take the Cessna 182, for example: Put four people in instead of two, or throw in an unexpected thunderstorm, or toss in some mechanical problem, and see what happens. Accident reports are filled with such cases of pilots who either panicked or plainly didn't *know* what to do.

"Aerobatics should be a must for a pilot. Knowing how an airplane feels upside down or doing a loop is important to a well-rounded pilot. You can't imagine what it's like until you've done it; for one thing, all of the controls are backwards when the airplane is upside down. And it's important to have a feel for that in case you get into the unusual situation because of storms or whatever. There have been many accidents where people have been upside down and they simply didn't know which way to go, because they've never been there before.

"Knowing these things is important, I don't care what you're flying," Scariot emphasizes. "It makes you a smoother pilot, and that's a comforting factor, even if you're a passenger on a commercial airliner. You certainly don't want the pilot jerking the controls around on a DC-10."

Florida Civil Air Patrol colonel, flight instructor, and former World War II bomber pilot Jack Moore agrees with Scariot. "The outstanding pilot," says Moore, "has to have extremely quick responses; he has to come to a state where things are almost intuitive. Mechanical. He has to be a machine. And, you know, that part of it is not something you can teach. I've always said I can teach anyone to fly so long as he has a modicum of judgment.

"Here's an example: I have a friend whose judgment is so poor that he's going to kill himself someday. There's no doubt in my mind. Hell, he's had five accidents already. Listen to this: A couple of years ago he went up to Vero Beach to pick up an airplane that had been on the ground for six months. He gets in the airplane and takes off. He doesn't even get to five hundred feet and the engine quits. Why? Because it had water in the fuel. Any damn fool would have known that. I mean, it doesn't take much gray matter to figure that if an engine has been sitting around for six months, you've got condensation in there. It's simple. You drain it.

"The whole thing is frightening," relates Moore. "When I got out of the military and returned to the area of civilian pilots, I was absolutely amazed at the low level of proficiency. Civilian pilots, by and large, are lousy flyers. A few are good but most aren't. And the ones who own their own planes are the worst; they fly the hell out of it for the first few months and then it's like the guy who owns a boat: they use it once a month for a while and then every other month and then . . . you know the syndrome.

"The FAA has tried to make it better with the biannual [checkup], where you have to fly with a flight instructor, but the hole is that the F.I. can't fail you. Isn't that a hell of a note? Here's this guy who says, 'Jack, I need my check ride,' and I take you up and say, 'Bill, you're weak; your landings are poor and you need some work on a lot of things.' I can fail to pass you but I can't flunk you. I can't ground you.

"I can put in there that you've flown a Cessna 172 successfully, but I can't put in that you've flown it *unsuccessfully*. So you simply go to another flight instructor who may be more lenient and he passes you. Try that with a driver's test.

"A conscientious pilot will work with an instructor to get his proficiency back. You have to have that attitude or it will destroy you. And I'll tell you this, if you don't have that attitude, you'd better get out of the business."

Moore likens it to combat flying: "The best pilots are the ones who can go out day after day, not worrying what happened the day before or how many planes were lost, and fly exactly the same way as they always have. You have to have the outlook that it's not going to happen to you. I've seen friends go down in flames who were better pilots than I and, sure, I've grieved, but I never felt my time would come. It's the guy who panics that you lose."

There is little doubt in most flight instructor's minds that first-minute foul-ups account for too many accidents. Here's an example:

There were four people aboard the Cessna 182 as it taxied toward the runway at Houston's Hobby Airport. The pilot had filed a flight plan for New Orleans, had taken what he was sure were all of the precautions he could for a safe flight. The weather was clear and warm, the plane had been serviced regularly and properly. Everything was in order. At least he thought so.

The takeoff was routine and the airplane climbed out at a proper angle and speed. But when they reached about five hundred feet above ground level, the engine quit for no apparent reason. The reason became clear when the startled pilot checked his gauges. The right fuel tank, the one on which he was operating, was indicating empty.

During the preflight, the pilot had become engrossed with the talking and joking of his passengers, and he had not noticed the position of the fuel selector. The unexpected loss of power at a crucial time came as such a surprise that he did nothing but sit there. The nose of the plane dropped some and he felt it was in a normal glide, so he continued to sit there, trying to gather his wits and, at the same time, trying desperately to remember anything that might have been told him. It was useless because his training had not included simulated forced landings on takeoff.

Without initiating a glide at the proper speed, the plane continued to mush at an alarming rate of sink and crashed. Miraculously, the four people escaped with only minor injuries, but the 182 wasn't so fortunate. All that could be salvaged was the tail section and the instruments. And the fuel selector handle.

Had the pilot been taught to lower the nose sharply, flying speed would have been recovered immediately. Additional adjustments in the pitch attitude could then be made to maintain a normal gliding speed.

It was a classic case of inexperience and passiveness. But at least three flight instructors who do give students simulated forced landings on takeoff verified the fact that most of the students reacted in exactly the same way. It proved a point made by Lou Scariot: "Many times a pilot learns just enough to be dangerous."

Embry-Riddle Aeronautical University is one of the largest and oldest institutions of its type in the world. With campuses in Florida and Arizona, more than seven thousand students annually learn every aspect of aviation, from basic to advanced flight instruction to air-traffic control.

Most of the students wind up flying with major air carriers or the military. The campus at Daytona Beach, for example, is much like that of any other university, the major difference being that all of the students have flying as a common goal. Another dissimilarity lies in their enthusiasm and motivation. The wild parties for which many college campuses are noted are conspicuously absent. The students rarely drink and the presence of drugs is almost unheard of. Either of these are considered distractions; it would hamper their judgment and reaction times, and none of them want that. Instead one finds students totally wrapped up in their chosen vocation; they study flying, they work at flying, and in their off-hours, they rap about flying with one another.

Pat Mack, a sophomore, who plans a military career after his Embry-Riddle degree, remembers a photo of himself at five years of age, sitting on the wing of a World War II fighter plane.

"My father was an Air Force pilot and as far back as I can remember, all I ever wanted to do was fly. Oh, I went through a period of wanting to be a policeman or a fireman, but by the time I got in grade school, I knew exactly what I wanted to be—a pilot," he maintains.

"I read books about flying, saw movies, made model airplanes, and completely wrapped myself up in airplanes. When I became a Boy Scout, the first merit badge I got was aviation.

"But the feeling really hit me when I got here, and when I first got my hands on the controls of an airplane. I walked around the Piper Cadet with the instructor, paying close attention to his preflight inspection. When we took off, he told me to put my hands on the wheel and my feet on the pedals, just so I could feel a takeoff.

"I wasn't even working the controls, but I could *feel* what was going on. It sent chills throughout my entire body. I don't have to tell you what it was similar to.

"When we were airborne, the instructor said, 'It's your airplane.' Of course, I had been through ground school and I basically knew what to do, but the knowledge that I was flying the plane was almost more than I could handle. I'll never forget that feeling; it was one of strength and independence and serenity; I guess those are the right words. I didn't even know the instructor was there. I banked the plane right and left and dropped the nose and climbed. As far as I was concerned I was in heaven."

Mack's fervor is matched by nearly every student at the university. "One day we were sitting around with nothing to do," Mack said. "Classes were over, the sun was shining, and we were talking about flying—that's all we ever talk about—so someone suggested we rent a plane and have a landing contest.

"We had been working on soft field landings, where you don't want the wheel to sink in the mud. You know, you have to keep all the weight on the wings; you have to keep the airplane right above the runway in a ground effect, so we spent a couple of hours, taking turns at the controls, seeing which one could come closest to the runway.

"We do things like that all the time, but we know the bounds we have to stay within. We push it to the limit, but we ride the edge of the envelope," he said.

The basic philosophy at Embry-Riddle is to teach students all they possibly can within the time frame they have to work. With many it is longer than a normal college stay; they stick around for advanced training and supplementary ratings.

"Pilots need to know only seventy percent about flying," says General Kenneth L. Tallman, president of Embry-Riddle and former superintendent of the Air Force Academy. "That's the low grade. But what if the thirty percent they don't know becomes vital? That's why we try to keep them here as long as we can; we want to cram as much in as possible."

Erin Slaney, one of the fifty or so female students at Embry-Riddle, differs from most in one major way: She did not grow up dreaming of becoming a pilot. "My dad works for USAir, so I can't remember the first time I flew; I've *always* flown. But the bug never bit me until I came down here to visit my brother, who was about to finish his degree at Embry-Riddle. He took me up to show me what he had learned, and I had this unbelievable revelation: Here was something that I could really enjoy and get paid for it.

"I got to thinking, what job am I going to have that's going to make me want to go to work every day? And not be in the same place and sit behind a desk? That day I found it.

"My long-term goal is to work for a commercial airline, have an established route. And have a family.

"I've heard so many of the guys say, 'I've wanted to fly since I was real little,' but I've never heard any girls say that. I think most girls are so psyched that all they think about is getting to wear nice clothes and be a secretary and wear high heels. They're brought up that way," she says.

"But women pilots think the same as men pilots. And I really think some of them have an advantage over men, because they have a lighter touch. That's what it takes, you know. You don't need to be in there muscling things around anymore. When we're flying, we don't manhandle the plane, and with some of the sophisticated equipment we have today, that's a definite advantage."

Gerald Gibb, who is director of Embry-Riddle's Airway Science Simulation Laboratory, says, "We try to turn the students on not only to flying, but to math, science, weather, and a well-rounded curriculum. We figure that if they understand how the factors of weather interlace with each other, for example, they will make better and safer pilots.

"They can *predict* the weather by the time we're through with them," he comments. "They do homework assignments based around the weather; they use it in the lab and in the cockpit."

Laboratory time doesn't stop with weather. Embry-Riddle has a comprehensive simulator program, ranging from a single-engine Cessna to a three-seat cockpit 707. While students are flying the simulators, Gibb and his assistants take the information off it and put it in a computer, which in turn puts it on an air-control screen. So while they are training pilots, they also train air-traffic controllers. More importantly, these students are getting one hell of an experience because they are not really dealing with an instructor, they are flying in air space. They are actually sharing that air space with other simulators, inside a system.

"If I cause an engine failure, since they're all linked together the student has to deal with it as it relates not only to himself but to the tower and to the other planes around him," says Gibb. "As far as training pilots, this is more realistic than anything you could do; I can do things here you can't do in the real world, where it's not safe or practical. It just doesn't seem to be imaginary to any of them when I take away the guy's engine and watch all of them respond to it.

"I can simulate the weather. We have archive data upstairs that stores intense weather situations. We can put [Hurricane] Hugo on the screen. Or I can give an air-traffic control failure. I can shut down the guy's runway.

"We'll go for the worst and say that a plane has just crashed and the runway's closed. The controller still has all these planes out there; they're running low on fuel, the weather is turning sour. They all have to deal with it, and, I'll tell you, I've seen them actually sweat. We've turned off the lights and they become so involved that it's eerie. I've actually seen some guys get sick when it was all over. But I can tell you, they landed the plane and taxied back to where they were supposed to be before they got sick. There's nothing wrong with that. I know they would have done the same thing if it happened in real life, and it makes me feel like it's all been worthwhile."

The 707 cockpit simulator is exactly like one in a 1990 Avianca crash that happened when the plane ran out of fuel. They have all of the data stored in their computers and can program this entire incident into the simulator. "And, you know what?" Gibb asks. "Not one of my students has ever made the same errors that were made in the Avianca crash."

"When I started to fly, we didn't know anything about the tower at all—or they about us. The tower was just something you tried not to run into when you were landing. There was almost a natural animosity. Now they're our friends.

"In the days before computers, the only tool a controller had was communication. He knew the air-speed and wind direction, so he could pilot an airplane's course via radio beams. The pilot would call out that he had just passed over such and such NAVAID (navigational aid), so the controller basically could tell how much time it would take to get to point B. We still teach that to pilots and controllers as a backup emergency procedure, but only after we have moved them into a radar environment. Our pilots leave here with a pretty good basis in air-traffic control; they know what's going on and why; they know the theoretical foundation of the whole thing—weather, air control, and everything that's important to a good pilot," declares Gibb.

After a pilot solos, there seems to be little danger of problems caused by overconfidence. Most statistics and accident reports show that overconfidence comes at about three thousand hours, when the guy thinks he really knows it all.

"Most private pilots have a high confidence level but their caution level is much higher," says Lou Scariot. "They are very methodical about going over their checklist and studying weather and asking people and, in general, trying to find out as much as they can before they even think of taking off.

"Then the guy gets to about the three thousand–hour level and there's *nothing* they can't do, nothing's impossible; the airplane is indestructible, and they think, I can handle this. That's when a lot of the accidents happen.

"You wouldn't believe some of the basic things experienced pilots do, like failing to put the landing gear down. It usually happens when they go from a fixed-wheel plane to a more complex one. I know it's part of the checklist, but it comes at a time when you're very busy flying the airplane. You're in a traffic pattern and you're talking to someone in the tower, and here's this warning buzzer in your ear, or lights flashing. But you're so busy doing other things, you think, What the hell's this horn blowing in my ear? Shut it off. Get that circuit breaker."

Mickey Rupp, a former Indianapolis 500 driver, has owned and flown P-51 Mustangs for twenty-five years. In fact, he's flown almost every type of plane available; he's competed in the Reno air races; he's done it all. He's also landed a plane with the gear up:

"It was a beautiful Florida day and I had been up for an hour or so testing a new engine. I was doing loops and spins and everything it takes to get my heart pumping. It had been a perfect day. I guess I had my head up my ass, thinking about how the new engine felt, and all that.

"I came in to my grass strip and did a 360-degree breakaway, just like I do every day. I was on the brakes and talking to the guy on the ground. The Mustang settled down for what I expected to be another smooth landing. It's a helluva plane and so damn easy to fly, once you're used to it. And, believe me, I'm *used* to it. I casually looked at the grass below me. It was about four feet beneath me. Why the hell hadn't the wheels touched? I kept thinking I was awful low not to be touching the ground. And then I knew. I said the same thing I've said so many times in an Indy car when I was going to crash: 'Oh, shit!' I hadn't put the rollers down.

"I just held my breath and let it happen. There wasn't anything else I could do at that point. The minute you start to touch down it's too late; once the prop has slowed down that much you don't try to power your way out of it. That would only cause more problems. The plane finally came to a stop at the end of the strip. The prop was torn all to hell and there was some damage to the underside of the fuselage, but I was pretty lucky.

"I never forgot again, and I can promise you, I never will," he said, with a sheepish look on his face. "You know," he added, "there are two kinds of pilots: those who have forgotten to put down the gear and those who will."

Flying today is entirely different than it was in earlier days—as are most things, for that matter. Then, the sky was all but free from other aircraft; rules and regulations were just about nonexistent, and new pilots had far less to worry about in terms of licensing. There were fewer types of airplanes to worry oneself about learning to operate. "It was," as octogenarian pilot Dorothy Stenzel put it, "a delight to fly, back when I started. Everything looked so neat from up there and you felt so free. You were your own boss and you could get up there *alone*."

Dorothy Stenzel started to fly in 1927, one day after her seventeenth birthday. She recounts the experience: "I found this place where I could go for a ride, so I took my birthday money and up I went. The biplane was a Waco 9 with a Curtiss OX-5 engine, and I'll never forget the thrill as I sat there in that open cockpit and felt the rush of air sweep over the top of my head when the engine started.

"When we lifted off the ground, my heart swelled and I felt like

I was in heaven. It was the most wonderful feeling I had ever had, and I decided right then that I had found my calling. After we landed I asked Tex Rankin, who owned the Rankin School of Flying, if he could teach me to fly. 'Of course,' he said. I was going to fly, and I didn't even have to be a boy."

The only problem was that she had to have $250 up front to pay for the ground course, and that was a lot of money in those days. It didn't matter, Dorothy was going to fly. But she knew that a part-time job would take far too long for her to save the money; she wanted to fly right then. So she asked Mr. Rankin what she could do to raise the money.

"If you were a boy," he said, smugly, "you could do some parachute jumping in my air show." Then he added the final barb, one which caused Dorothy to rise to the occasion. "But you're *not* a boy," he said as he walked away.

"Wait a minute," she yelled. "What makes you think *I* can't jump out of an airplane?"

The look in her eyes was one of indignation and determination. He didn't even question her. He had met a girl who might damn well do it. Besides, as he told her later, a girl sky jumper might be just the crowd-pleaser he had been looking for.

So Dorothy Stenzel became the first girl in Oregon to parachute during an aerial show. She got a hundred dollars a jump.

"I would be lying if I didn't admit that I was scared on that first jump at the Portland Airport," she confesses. "My knees were shaking so bad that I had trouble climbing to the edge of the cockpit, but I was going to show them. Mr. Rankin had told me what to do, so I went over every part of the instructions as I sat there on the edge of the cockpit."

Rankin turned to her and pointed downward with the index finger of his left hand. It was time. She jumped. Emergency chutes weren't used in those days, so the thought of what would happen if the main chute didn't open never entered a parachutist's mind. It *had* to open.

"Much to my surprise, I *liked* the feeling of floating down through the air," Stenzel declares. "I was going down a lot faster than I had expected, but it was an exhilarating feeling. When I hit the ground I thought I had broken both my legs, but I wiggled them around as I sat there with all the chute cords wrapped around me and everything seemed to work so I pulled myself to my feet. I had landed about where I was supposed to, so I could hear the cheering of the crowd. I had a job. And I would have the money for what I wanted most," she said, with possibly the same gleam in her eyes that was there when she was a tenacious lass of seventeen.

Dorothy made several jumps, "just so I would be sure to have enough money to get me all the way through instruction."

Rankin gave a pep talk every day in ground school, but it wasn't one that excited Dorothy Stenzel. He constantly reminded the boys that they could do anything they wanted. "Why, you can even fly the mail in Alaska," he told them. And then he said, "Dorothy, you can work in the office."

"It got my hackles up again," she says, still with a tinge of indignation in her voice even after all these years. "There was no way I was going to work in an office, particularly after I had jumped out of an airplane to get the money to fly. I hated that man! And I guess that was the best thing that could have happened to me, because I tried harder than any of the boys, and I'll have to tell you, I was good—good enough that I wanted Mr. Rankin to go up with me and see for himself. 'Okay,' he said, 'we'll see.' That's all I wanted."

Mr. Rankin must have been impressed, because he said the five most placating words he could have chosen, as far as Dorothy Stenzel was concerned: "You fly like a boy."

Few, if any, of these journeys into the past give an idea about flying today. Now it is a more structured affair—this thing of flying. In fact, it is somewhat cut-and-dried. No longer is it possible for a kid to barter for flying time. But it *is* possible to learn at any pace and to any degree.

Now there is a formula most beginning pilots follow: Forty hours instruction, a solo flight, and approximately $2,500 in cost, including renting the airplane. Or one can enroll at a school such as the North American Institute of Aviation, and live right there for six months. And for $21,605, one can fly away with a pilot's commercial, multi-engine and certified flight instructor's license. All in one neat package. Of course, the package is one of intensity—seven days of flying each week and five days of ground school.

The days of "doing it on your own" are well in the past.

But the spirit of the aviator of old lingers in the hearts and minds of every pilot in every plane in the sky, no matter if he's a graduate of Ramp 66 Flying School or Embry-Riddle Aeronautical University. They have that same free-flying vitality that beat in the heart of Orville Wright. It's just that the equipment has changed. And the cost.

The one thing that has remained constant, it seems, is the essence of the pioneer aviator which lurks somewhere inside each new pilot.

Chapter Two

Air racing may not be better than your wedding night,
but it's better than the second night.

— MICKEY RUPP, AIR RACER

I t wasn't long in coming: The excitement of the airplane in-
stantaneously drew the intrepid soldier of fortune like a moth
to a candle. Scarcely had the canvas covering of the first
planes been put in place before there were stouthearted men
hurtling through the air at speeds near the airplane's breaking point.
Fueled by a rebellious desire for fame and fortune, driven by speed
as much as anything else, a new band of celestial heroes emerged—
the mercenary.

The excitement of the Mexican Revolution was more than some
American pilots could handle. It was the first opportunity to fly an
airplane *and* defend a cause, making some money along the way.
Although most pilots weren't even sure exactly what the cause was,
this was a chance to leap in on the side of revolutionists such as Pancho
Villa and Emiliano Zapata.

One of the first mercenaries was John Hector Worden, who was
to become the archetypal fight-for-pesos aviator. He was one of the
first pilots to successfully carry an air strike against guerrilla forces.

Worden had all of the theatrical attributes of a celebrity. He was
a Cherokee Indian who had gone to France to study aviation at the
celebrated Blériot School of Flying, and had returned to the States
to become an instructor and stunt pilot for the Moisant Air Shop,

first on Long Island and later in Texas. The latter move obviously put him within earshot of the South of the Border skirmish. And it made the adrenaline surge through his body.

If there is a thread that runs through pilots that makes them more daring than, say, florists, it also is the desire to carry their aggression into an aerial command post. So when Moisant sent Worden to Mexico to demonstrate the fledgling airplane to the Mexican officials, it was as easy as pie for the Federales to keep him there to fly scouting missions against the rebels. The year was 1911.

As illustrious World War II bomber pilot Charlie Brown was to put it many years later, "The real pilot—I mean, the guy who doesn't give a damn about his neck, but thinks about the thrill of combat—never worries about adversities. The only thing he worries about is finding a suitable parking space when the engine quits." Worden fit, or perhaps *cast*, the mold. The French Blériot that Worden flew was adequate for a pioneer aviator who was participating in actual warfare. But maintenance of the aircraft left a lot to be desired; there were no trained mechanics or ground crews, and gasoline was so poor that engine problems were the norm rather than the exception.

Worden's plane was a welcome target for ground troops and it was not uncommon for him to return to the craggy airstrip with the canvas well-ventilated from rifle fire. To combat the aggravating potshots, Worden suggested that he "throw" bombs at the guerrillas. "If it doesn't do anything else it will *scare* the hell out of them," he had said in broken but logical Spanish.

The whole idea of aerial bombing was highly attractive to the Mexicans, so up he went. Although he was kept busy flying a plane whose engine frequently cut out due to bad fuel, he managed to hurl bombs at what he considered strategic targets. It would be romantic and exciting to report that his accuracy crippled the enemy troops, but that wasn't the case. All he did was to thoroughly provoke the revolutionists; they hired Didier Masson, a French-born American air star, to fly for *them*. They even bought him a five thousand dollar–Glenn L. Martin pusher plane, which was expensive for the day.

Complete with homemade bombs, a drafted bombardier, and a makeshift bombsight, the plane, dubbed the *Sonora*, was the first real bomber ever used in the Western Hemisphere. With the plane, Masson wreaked havoc on the Federales, as the pair of airmen dropped their three fifty-pound bombs from the embryonic bomb rack on scores of crucial targets. Meanwhile Worden was literally "tossing" pipe bombs at whatever looked good to him, and, after a great deal of practice, he was doing it with a certain *savoir-faire*.

Worden and Masson never met in direct combat, but their efforts for their respective employers made the war a more exciting one, and certainly a more sophisticated one.

Driven by an uncontrollable desire for airborne stimulation, but tempered by a small amount of horse sense, Worden and Masson realized were they to continue the aerial insanity, it was only a matter of time until their numbers were up. Totally without the motivation of patriotism, the protagonists retired and looked for other exciting ways to make money and to prolong their working lives.

Following the Mexican conflict, many other American pilots followed insurrections throughout the world—Spain, Poland, wherever there was a lunatic need for men to fly for a cause, which in nearly every case was money. One of the most famous avaricious aviators was Bert Hall, who became a sort of offbeat hero to the world. Hall roared from the Balkan wars to the Russian Revolution to a stint with the fabled Lafayette Escadrille and to command of the Chinese air force. He became the self-proclaimed "gay-dog hero."

His braggadocio attitude, linked with a skill almost unsurpassed, not only made him front-page news but the topic for a 1919 motion picture, *A Romance of the Air*, at which he made personal appearances at "each and every performance."

For a brief period, the age of chivalry returned with the advent of World War I, as aerial jousts electrified the entire globe. A British journalist fittingly referred to the battles as "dogfights," because that's precisely what they resembled. Predictably, the name stuck.

A vehicle that had been born in the peaceful sands of a Carolina beach swiftly became the perfect weapon of war. The foundling airplane was first thought of as a reconnaissance vehicle. Both sides were sure that airplanes would bring a speedy victory, because the flying machine provided a perfect platform for studying the movement of enemy troops and determining the proper deployment of one's own soldiers.

But it was only a matter of time until someone bolted a gun onto one of the biplanes; and then one of the guys on the other side did the same thing, and the aerial street fight was born. Suddenly pilots could not only defend their comrades on the ground, they could shoot down their adversaries.

One of the exciting things about it lay in the fact that the pilots made their own rules. Since there had been no precedent and there was little training, the individual personality of the aerial ace manifested itself in his tactics. The airplane was an extension of each pilot's personality. Sitting there in the open cockpit at eighty miles per hour with the wind blowing in their faces, the new gladiators could feel the heat from the engine and could smell the oil and burned gasoline.

Riding the winds of war in a flimsy contraption made from wood and canvas, with feet planted firmly on the pedals and the wooden stick grasped tightly in their hands, these lofty heroes flew straight into the hearts of those back home, and the relative few who returned did so amidst the hoopla of their countrymen. Not since the knights of old had there been such conquerors.

The planes themselves were marvels, even by today's standards, but it was the men who flew them who deserved all of the plaudits. There were precious few gauges and the few that existed didn't work most of the time. An altimeter, for instance, might be off by several hundred feet, which, in itself, was risky because most of the dogfights took place at very low altitudes. The compass might point due north when the plane was actually traveling south, or it might spin uncontrollably in its case. The only fuel gauge the pilots had was a watch; they knew how long the fuel was supposed to last and, if they had time to check the watch, they could tell when they should head for home. The entire business of aerial combat was far from sophisticated.

But, despite the fundamental nature of the aircraft, champions were born. Captain Eddie Rickenbacker, who had thrilled an entire nation with his Indianapolis race car, pitted it long enough to become America's leading ace in World War I, shooting down twenty-six-German planes in less than six months. His smile was plastered on front pages of newspapers and magazines across the country, and the familiar Hat-in-the-Ring identification on the side of his Spad—the emblem of the 94th Aero Squadron—became the symbol of a victorious cause.

The Royal Air Force had as its ultimate hero Billy Bishop, the White Knight of Canada, who had seventy German planes to his credit. On the other side, Captain Oswald Boelcke was the first great ace. So respected and honorable was he that when he was killed, Allied planes flew over his funeral and dropped a wreath.

The skill and daring of the pilots was only matched by their *esprit de corps* and sense of fair play; hence the link to chivalry. Pilots from each side fought with a vengeance, but refused to take advantage of an opponent's misfortune. If a machine gun jammed or if for any reason the combatant was unable to fight back, each waved a gloved hand and then returned home and prepared to fight another day.

The planes themselves reflected the philosophy of the nation. British fighters were regulation, with no special markings. Their pilots were not allowed to carry chutes for fear that one might abandon government property unnecessarily when perhaps the plane might be saved. You can be sure the British pilots did everything within their power to get damaged and ailing planes back home. In typical British fashion, when the ruling was reversed and pilots were allowed to carry chutes, most declined. It would be cowardly, they felt, and they proclaimed they would rather go down with their ship.

Unlike their conservative enemy, the Germans began marking planes vividly and boldly so all would know who the pilot was. So radiant were the planes that they became known as the "Flying Circus." One Fokker D-1 triplane was painted vibrant red and was readily identifiable as the mount of the Red Baron. The supreme ace of the war was Baron Manfred von Richthofen.

Von Richthofen had eighty downed planes to his credit, and the entire German nation mourned when he was killed in his fierce red plane. The Red Baron went the way of most World War I aces. Few lived to tell their tales.

Following the war, planes got faster and metal skins replaced the canvas, but the likes of the dashing aviators in mortal combat, with the wind blowing in their faces and their scarves flowing in the breeze, would never pass this way again. But they did hand down their mantle to scores of other daring men. After the war the nation seemed to explode with crazy antics in the air—air races, barnstorming, and a dozen other offbeat aerial adventures.

• • •

Since its inception, flying had generally been a fair-weather pastime or profession. Even military pilots were grounded at times by weather conditions in World War I. But with the advent of the mail service, a handful of pilots were forced to follow the words of Herodotus chiseled over the entrance to New York City's main post office: "Neither snow nor rain nor heat nor gloom of night stays these couriers from the swift completion of their appointed rounds."

Flying the mail became the dream of the Post Office Department. Although irregular and unofficial mail flights had become a part of some airplane meets, there was no formal approach until someone went directly to the U.S. Army with the suggestion that "flying the mail would train pilots for the war effort." Reluctant to free pilots *or* planes, the army, in typical fashion, dragged its collective feet. But early in 1918 the War Department agreed to cooperate with the new Post Office Department.

The first flights were scheduled between New York to Washington on May 15, 1918, with planes taking off from each location and stopping in Philadelphia, where fresh pilots and planes would continue the delivery of the mail. The 204-mile trip was expected to take three hours and would open the channels for delivery of mail the "same day if posted by noon."

President Woodrow Wilson led a host of dignitaries at Washington's Polo Grounds as they watched the Post Office Department's employees transfer 140 pounds of mail from the truck to the Curtiss Jenny, which was to be flown by army pilot George Boyle.

The first of a tidal wave of postal glitches that would follow in ensuing years caused many red faces among the officials. When repeated attempts at starting the plane failed, the mechanics checked everything. Except, of course, the fuel. When all else had failed, they looked in the tank. *Voila!*

Using gasoline drained from other airplanes, Boyle finally took off. Had he flown north, he would have reached Philadelphia on schedule. But it was not to be; Boyle headed south instead, landing one hour later in Waldorf, Maryland. The mail had to be loaded back into a truck for delivery to Philadelphia, an ignominious ending for the first leg of the celebrated mail flight.

The U.S. Army/U.S. Post Office partnership lasted little longer than three months. The army, reluctant to risk its planes and pilots in time of war, relinquished its services. The Post Office Department ordered six new planes from the Standard Aircraft Corporation in New Jersey and began plans to fend for itself. On August 6, the airmail service without army assistance was inaugurated. The army returned to defending the nation, and the Post Office optimistically started doing what it thought was its forte—providing speedy mail delivery.

The service was extended westward from New York to Cleveland and Chicago. Two pilots, Ed Gardner and Max Miller, were selected to fly the route in test flights. It would be the first time pilots were to encounter the Allegheny Mountains, a range that appeared to be placid but proved to be a challenge. In fact, the mountain chain was later to be referred to as the "Hell Stretch."

From those first flights came airmail routes that stretched north-ward to Alaska and westward to California, as the Post Office pressed on in its rigid determination to provide rapid service anywhere it was needed.

In providing the service, the mail pilots did so at great peril and valor. Inexperienced ground crews and airport workers, and cantan-kerous aircraft, dogged them all the way. These pioneer aviators will always be remembered as the heroes they actually were. Their charge was an arduous one, as they often operated on courage and stead-fastness. But, after all, that's what was expected in this primitive time of flight.

One early pilot, upon a forced landing at North East, Maryland, cabled his backup: "Forced down. Four miles southeast of northeast. Send help." The standby pilot read the telegram and said, "That fellow had better sober up and come home."

The Roaring Twenties was just that so far as aviation was concerned. Every day seemed to bring new and more exciting challenges aloft. The reason for the wildness stemmed from the fact that there were so many out-of-work aviators and so many idle airplanes follow-ing the war. With nobody to shoot at and nobody to bomb, these men looked for employment and, as one might imagine, the profes-sion, by the very nature of the pilots, embraced excitement, if not downright risk. Pilots began barnstorming, a combination air show and carnival.

Barnstorming was so named because a few pioneers of the mania actually flew through barns open at either end. One pilot unceremoniously flew into the side of a barn, destroying both the structure and the aircraft, but he hobbled triumphantly away. To these bands of mostly ex–World War I aviators, barnstorming was just what the doctor ordered. It was a way for them to display their skills as they had done over German terrain, but this time there was someone to applaud them. And the roar of the crowd spurred them on to greater, although often absurd, heights of dauntless feats.

The first aerial stunt had come in 1913 in France as Adolphe Pégoud performed a stunt thought impossible. He had flown his Blériot monoplane up in an ascending arc until he was flying upside down, and he then dove to close the circle. He had, unwittingly, invented the loop. When American daredevil Lincoln Beachley heard the news, he hopped into his Curtiss biplane and, not to be outdone by some upstart Frenchman, completed three loops, and then in a final gesture of victory landed his plane inside San Francisco's immense Machinery Palace.

But barnstorming was mostly an American craze. Aviators took the loops and stunts of earlier pilots and added to them, inventing new and zanier tricks. Some of the tricks required more than one person aloft, so one of them flew the airplane while another walked on its wings, or hung precariously beneath it by his teeth at the end of a rope, or slithered from one plane's wing to another while in flight. From speeding cars and trains they grabbed ropes hanging from the plane, and, in short, did everything that popped into their fertile showbiz minds.

The plane that made all of this possible was the ubiquitous Curtiss JN-4D—the flying Jenny of combat days. The Jenny was the preeminent American fighting machine of the war and, at the end of the fighting, there literally were thousands of them to be had. The Jenny, with a somewhat temperamental OX-5 engine, was an enigma. Its trim good looks were deceiving, for beneath its canvas skin and braces lay many problems. Precarious landings had forced Curtiss to install semicircular skids at the tip of each bottom wing; the thin wings had to be braced with scores of turnbuckled wires; the engine, when not overheating, spewed oil and hot fumes which occasionally ignited the nitrate dope-covered canvas cloth over the wings, creating an unplanned, show-stopping finale. During the Great War, the Jenny was said to have been a battalion of parts flying in formation. Even though the Jenny had no brakes, it still had many redeeming features. It could be landed at thirty-five miles per hour, which meant there were unlimited places to put in when things went sour. It could be stuffed into a haystack if all else failed or dropped into a treetop, with little more than a bruised nose for the pilot and some broken airplane parts, which were readily and cheaply available. Used, recovered wings were about twenty-five dollars, and most other parts ranged from one to five dollars. The most expensive replacement item was a rebuilt OX-5 engine which went for a staggering seventy-five dollars.

To the rollicking aviators, it was all part of the act; this was, after all, show biz. The Jenny added yet another dimension to what might be referred to as the great American thrill show. Pilots were the cowboys of the sky. As they ran out of tricks, or as others emulated the latest discovery of what could be done with a plane, they created newer and more daring exploits.

The original barnstormers were little more than fast-moving gypsies. They moved around the country like the wind itself. A pilot would blow into town, make a deal with a local merchant or filling-station operator for gasoline and some food, and after allowing for a day to draw a crowd—who donated maybe ten cents apiece—the guy would put on his show. If he landed in a field near a barn, he might have a straw bed for the night; otherwise, he slept beneath the wing of his plane. For food, many a pilot depended on a midnight harvesting of a farmer's vegetables or, if he was lucky enough and a henhouse was nearby, he might have eggs for breakfast.

They hopscotched across the country, staying a day or so here and perhaps a week there, if the crowds for their stunts were good.

Emerson Lockhart had been an American aviator in "the war to end all wars." Although he wasn't an ace (five kills), because he entered the conflict in its waning stage, he did see aerial combat, and when it was over, he—like most of his compatriots—longed for more airborne ecstasy. So he began barnstorming in 1923. At age ninety-two, Lockhart vividly remembers his first barnstorming adventures:

"I had bought a Jenny for a hundred and seventy-five dollars from this guy who ran the Albany airport. This, by the way, was about all the money I had in the world. I had saved it while I was in the army, and I knew damn well I'd piss it away if I didn't do something useful with it. Now that I look back at it, I guess buying a beat-up airplane wasn't exactly *useful*, but it sure seemed like a good idea at the time.

"Once I had the airplane, I went all around Albany, trying to find someone who would sponsor me for a thrill show. I couldn't find a damn person, so I told a guy I knew who had a filling station that if he would give me enough gas to fill my plane, I would park it beside his station so it would draw a crowd. He agreed, so I left the plane there for three days while I got my things together and mapped out a route across the country. I was going to go to California, where I was sure there would be plenty of flying work for me."

The ramrod-straight, steely-eyed Lockhart speaks softly as he recalls that perilous journey, gesturing with his left hand and pointing from time to time with his cane. It becomes a magic wand, taking him back to simpler and surely more enchanting times: "I left Albany one morning with my things stuffed in the back cockpit and tied down with a couple of bungee cords, and I flew up to Schenectady. It was the same damn thing up there—nobody would give a dime, so I got a job delivering milk just so I could make some money and get on with my 'air show.' Hell, I had gone from being an aviator to driving a horse-drawn cart. But I saved enough to get along for a while and to get a sign painted."

Lockhart's sign said simply: AERO THRILL SHOW—A STUPENDOUS EXHIBITION OF FLYING SKILL. Emerson Lockhart had confidence, if nothing else. With the plane to draw onlookers and the sign to hook them, he planned to find a local kid to go through the crowd, passing a hat, and bringing in the money.

"The next Sunday, I got permission from a local farmer to use his pasture, which was right alongside the highway. I parked the plane there and, sure enough, I drew a big crowd after an hour or so; there were maybe a couple of hundred people, so I took off. I did some loops and buzzed the parked cars half a dozen times and then wrapped it all up with a dive from three thousand feet, pulling out about a hundred feet above the pasture; then I banked it sharp, did a roll, and brought it in. The crowd was clapping like mad, and the kid had taken in eight dollars and seventy-five cents. I gave him fifty cents. It was big business."

"From Schenectady I flew to Utica and then, town by town, began to work my way to California," he says. "But it wasn't always successful. In Pittsburgh, for instance, I waited and waited beside the road and only a handful of people showed up. I had a kid out there trying to flag down cars, but only a few stopped. I taxied the airplane up and down the pasture a few times and that drew maybe twenty or twenty-five cars, so I figured I might as well go on up there and see if that would help.

"When I got up I saw what the problem was; there was an automobile race just a couple of miles away and there were cars everywhere. But I went ahead and did my show and when I landed, there wasn't a single car waiting for me. The kid who was flagging traffic and collecting money was sitting on a fence post. When I taxied over and got out of the plane I asked, 'Did ya take in any money at all?' He looked at me, half pissed-off and half sorry, and said, 'Two quarters.' And then he added, 'I coulda gone to the car race for all the better this turned out.' I asked him how much it cost to get in the race. 'A quarter,' he replied, I gave him *both* quarters and said, 'Here, go ahead and go to the race. And get yourself something to eat and drink.' Then I got a delivery job at the South Hills Dairy for a couple of weeks.

"It took a lot just to keep that old plane flying. It seems like there was always something breaking on it. It was rickety as hell," he says, and a wide grin spreads across his weathered face. "But, you know, it had a lot of charm. It was like a woman; it was a lot of trouble, but it sure was a lot of fun. Yes sir, a *lot* of fun.

"You could land it almost anywhere because you could slow it down almost to a stop before you touched the ground. One day outside of Scranton the damned engine quit completely, and, damn, there were trees everywhere. I was in the foothills of the Poconos, so I glided around until I found a spot where the trees were a little further apart. I slowed 'er down to probably twenty-five miles an hour, and I guided it right between two trees, just far enough apart that it clipped the ends off all four wings. But the airplane just sat down on the ground after I got past the trees. Sure, it cost me about a hundred bucks to repair it, but it was better'n bustin' my butt, so I wasn't too upset. I got a job delivering milk and got it put back together in a few weeks." I assumed he still was talking of the airplane.

"In Akron, I had a helluva crowd. There was cars parked everywhere, so I got two kids to work the crowd. There must have been three hundred people there. I put on an extra special show because I really needed the money; I had only the gas that was in the plane and a dime in my pocket.

"I taxied the plane to a stop and most of the cars had started to pull away. They were waving and people were clapping like mad. I felt like Eddie Rickenbacker. I looked around for the boys to see how much money I had made. There wasn't a kid in sight. Do you believe those little bastards ran away with all my money? I have no idea how much they had taken in, but I'd be willing to bet it was close to twenty bucks.

"I had to get a job again, so I went to the Standard Dairy in Akron and asked if they had any openings for a driver. 'You got any experience?' the man asked. 'You got no idea how much experience I've got,' I told him. I worked there for a month and lived at the 'Y' before I decided to move on, and with some of the money I had saved, I bought a 'toothpick' propeller for the airplane. It was tapered real sharp at each end and was supposed to make the engine run faster."

There were all sorts of "improvements" advertised for the airplanes, but most of them merely caused more problems. The engines were highly unreliable at best, and by then most of them had far too many hours on them, so Lockhart spent as much time behind horses as he did behind propellers. Before long there weren't two Jennies alike; each had been modified to the hilt and most were held together with wire and string.

"I didn't know a damn thing about navigation," Lockhart exclaims. "Nobody did. There weren't many road maps so I followed highways and guessed a lot. For weather conditions, I used every trick I could think of. One pilot told me to use cows as weather vanes. 'You know,' he told me, 'cows always turn their tails to the wind, so it's simple.' One farmer also told me that if the cows were lying down, it was going to rain. I still believe that, mainly because I didn't believe it then, and I'll have to admit, I got wet a lot.

"There weren't many airports, so I seldom landed on a real run-way. I'd just try to spot a field close to a filling station so I wouldn't have to carry the gas too far. I had two five-gallon cans and, even though gas only cost twenty cents or so a gallon, ten gallons was usually all I could afford. And there were times when all I could buy was a couple of gallons or just what it took to get me to the next town, where I could draw enough of a crowd to fill 'er up."

It took Lockhart four months to get to California, and when he arrived he found, much to his frustration, there were so many barn-stormers there that a loner couldn't make the price of a cup of coffee, let alone a tankful of gasoline. Big-time air shows had incorporated the barnstormers into actual aerial acts, so in typical show business fashion Emerson Lockhart joined a flying team for the astronomical sum of twenty-five dollars a week.

"Somehow it all seemed worthwhile," he says, as he gazes fondly toward California. "At least it beat the hell out of looking at the south end of a northbound horse for the rest of my life."

Throughout the country, barnstormers had become romantic fig-ures; they were purposely crashing planes into dilapidated, burning buildings and doing a thrilling variety of stunts on wings, from mock tennis matches to all sorts of acrobatics to setting planes on fire or blowing them up after the pilot had parachuted to safety. And, while all of the crowd-thrilling episodes were unfolding above the throngs, pilots were fine-tuning the art of aerobatics. They were experiment-ing with new and more daring feats, and their skills were honed to a fine edge. There is little doubt that much of the skill and all of fro-lics of flying were born out of necessity. And it is just as true that the pilots were not grounded by weather nearly so often as by lack of cash.

Emerson Lockhart was far from the best-known barnstormer. Nearly every town had one. They were part of what ushered in the madness of the Roaring Twenties. Perhaps it is a tribute to their tenacity from the very beginning; maybe they refuse to take that final flight. Whatever the reason, there are a *lot* of old-time barnstormers left. Bryan Quinlan is another who was cut from the same cloth as Lockhart.

Quinlan was somewhat of a latecomer to the art—or madness— of barnstorming. He was a bright-eyed kid of fifteen when Emerson

Lockhart was alternately delivering milk and thrilling crowds. It was 1935 before Quinlan ever flew a plane, and even that first flight was an exciting one.

He worked around the airport in New Orleans, sweeping up and keeping palm fronds off the runway in any and all odd jobs that needed to be done. He also paid rapt attention to what was going on about him. He studied where the planes lifted off the runway and how they approached it when coming back. He asked questions. Incessantly. "I asked so many questions," he said casually in his Louisiana home, "that I was a pain in the ass. But damnit, I wanted to fly."

Occasionally, just to shut him up, one of the pilots "gave me a flight," he related. It shut him up, but it certainly didn't shut off his mind. He watched intently every move the pilot made. What they regarded as "placating" the kid was in actuality a learning process. He was taking *lessons*—although nobody knew it at the time.

The first flight came one afternoon when everybody was watching a Memorial Day parade in town. There was nobody around the airport but Quinlan. But there *was* an airplane, a Ryan; and it was sitting right there, beckoning to him.

"It must have taken me half an hour to muster up enough courage to get in the plane," says Quinlan, with a devilish look in his hazel eyes. "And it was another half hour before I really decided to fly it. I just sat there and studied everything, and I went through the motions.

"Finally I made up my mind to have a go at it. Hell, it wasn't all that tough. Oh, I admit the takeoff was far from perfect. It was lousy, if you want to know the truth, but I got it in the air, and after that, it was easy. I flew all over the place—except over downtown, because that's where everybody else from the airport was, and I sure as hell didn't want *them* to see me."

After Quinlan's "solo" flight, there was no holding him down. He saved every cent from that day on until he had enough money to buy a Curtiss Jenny that had been all but used up by a couple of barnstormers all over the Southwest.

The craze had died down somewhat by the time Quinlan was ready to "thrill the crowds," so he had to come up with a fresh approach. His idea was simple: He would crash at each performance. At least he would *appear* to crash.

To accomplish this, Quinlan would perform all sorts of stunts—which, like his pilot training, he had learned himself from trial and error and from watching and talking with other stunt pilots. At the end of his show, he would throw the plane around wildly and disappear over the horizon. On board he had a smoke bomb, which he threw over. The whole thing appeared to the crowd as if he had gone out of control and crashed on the other side of the hill. All they saw was a cloud of smoke and no airplane.

They sat in horror. Until, after a few minutes of flying around over there, he would reappear over the horizon. The crowd went nuts.

"Hell, I did this for three or four years," he says wistfully. "I billed myself as 'The Man Who Flies Back from Death.' "

Quinlan, who in his seventies is still flying, remembers the era of the barnstormers:

"I suppose barnstormers were so popular because in those Depression years there wasn't much else to do. We didn't make much money, none of us—not even the guys who were a helluva lot better known than me—but then nobody else did either.

"If I made ten bucks a show, I figured I was doing well, because, after all, people could sit down there and watch it for nothing if they didn't feel like giving a 'donation.' And the only ones who did give anything at all were the ones who felt sorry for us, up there working our asses off for a few bucks.

"And, you know, to this day, I never pass a guy on the street who's playing a guitar or dancing or even selling pencils that I don't give him something." A look of pensiveness spreads over his face. "There's a Depression for everybody, sometime in his life."

In addition to courage, barnstormers apparently had a lot of heart.

Since the advent of the *second* airplane, the quest for speed records has endured. It clearly was a chance for one person to be "the fastest man alive," a phrase that brought wistful looks to the faces of nearly every pilot who followed in the footsteps of the very first aviators—from the beginning to the 1930s.

Glenn Curtiss's pusher biplane was the fastest in 1909. In fact, at the world air races that year in Rheims, France, Curtiss was the only

American aviator. The underdog Curtiss beat the favorite, France's Louis Blériot, who only weeks before had astounded the world by flying across the English Channel. Curtiss beat him by six seconds and reached the astounding speed of forty-six miles per hour.

By the late twenties the speed record had soared and, while the tattered barnstormers risked life and limb in patched-up war planes, a new champion was born—the speed king. And America looked to yet another superstar—James Harold Doolittle.

Jimmy Doolittle was a military pilot foremost, but a speed merchant at heart, so he shocked nobody who knew him when he became the country's major advocate of aerial speed. But Doolittle wasn't the only speed-crazed pilot around. Even women took to the air-racing circuit. Mary Haizlipp, a pioneer air racer, summed it up for all of them: "Racing planes didn't necessarily require courage, but it did demand a certain amount of foolhardiness and a total disregard for one's skin." And then she added pensively, "I would be flying now but there's precious little demand for an elderly lady air racer."

Jacques Schneider, the son of a wealthy French armaments manufacturer, was only happy when traveling at high speeds. But it was his speed on water that relegated him to the role of "spectator" in air races, despite his strong desire to fly. Schneider had crashed in a hydroplane and was never again able to race anything, so he did the second best thing: He conceived the La Coupe d'Aviation Maritime Jacques Schneider, or as it was to become known, the Schneider Trophy, a race designed to foster the development of commercial seaplanes. The first Schneider race was held in Monaco in 1913 and was won by Frenchman Maurice Prévost.

The Schneider race quickly pitted nation against nation. At first the French excelled, and then the British and the Italians. But in the early 1920s Glenn Curtiss produced a series of outstanding aircraft, and stringent competiton between the U.S. Armed Services created some outstanding pilots, making America a strong contender to what had been a European-dominated sport.

The U.S. team in the 1923 Schneider race was made up of experienced pilots and sleek, powerful airplanes. So powerful were the planes and so experienced were the pilots that Lieutenant David Rittenhouse sped home the victor, averaging more than 177 miles per hour in a Curtiss CR-3.

Since the race was traditionally hosted by the victor, the 1924 race was held in Baltimore. The French and Italians, fearful of being outclassed, withdrew, but the British steadfastly stayed in the competition. Before the race their chief contender "porpoised" just after touching down; that is, it flipped over and sank. It left the U.S. Navy team in the enviable position of being able to glide leisurely around the course to victory. But the Europeans were flabbergasted when the Americans canceled the race. The Royal Aero Club immediately cabled "warmest appreciation of this sporting action."

In 1925 the Europeans finally made it to Baltimore, only to find that the most serious challenger was a Curtiss R3C-2, flown by a young army lieutenant by the name of Doolittle. And the confident Californian roared home the victor, with a speed of 235 miles per hour.

The Schneider Trophy Race came to an end in 1931. If anything, it proved that brute power alone was not the answer to aircraft speed or safety; there must be a parallel advance in the principles of drag reduction. Early planes had been squarish, but mainly because of Schneider competition, government funds helped designers develop more streamlined airplanes. It was hard even for the designers to imagine that airplanes encumbered with huge floats could attain speeds of over four hundred miles per hour—but by the time the Schneider was history they did. And the Royal Air Force credits their own competition as part of the foundation which enabled them to defeat the Luftwaffe in the Battle of Britain.

In 1936, the same year the Schneider Trophy was retired to Britain (they had won it the required three times in succession), Jimmy Doolittle turned to transcontinental air racing, winning the inaugural Bendix Trophy Race in the speedy Super Solution, which was powered by a Wasp, Jr., radial engine. Moments later he hopped back in the plane and established a new coast-to coast speed record. Jimmy Doolittle clearly was of heroic proportions.

Meanwhile, air race fans were turning their eyes and their attention to Cleveland, where the National Air Races were beginning to attract vast throngs annually. They became to Labor Day what fireworks were to the Fourth of July. In fact, so great was the spectacle in 1929 that pre-race ceremonies included daredevils of all of the U.S. service organizations, with Charles Lindbergh putting on daily demonstrations for the Navy team. The Canadian air force team petrified the crowd by screaming their metal-skinned fighters just a few feet over the heads of spectators. A cumbersome Ford Tri-motor was flown through a series of loops, rolls, and inverted maneuvers, causing one spectator to quip, "It's a lot like watching an elephant skipping rope."

Goodyear blimps and the Navy dirigible, U.S.S *Los Angeles*, floated overhead, while war heroes from both sides walked through the crowds. At night there were marvelous fireworks extravaganzas. All in all, it was as festive an aeronautical occasion as anyone had ever seen.

Of all of the experimental and specially built racers, clearly the most dramatic in Cleveland Air Race history—or *any* air races, for that matter—was the Gee Bee, an impish plane with a dramatically shortened fuselage and a mighty engine. The Gee Bee was tested by racer Jimmy Haizlip, who said of it in his only flight in the cantankerous ship, "My first shock came when I touched the rudder. The thing tried to bite its own tail. The next surprise I got was when I landed; she stalled at a hundred and ten miles an hour."

The Gee Bees, although notoriously hard to handle, were the real crowd-pleasers of air races, because they resembled an enraged bumblebee. But they were to "sting" all but one man who flew them. The lone pilot to survive Gee Bee flights was Jimmy Doolittle, who won the 1932 Thompson Trophy in one.

"A combination of things enabled me to fly the Gee Bee when most couldn't," mentions Doolittle. "When I first flew it I could tell it was going to be hard to handle, so I took it up to two thousand feet and made some sharp turns. I was high enough that a problem could be corrected if necessary. When I did a double snap I realized the plane was extremely critical. If I had been at the customary two hundred and fifty feet I would have crashed. With most airplanes you can trim them to the point where they will almost fly themselves; with the Gee Bee you had to fly it continuously. If you let go of it, it took over, apparently in an effort to destroy itself.

"What happened to the other guys [who flew the Gee Bee] is that they got a little careless. But I found that if I climbed a little during the straight leg and sort of dove through the turn, I not only had more control but I didn't lose much airspeed."

Doolittle not only won the 1932 National Air Races but he set a qualifying speed record of 296 miles per hour in the Gee Bee. "I gave her the gun and she flew like a bullet," he said.

Air races became a national mania and the names of the men and women who flew in them became as much a topic of conversation as Indianapolis race drivers or baseball players. As air racer Mickey Rupp put it, "[Air] racing might not be better than your wedding night, but it's better than the second night. The adrenaline is a naturally induced narcotic and once you get it moving around in there, it's a rush that's hard to describe. You get it the minute you get the plane moving."

Nobody ever said it better.

It goes without saying that "Dusty" McTavish was a crop duster, back in the days before and after World War II, when pilots flew by the seats of their pants, and luxuries such as radios and sophisticated instruments were a long way in the future. Between his periods of crop dusting he taught army pilots.

As did most pilots who started flying in the twenties and thirties, Dusty mostly taught himself. "I had a total of an hour and forty minutes of supervised flight time when I soloed, and that was with an instructor who I found out later didn't have any license at all. But that didn't matter; I flew every day and, you know, I finally got to where I thought I was pretty good. So when the war came along, I knew I had to be a part of it. I was living in Florida, so I went up to Carlson Field and got a job as an instructor.

"We used Stearmans most of the time; it was a great plane. I mean, you weren't afraid of tearing it up. We did a lot of aerobatic instruction back then and it was one of the best training planes ever made. Hell, we dove at terminal velocity and did all sort of things. Of course, the engine quit when you rolled it on its side but still it was a great plane; when you rolled it back over, the engine ran again.

"We got up at a high altitude and tried to do lazy eights. The engine would quit and when we were gliding down, we'd get it restarted. Nobody thought a thing about it. There was one thing about the Stearman: It would take about anything you wanted to give it. Damn, those planes were tough, but they didn't have enough power to do an outside loop.

Dusty got a job dusting crops in South Carolina. "There wasn't anything to it at first," McTavish insists, "but then electricity found its way there; every little farm and every shack got it. There were wires crisscrossing through cotton fields.

"You might fly over a farm one day and the lines weren't there, and the next day, just when you swooped down to start dusting, there they were. It was tougher than hell to keep up with it. You have no idea how many forced landings I made because I hit a lot of those damn wires.

"One time I was in a J-4 [Piper] Cub and the engine started coughing and was just about to quit. As was the custom, I looked for a road to land on; we did it all the time. I had started to watch for poles because you couldn't see the wires until it was too late. If you could spot the poles you could duck down under and miss the wires.

"There were big cross-country power lines along one side of the cotton field and a hedgerow along the other side. I was watching the poles and the hedgerow, and I'll be damned if I didn't hit another wire that ran across the field. It knocked one end of my prop off, and the plane was shaking like mad. In a matter of seconds the action of the unbalanced prop shook the compass right out of the instrument panel; gasoline was spraying all over me from a broken fuel line.

"I pulled up and shut off the engine," says McTavish, as unemotional as he probably was when it happened. "And then I started looking for a place to land. There was a straight stretch of dirt road over behind some buildings so I glided over there and landed. The second the plane stopped rolling I got out and ran like hell because I was afraid it was going to catch fire and blow up. After a couple of minutes I went back to the plane and saw that the engine mounts were broken. The whole engine would have fallen out in another thirty seconds."

It was pretty much a routine day for McTavish, and for the scores of other pilots who were dusting crops throughout the South and Midwest. It was a profession that appealed only to the stout-hearted—or to the foolhardy.

"One day up near Cheraw, South Carolina, I dropped down from the north end of a big cotton field only to find a new power line. In a case like that, when it was too late to miss one, I always gave her full power and cut right through it, but when I hit that damn thing it stretched out for about three miles. It just wouldn't break. When I had stretched it as far as it was going to go, with the airplane straining like the very devil, it shot me backwards like a giant slingshot. I ended up in the top of a peach tree. And do you know, I didn't get hurt a bit until I climbed out of the airplane and stepped on a broken limb and fell out of the damn tree."

What did crop dusters do in their spare time? They flew stunt planes, of course. It's no surprise that men who do strange and wondrous things in an airplane for a vocation also have a perilous avocation.

"I flew the first Pitts Special," states McTavish proudly. "It was up at an air show in Charlotte, and I had gotten there just before dark on the evening before the show. There was a low ceiling, but the guy insisted that I fly it right then, so up I went. I could only get up about a thousand feet, but I found out real quick that the plane had a very high stall speed. It only had an eleven-foot wingspan, so I wasn't too surprised at this characteristic."

McTavish's Scottish eyes sparkle as he relives those simpler days of flight. "The airplane would snap-roll like nothing you ever saw. I thought, this is wonderful, so I tried half a snap and an outside half snap. When I did the outside part of the snap the engine quit and the prop stopped. I had the big airport right below me, so I thought, I'll dive it and if it doesn't start, I'll do whatever it takes to land it. It didn't start, so I got up to about one-forty and I pulled it out and did a wing-over to land it. Then the prop turned once so I dumped the stick again. The only problem was, I had gone past the runway and I was about five feet off the ground. I had to put it down.

"He had built the airplane with Cub wheels and no shocks, so when I put it down in the grass I was going so fast that it literally bounced across a ditch, and I landed it perfectly crossways on the other runway, crow-hopping to a stop. None of the guys who were watching me had any idea that it was a forced landing. They were applauding me when I taxied back. They said it was the greatest stunt they had ever seen. I never told them any different."

Nobody ever said crop dusters were stupid.

"The thing is," McTavish says, as he touches on one of the threads that runs through pilots who do chancy things, "really good pilots don't panic in situations like this. I've read that some people have quicker reaction times than others and I really believe that. Most of the good pilots I know were good athletes as well."

McTavish reflects he has been "pretty apprehensive at times, but never experienced absolute fear." And this is a man who has made forced landings on back roads and golf courses and main streets of small towns. It also is the man who, at seventy, flies his own Czechoslovakian Zlin, a vintage low-wing stunt plane.

Although his flying consists mostly of taking friends for rides these days, one can detect the far-off look in his eyes, as if he were looking just over the horizon to another era, one when a man could fly by the seat of his pants—a time when there was no talk of exhausted ozone layers and pollution. When you *owned* the airways. The trace of a smile on his lips indicates that the time journey has been a good one, even if only in his own shadowy perspective.

The first black mercenary pilot surely was Hubert Fauntleroy Julian, who was hired by Ethiopian Emperor Haile Selassie to perform aerial stunts at the African leader's coronation in 1930.

So impressed was the emperor that he hired Julian to command his three-plane air force. The only plane Julian was not supposed to fly was the emperor's prized de Havilland Gypsy Moth, which Haile Selassie wanted held until *he* was ready for Julian to take him on a quiet personal flight. But the lure was too great for the stunt pilot. He purloined the plane and put on an impromptu air show for a crowd massed for one of the ceremonies surrounding the emperor's inauguration.

It wouldn't have been so bad had Julian not crashed the plane, thereby receiving not only his flying papers but his "walking" papers as well. Seemingly unruffled by the dismissal from command of the Ethiopian Air Force, Julian announced upon his arrival at New York City, "When I left, the emperor and I were the best of pals."

By their very nature, mercenaries are long on utopian dreams and short on reality.

By the mid-1930s the war plane had become the "pursuit" plane, and it bore little resemblance to its flimsy predecessor. For one thing, its skin was metal, its engine was much more powerful, and its design was far sleeker than the boxlike creations that predated it. It was faster, more maneuverable, and more deadly than the planes of World War I.

One of the first successful pursuit planes, designed in 1934, was the Curtiss-Wright Hawk 75, labeled the P-36 by the Army Air Corps. Its speed of three hundred miles per hour made it attractive to the army, but with clouds of war once more looming on the horizon, they looked for improvements to the plane, which was sleek save for the boxlike frontal area surrounding the air-cooled Pratt & Whitney engine.

Curtiss adapted a liquid-cooled, much narrower Allison engine to the plane, giving it a sleeker design. It was designated the Hawk 81. The Army called it the P-40. The world would never forget it. With a top speed of 350 miles per hour and hefty armament, the Warhawk would be a formidable protector of the sky over our nation.

But it was another nation that made the P-40 "king of the air" for a while. The outbreak of the Sino-Japanese War in the summer of 1937 sent China scurrying for a man to lead its rickety air force. They chose a leathery-faced, hard-nosed captain of the Army Air Corps who had been ostracized because of his outspoken belief that bombers weren't worth a damn when a really good pursuit plane was around. So it was with mutual satisfaction that Claire Lee Chennault resigned his commission in 1937 and took the nebulous job as aviation advisor for the Chinese Nationalist Air Force, under the leadership of Generalissimo Chiang Kai-shek.

Through some high-powered diplomatic maneuvers, China obtained one hundred of the new P-40s, and Claire Chennault had an air force. Anticipating a Japanese victory, an alarmed President Franklin Delano Roosevelt issued an executive order, allowing American service pilots to go to China to fight Japan for one year before they had to return to their former positions.

By 1940, Chinese recruiters, armed with attractive monetary contracts, lured scores of fighter pilots to fly for the newly formed American Volunteer Group. The AVG, because of their soldier-of-fortune bearing and their fierce P-40s, became so feared by Japanese pilots that they became known as the "Flying Tigers."

With razor-sharp shark teeth and sinister eyes painted on the nose of their P-40s to "frighten the Japanese," the Flying Tigers quickly became *bon vivant* fearless heroes. Chennault advised his men to use the superior diving speed—up to five hundred miles per hour—to "make a pass, shoot, and break away." So successful were the Warhawks that they shot down an average of twenty-three Japanese planes for each P-40 lost in combat.

The superior diving speed of the P-40, combined with the heavy armor surrounding the cockpit and the self-sealing fuel tank, enabled the AVG pilots to dumbfound their adversaries completely. The P-40s could dive on the Japanese planes, cut them away from their group, and destroy them, a tactic seldom used before in aerial warfare.

The Japanese planes, although not as fast, were highly maneuverable. Their lack of armor made them light and as quick as a bumblebee, so the plan of the AVG from that point was to draw away the fighters from their bomber groups and cut them down one by one. With this ploy, the Tigers could then move in and methodically devastate the larger, more vulnerable bombers.

One of the most famous of the Tigers was Gregory Boyington. But Boyington was to run afoul of both Chennault and Generalissimo Chiang more than once. His desire to destroy the enemy, combined with a fanatical urge to clown, kept him in constant trouble. The colorful Tiger ace finally resigned from the AVG and returned to the Marine Corps, where he led an assembly of pilots nicknamed the "Black Sheep" Squadron. The pilots under the command of Boyington were younger, so they dubbed their leader "Pappy." As a group, they were close to being a reincarnation of the Flying Tigers.

Pappy Boyington's intense desire to "show" his former critics led him to such courageous heights that he was awarded the Congressional Medal of Honor.

Combat-weary and with planes that were nearing their demise, the Tigers followed Boyington one by one and returned to the American Army, but they left behind a legacy that generations of Chinese will never forget. They would forever remember the shark tooth–painted airplanes and their pilots who wore leather flight jackets bearing cloth patches with Chinese symbols on the back, identifying them as allies to a nation of people, most of whom had never before seen an American. They left memories of high jinks in Rangoon and in the skies over Burma.

In July of 1942, with America needing every pilot it could muster, the American Volunteer Group officially disbanded. There surely will never be as illustrious a band of mercenaries again. This spirited group of daring men was one of the most amazing and hardened fighting forces of World War II. And one of the most effective, as they destroyed 297 enemy planes and unofficially downed 300 more. The extraordinary testimonial to their effectiveness lay in the fact that they lost but four men in the year's combat.

Chapter Three

Anybody who tells you he was never afraid going into combat is either a damn liar or a damn fool.

— Colonel Jack Moore, USAF Retired

I t wasn't so much the airplane as the aircraft carrier that gave the Japanese the ability to deal the swift blow to American forces at Pearl Harbor on December 7, 1941. The stage, however, was set many years before the surprise attack—1910, to be exact; on that date a bold flyer named Eugene Ely lunged an airplane off a makeshift wooden deck of the USS *Birmingham*, skimmed the water, and surprisingly, got the plane airborne. Several weeks later Ely took off from San Francisco and landed on yet another contrived carrier, the USS *Pennsylvania*, as it lay at anchor in the bay. With uncanny accuracy, he had opened up a new use for the airplane in war.

Ely, with predictable optimism, didn't think it was all that difficult, but everybody else on board the ship felt it was possibly the most important military flight in history.

Whatever, the stage was set for the use of the aircraft carrier. Oddly, it wasn't until 1938 that a whole lot more happened with what was to become one of the great weapons of war. Admiral Ernest J. King conducted extensive exercises with carrier landings, takeoffs, and the disposition of airplanes when a bevy of them returned, all at once, to the mother ship.

King practiced sneak attacks from the decks of the carriers *Saratoga* and *Lexington* in an attempt to convince the War Department of the importance of both sea and land missions. Ironically, one of the first mock targets was the U.S. Navy base at Pearl Harbor, and watching from the wings was Admiral Isoroku Yamamoto of the Imperial Japanese Navy. For additional information Yamamoto studied the Royal Navy attacks on the Italian Navy in the Mediterranean. He was understandably impressed with the fact that a flock of fragile British biplanes sent half the Italian Navy to the bottom of the sea.

On May 26, 1941, Yamamoto became convinced that carrier warfare could work. On that day planes from the Royal Navy destroyed the *Bismarck*, which was the pride of the German fleet.

Nearly three years from the day Admiral King staged his mock attack on Pearl Harbor, Admiral Yamamoto duplicated the exercise of 1938, but this time with real bullets and real bombs, and took the entire world by surprise. If there was a positive side to the attack, it lay in the fact that all of the American aircraft carriers were at sea and would be able to strike back quickly. Otherwise the very outcome of the war in the South Pacific might have been jeopardized.

While the war in the South Pacific depended heavily on the mighty aircraft carriers, the war in Europe was just the opposite. American airplanes were not only helping to stave off the Luftwaffe in the Battle of Britain, they were taking the confrontation directly to German soil. American planes based in Britain were making daily bombing raids on strategic enemy targets.

B-17 Flying Fortresses were inflicting destruction on the German homeland, and many of the American fighter pilots were becoming aces. They were doing it at much faster speeds and with far superior airplanes than their World War I counterparts, but with much the same valor.

One such ace was Lieutenant Colonel Francis Gabreski, a P-47 Thunderbolt pilot with the Eighth Air Force's 56th Fighter Group. When the war ended, Gabreski had twenty-eight kills, two more than America's leading World War I ace, Eddie Rickenbacker.

One of Gabreski's first encounters with superb German fighters was over Holland in 1943. He sighted a formation of twelve twin-engined Messerschmitt 110s, which were taking dead aim on the B-17s. The Me-110s appeared to be ready to unleash their rockets on the Fortresses. To make matters worse, the 110s were escorted by the deadly Focke-Wulf 190s and Messerschmitt 109s.

He dove toward the 110s with full power from his 2,000-horsepower Thunderbolt and all eight .50-caliber machine guns blazing. The surprise action scattered the 110s and temporarily thwarted their fateful aim on the B-17s. He knew he was wasting ammunition, but he kept firing.

It paid off as he swooped near one of the 110s. It was only about a hundred yards from Gabreski's airplane when it exploded, sending pieces of the plane in all directions, some into his own plane. He tested all his controls to see what damage, if any, had been done to the controllability of his P-47. Feeling that he could still do battle, he took after another 110 which was moving into range for a rocket-launch at one of the B-17s. Gabreski blasted the 110 out of the sky.

Within minutes, the rest of his fighter group had joined in the fray, and with precision and courage had dispatched the German warplanes back to their homeland.

Jack Moore is in his seventies and divides his time these days between talking with old buddies around Lake Worth, Florida, about flying, and teaching young pilots what the Civil Air Patrol is all about. Moore is a colonel in the CAP, but during World War II his duties as pilot of a B-17 were far more exciting, if not downright precarious.

Like most pilots, Moore began to dream of flying as a youth. "And it's probably a good thing I got an interest in *something*," he says, "because I got in so much trouble running the streets that I ended up in reform school.

"As part of the punishment we had to root out palmetto patches, and it so happened that one of them was right near a place where a man named Engle was grubbing out a little air strip. Every time a little plane came in or took off, my heart pounded. I made up my mind right there that I was going to make enough out of myself to get the money to fly an airplane.

"After I got out of reform school I got a job helping finish the airport. Mr. Engle had a Stinson 105 and I took out most of my pay with rides in it. Hell, I'd grub out those palmettos with an axe and an adz all day just for a ride in that plane," Moore mentions, as he remembers the time when his life began to turn around.

"I still remember the feeling of flying in those first days," he says.

"It was even more than I expected it to be; there was a sense of exhilaration, but on top of that was a little feeling of fear. My subconscious kept telling me that I was out of my element; it kept pounding at me: You're in the air. You shouldn't be here. You're a land animal. You're going to get killed.

"Part of this, I think, is why some people get air sickness. But for a nut of a kid like me, it was like a bird being let out of a cage. There was complete freedom, and when I looked at the ground from up there I felt like I was the ruler of all I surveyed," he relates.

Moore followed the air currents right into the Army Air Corps and into England, where so many American pilots were based.

He couldn't wait to get into combat, and it didn't take long after he got to England. Two days after he arrived, he found himself in the briefing room with a bunch of other B-17 pilots awaiting word of their mission. It was still pitch dark outside when the map was uncovered and the target displayed. Berlin! Somehow he knew it would be like this: He felt all of the old thrills and chills of his first flight, of his solo flight, of his first flight in the Flying Fortress. It was a mixture of pride and apprehension.

"I remember how cold it was as I walked toward the plane," he says. "I had heard about the thick fog that England was noted for but I didn't expect it to be so cold in April. I was shivering but I kept telling myself it was because of the piercing coldness. Now that I look back at it, I'm not so sure it was the cold.

"Once we got in the air, the shivering was gone and the flight across the English Channel was much like any other flight I had made—except the thought of my plane dropping bombs on innocent people began to creep into my head. And then I remembered how London had looked to me when I got there—the churches and the historic buildings and the homes that had been reduced to piles of rubble by the Luftwaffe. I pushed any concern I had right out of my mind and it never came back.

"I had a job to do, and damned if I wasn't going to do it, to the best of my ability. Which I thought was pretty good," he says, with the confident smile of an aviator. "And, you know, I never had any concern about the bombs we were dropping, particularly in that war. If there *is* such a thing, World War Two was a righteous war. If you're a professional, you go ahead and do your job. You may complain, but you do your job. Hell, I would have dropped the A-bomb if I had been told. And not worried a whole lot about it.

"I couldn't believe how much antiaircraft fire there was over Berlin and how many German fighter planes kept diving at us. But fortunately we had our own guys out there in P-47s and they kept the Jerries off our tails so we could complete our bombing run," Moore remembers.

The flight home seemed like the longest he had ever been on, probably because the anticipation of battle was gone. It was like a milk run back. Mission after mission reeled off, and Moore began to realize that "You shake the most when you get back." There were lots of times when he looked at the airplane and saw a hundred holes in it, and his knees got weak and he would have to sit down on the tarmac.

"One day we came back with four hundred twenty-two holes in the airplane, but it had been flying fine," he recalls. "Of course, the B-17 was one of the sturdiest planes ever built. The B-24, for example, wouldn't take as much as the 17. With the Fort, all the control cables were electric, and redundant to boot—the gear, the flaps, everything. On the 24, the controls were hydraulic and if you got one hole in them, that was it.

"The 17 would take a tremendous beating and bring you home," Moore exclaims. "Jesus, I brought one back from Munich with two engines gone. And I wasn't even concerned. Oh, don't get me wrong; there were plenty of times I *did* have time to be scared. We were up against the Abbeyville Kids, one of Goering's pet squadrons. They had yellow-nosed FW-190s, and if they didn't scare the shit out of you there was something bad wrong in your head.

"Anybody who tells you he was never afraid going into combat is either a damn liar or a damn fool. But you get a little used to it, especially when things go as planned, which they always did. Until number fifteen. We were over Czechoslovakia and everything was right on schedule. Our target was Stuttgart. It was like the other fourteen missions: We were keyed-up but confident and routinely heading for what we were sure would be another successful mission. The one thing we all had plenty of is confidence. Sure, a lot of the planes didn't come back, but I always told myself that it would never happen to me.

"And then all hell broke loose. Right out of the sun came about a dozen Focke-Wulf 190s, with guns blazing," Moore says, as he rubs the knuckles of his left hand with the palm of his right. "We were hit bad, but I was still determined to get out of the trouble.

"I guess my copilot had different ideas. But then he was a flat-assed coward. I don't know, maybe that's too harsh, but damn it, that's the way I felt at the time. Later I realized that all of us are cowards to one degree or another, but this guy couldn't even function. Here were the rest of us doing our jobs as best we could under the extreme circumstances, and my copilot was running true to form. He had been so bad that I could never let him fly the airplane over the target. He sat with one flak suit on and two more over himself, and he grabbed the microphone and ordered the crew to bail out. I immediately rescinded the order and went back to trying to save our asses.

"Both engine three and engine four were on fire. I had full left aileron but it was so damned hard to hold that I had my leg hung over the yoke. I had full left trim and reduced power on one and two, but we were still in a steep spiral to the right." He rubs harder on his knuckles and a far-off, foreboding look spreads over his face. He is reliving, probably for the thousandth time, the moment of greatest anxiety in his life.

"The whole plane was on fire, so then *I* got on the intercom and ordered everybody to bail out. When I was sure they had time to get out, I tried to get up and follow them out of the burning plane. I couldn't get up because of the spin.

"You don't have time to be afraid in a situation like that. I mean, your mind is racing so fast trying to figure out what to do that there isn't time to just sit back and say, 'I'm going to die.' Sure, I figured I *was* going to die, but my life didn't flash before my eyes or *anything* like that. All I was concerned with was getting out. And I sure as hell didn't give up.

"The B-17 had a characteristic of spinning tight for a while and then it would flatten out. Thank God it did just that, so when it flattened out for that moment, I was able to get up. In all our training we had been told to go out the bomb bay, but for some reason I decided to head for the forward hatch. I don't know why I did it, but when I got there, I was glad I had. The bombardier was stuck in the hatch. His chute had gotten wedged in, and there was nothing for his hands or feet to grab onto to pull himself out.

"He didn't even know I was behind him when I kicked him in the ass, but he went out the hatch and I saw his chute open. I followed him, but just as I left the plane, it exploded in a ball of fire. My chute had already started to open and pieces of the flaming debris caught it on fire. I was going down a lot faster than I should be, and I knew I was going to hit hard.

"It felt like I had driven myself into the ground like a tent stake when I hit. There was nothing but numbness for a while. I just laid there and looked around to make sure there wasn't somebody getting ready to shoot me. Then I tried to get up. I got about halfway up and went back down like a load of bricks. I couldn't stand up. Every time I tried, I fell down so I just laid there for another minute or so. And then I began to check my legs. The left one was bleeding badly, apparently from the pieces of the airplane; the right one was bent in so many places that I was sure I had multiple fractures.

"After what seemed like an eternity, I saw some people coming up the hillside toward me. I couldn't tell if they were soldiers or not, so I laid down real still. When they got closer I could see that they weren't German soldiers, so I raised myself up on my elbows and tried to look as friendly as possible," he says. His hands are in his lap and much of the tension has disappeared from his face.

"They talked to me, but when it was obvious to them that I didn't speak their language, they quietly and carefully lifted me up and laid me in the back of the cart. They took me to their tiny village, and, you know, I still don't have any idea what village it was. All I know is that they were friendly. They took me upstairs in an old building to a doctor's office. I'm not sure he wasn't any more of a doctor than I was, but he made a makeshift splint for my right leg and tried to stop the bleeding in my left. He poured some alcohol out of a bottle with no label; I guess it was alcohol, I don't know, but whatever it was, it burned like hell."

Once more a look of consternation overtakes Jack Moore. "What happened as I hobbled down the office stairs and out toward the car that waited for me was straight out of a B movie. I mean, you've *seen* it. Here came this open Mercedes touring car with swastika flags on each front fender and four soldiers in brown shirts with swastika armbands sitting in it. The car screeched to a halt in front of me and two of the soldiers got out and put me in the backseat between them. Not a word was said. Even in German.

"I had no idea where we were going but I could see clouds of smoke ahead of us. As we got closer, I realized we were going right through the area we had bombed. We had hit this synthetic oil factory and the flames were leaping about five hundred feet in the air. I guess I was grinning from ear to ear because when one of the guys in front turned around with a very grim look, I realized he didn't see any humor in this at all.

"They put me on a train in Pilsen and again it was like a movie. It was one of those kind of railroad cars with the aisle running down one side and the compartments on the other side, with sliding doors with glass panels in them. At Dresden an SS officer came aboard the train and when he saw my uniform, he jerked the door open and started shouting *"Schreckenfliegen! Schreckenfliegen!,"* which I later found out was German for "terror flyer." And then he started kicking the hell out of me. He broke some ribs and bloodied my face. The SS guys weren't very nice," declares Moore in an intended understatement.

From there, he was sent to Stalag Luft Three, about ninety miles southeast of Berlin, one of the main camps where most of the Allied air crews were sent. Their story was told in the film *The Great Escape,* shot on location.

"It seems like the whole thing was a movie, now that I look back at it," Jack Moore says, as he leans back and begins to think about the events that took place at Stalag Luft Three during the next year.

Detainment in a concentration camp is another potential outcome to aerial combat, one that rests uncomfortably between coming home and becoming a casualty. His time there was the only year since Moore had been eighteen that he didn't fly.

As Jack Moore speaks of the camp, he further illustrates the difference between being a good pilot and a mediocre one—both in and out of the air:

"Most of the Allied air crews were in either Luft One on the Baltic or Luft Three about ninety miles southeast of Berlin. I was at Luft

Three, when the Great Escape was attempted. There were ingenious things going on there. I mean, there were ten thousand men there and all of them were officers, so you had a fairly high intelligence level. I don't know if you remember or not, but all of the old paperback books—and we had a lot of those—had a red page in front. We found out that if you tore out those pages and boiled them, you had a good red dye, and we could use that for a variety of things from counterfeiting money to dyeing cloth for bogus German uniforms.

"On one occasion, the guys actually made uniforms and wooden rifles. To get the patterns one guy would strike up a conversation with one of the guards, and while they were talking, another guy would be measuring his gun from behind. The rest was easy: They carved out exact replicas. Once they had the uniforms and rifles completed, two Americans dressed as German guards marched twelve 'prisoners' right out of the front gate to freedom. Fourteen guys escaped in that one," says Moore.

"There was a lot of forgery, of course, and some of the guys became really good artists and engravers. It was incredible. But the tunnel caper was the capper. Albert [Red] Clark was the security chief for the secret operations. He had been moved to the south camp, where I was, sometime before the breakout in March of 1944. Granger McDaniels was the actual cooler king—the role Steve McQueen played in the movie—and between the two of them, they engineered the unbelievable feat.

"Just getting rid of the dirt those guys were digging was inconceivable. We filled our pockets and caps and everything that would hold dirt and sand and then we'd walk around the compound, dribbling the stuff evenly. They didn't notice that the ground around the barracks was building up. In fact, one of the guards said once that it looked like the whole damn building was *sinking!*

"The tunnels were called Tom, Dick, and Harry, and you know, they damn near pulled it off. When the Germans finally discovered them, they shot seventy-six of our guys. Even Goering had to figure nobody would believe they had shot that many men trying to escape, but that's what they said. Not one of those guys was shot trying to escape; they were executed.

"It was a helluva experience," Moore remembers, as a look of pride moves across his youthful-looking face. "None of us were sorry to get out of there when V-E Day came, but we all had sort of a fond spot for the stalag when we left. It had given us the opportunity to use our brains, even though we weren't flying."

He gazes into a memorable and exciting past. "You know," Moore says, "the one thing that kept me going was a faith that I would get out of there and bomb the hell out of Berlin just one more time. It was my one compulsion. Just one more time! It was the main reason I wanted my freedom."

Many things go through a combat pilot's mind on the morning of a mission. Lieutenant Colonel Charles L. Brown (USAF Retired) remembers them vividly. He was captain of *Ye Olde Pub*, a battle-weary B-17 flying regular missions over Germany in 1943. One particular mission stands out in his memory.

It was 4:30 in the morning and a numbing cold fog curled around the airplanes at AAF Station 117 in Kimbolton, England. The fire in the small stove used to heat the combat crew's Nissen hut had died out, and the cold of the English predawn penetrated the very walls.

"When my mind began to function, I realized the fear, to a large degree, was based on how I would perform during my first mission as a pilot/aircraft commander of a B-17 crew over Germany."

The target was Bremen, Germany, and the specific objective was to be a Focke-Wulf 190 plant in one of the outlying districts of the city. Brown had made one other mission over Bremen as pilot, but one of the deputy group leaders had been aircraft commander. The stress of flying close formation in an actual combat situation had kept him from observing too much of the combat environment. But he did remember that the flak had been extremely heavy and accurate, and he also recalled the helpless feeling of having to fly into the black shroud over the city.

At the preflight briefing, the intelligence officer pointed out flak areas to avoid enroute and finished with the fact that Bremen was protected by more than 250 flak guns manned by the best gunners the Germans had. He also said they would be subject to attack by more than five hundred German fighter planes. American and Royal Air Force fighters were scheduled to be available all the way to the target and return. *If* they were on time.

The group combat formation was to consist of the lead, high, and low squadrons, each made up of a three-ship lead element, followed by a second four-ship or diamond element, for a total of twenty-one aircraft. Brown's ship was to fly number three (left wing slot), second element, or low squadron—more commonly called "Purple Heart Corner." A low cloud cover restricted visibility so they were briefed to assemble in formation at seven thousand feet on the Kimbolton radio station.

With the briefing over, Brown and his crew made the short, cold truck ride to *Ye Olde Pub*, B-17-F, Number 42-3167.

"As I stood there, I suddenly experienced a quiet, almost tranquil feeling. My thoughts wandered. I had just celebrated my twenty-fifth birthday two months before. Well, really it was my twenty-first, but to impress my crew and give them some confidence in my ability, I had told them I was twenty-five. I thought a lot about the confidence that all nine of the crew must place in me and the tranquillity left as quickly as it had come."

All of them were Americans in England, on soil that had been a battlefield when lances and crossbows had been weapons, and they were preparing for battle with a modern weapon that would strike solidly into the German soil several hundreds miles away. Although the purpose of war never seems to change over the centuries, the lances and knives and swords had given way to .50-caliber machine guns, 20-millimeter cannons, and 500-pound bombs, all combined into a "Flying Fortress." The major difference still was the swiftness of a more modern warfare and a more efficient way of dealing out death.

Shortly after the men entered the cockpits, the first of a series of signal flares arched through the ground haze, indicating that it was time to start engines. The first three engines of *Ye Olde Pub* started without problem, but number four ran rough for the first few minutes. The quiet of the airfield was now brought to life by the rolling thunder of ninety-six large radial engines. (There were three spare planes in addition to the twenty-one scheduled to take part in the mission.) The semi-darkness was pierced by exhaust flames and the poor visibility was further restricted by the smoke from the starting engines. The smell of oil, gasoline, and smoke now penetrated all of the cockpits as they prepared to taxi.

Taxiing to the takeoff point was not easy, since the taxiways were narrow and the wings and engine nacelles of the aircraft overlapped on either side of the asphalt. There was no room for passing; falling in line in the proper position was a must. Due to the limited runway length, only three aircraft could line up on the strip at the same time. Starting with the group leader as number one, the other aircraft lined up according to their position in the formation. Except for the three spares, Brown was to be next to last, or number twenty, on takeoff.

"Takeoff in any aircraft is an exciting moment for the pilot, but taking off for the first few times with a full bomb load and full fuel load on a combat mission is nothing short of awe-inspiring," Brown says. "This was no training mission; the guns, bullets, and bombs were real. The game was over . . . We were playing hardball."

The runway seemed excessively rough because of the extra bomb and fuel loads, but the airplanes quickly gained speed on their takeoff roll. As the elevator trim was coordinated with a slight back pressure on the control column, they gently lifted off the runway and began a climbing right turn to follow the lead aircraft. Despite the poor visibility, they mostly were able to keep the aircraft in front of them in sight until they all formed into flights and squadrons, assembling into a group formation in the heavy cloud cover.

They completed takeoff by 8:42 A.M. and by 9:40 had formed the group at 8,000 feet. The other two groups completed the wing formation of sixty aircraft.

Due to the clouds, they were five minutes late as they left the English Coast just north of Great Yarmouth. It was 10:39 and they were at 24,000 feet. They were still five minutes late when they reached the enemy coast at 11:05.

The cloud cover over the continent was scattered to broken with most clouds topping at under 10,000 feet. Friendly fighter escorts of mostly P-47s were excellent until they reached the initial point for the bomb run at 11:32. They were at 27,300 feet. During the bomb run of approximately ten minutes, they would cover more than thirty miles in an essentially straight line, with some minor diversionary course changes to avoid heavy flak areas. Although the procedure gave the lead bombardiers adequate time to set up the bomb sights and correct for wind drift as well as smoke and cloud obstructions, it also gave the German defense units time to identify them as a target and to determine their flight path and altitude, the key ingredients in destroying an airplane with antiaircraft fire and/or fighters.

All Brown could see in front of him was the rapidly expanding black cloud from flak bursts, which gradually became a black oily carpet as they got closer to the target. A veteran combat pilot had told Brown that you were in serious trouble when you were close enough to see and distinguish the orange and red centers of the flak bursts.

"About two minutes before bombs away, immediately in front of us, I saw what appeared to be fantastically beautiful, although deadly, black orchids with vivid crimson centers. Oh, shit! I thought."

"We're hit! We're hit!" two voices rang over the intercom simultaneously. The nose section had been hit and partially destroyed. But the pilots, as well as the nose gunner, also had problems; oil pressure suddenly had dropped on the number two engine, so engine shutdown procedure was begun immediately. As Brown attempted to apply more power to the remaining three engines, number four began to run away. It was revving to the danger point of self-destruction.

At that point, the aircraft suddenly lurched skyward just as the bombardier called out the welcome "Bombs away!" report. With the sudden shedding of three tons of weight, Brown thought perhaps he could remain in formation, but it wasn't possible with number two shut down and the same procedures beginning on number four, which was necessary to bring it back into a usable power range.

At the precise moment the group started a left turn off the target, both the number four aircraft in the squadron—the original flight leader and *Ye Olde Pub*—were flying side by side.

"I looked out my window and my heart leaped to my mouth," says Brown, "but I kept my composure and nudged my copilot with my right elbow. I pointed to the other crippled B-17 flying our left wingtip. Both right-side engines of the other bomber were on fire. Hell, within a matter of seconds, the whole goddamn wing burst into flames and the plane went into a steep dive. As the plane spun toward German soil we didn't see one damn chute. Nobody said a word. I didn't, Pinky, my copilot, didn't; none of the other crew members uttered a word on the radio."

They could not dwell on the tragic loss because they also had serious problems as the formation slowly pulled away from them.

They couldn't even maintain enough speed to stay in sight of the rest of the air armada, so they were suddenly alone, a cripple with a feathered engine and another that worked properly only on occasion. Either condition normally attracted German fighters like blood entices sharks.

Brown's crew didn't have to agonize long. "Enemy fighters at six o'clock," yelled the tail gunner on the intercom. And then the intercom was alive with other frantic messages: "Bandits at twelve o'clock." "Six 190s at three o'clock high." They were being attacked from all angles.

Every crew member could hear Frenchy Coulombe open fire with the twin .50-caliber guns in the top turret, and then they heard Doc open fire with the gun in the nose. Both of them were trying to shoot down two FW-190s that were approaching in a coordinated attack from the ten and twelve o'clock positions.

"I saw the wings of the first fighter light up with machine gun and cannon fire," remarks Brown, "and for a fraction of a second I was mesmerized by the sight. It looked like all the movies I had seen back home. Then it hit me: This is no movie; we're up to our ass in trouble!

"I pulled up and headed directly toward the attacking fighters, on a collision course with the one attacking from twelve o'clock. I thought it might unnerve at least one of them. It must have worked because both planes broke off their attacks by rolling over and diving. 'Fighters attacking at six o'clock level,' screamed Ecky in the tail. And then he said, in a voice of panic, 'Get 'em, somebody, my guns are jammed. Jesus Christ, they won't fire.'

"I heard the machine-gun fire from the fighters, and I felt the vibration as the bullets and the subsequent cannon fire struck the aft portion of the airplane. I was scared. I don't give a damn who knows it.

"I got on the radio: 'Denver One! Denver One! Mayday! Mayday! This is Goldsmith [his code name] under attack south of Wilhelmshaven. Need assistance!' It was all I had time to transmit on the fighter frequency."

There was no response and no fighters came to the rescue. The cavalry did *not* arrive just in the nick of time. And, to make matters worse, it was to be the last radio call. The next wave of fighters hit directly on the radio room. And they also shot away the controls to the number three engine.

After the first enemy fighter passes, Brown found that the controls to number three were inoperable, but the oil pressure and engine temperature remained stable and the engine continued to produce a little more than 50 percent power. Had they totally lost number three, it probably would have been the end of the line.

The only defensive guns that weren't frozen or otherwise malfunctioning were the twin 50s operated by Frenchy in the top turret and the single gun in what was left of the nose. With these limitations in mind, Brown began to turn the nose of the 17 into each attacking fighter and for a while became a two-and-one-half-engine attacking fighter. This seemed to throw the German fighter pilots off their routine. As a consequence, due to the Fortress's climb, dive, and turn maneuvers, the enemy had shorter aiming and firing runs and faster rates of closure. They definitely were off balance.

Despite the best efforts, the American bomber was hit hundreds of times by the machine gun bullets and 20-millimeter cannon shells. It was bitter cold in the airplane as sixty-degree-below-zero winds swept through the opening in the nose and out the many holes left by the attackers.

"At some point during our twisting, turning, climbing, and diving maneuvers, their attacks finally ended, and the fighter escort of P-47s reappeared," says Brown. "Where the hell they had been we didn't know, because we hadn't seen friendly fighters for a long time.

"While I was trying to determine the full extent of our damage, I casually looked out the window and I was astonished at what I saw. There, not three feet from our wingtip, was an Me-109. For a moment I thought the heat of battle had been too much; I closed my eyes, figuring it would go away, but when I reopened them, he was still there. I nudged Pinky and pointed to the German plane. His mouth dropped open in amazement. Neither of us said a word.

"The German pilot nodded to us, but we didn't return the greeting. We assumed it was only a matter of time until he attempted 'the kill.' He appeared relaxed and confident, and with only one of our original eleven guns operating, I somehow felt he had a reason for his poise."

There was something different about this particular Messerschmitt. It was solid black. They had sent up a night fighter. And, in addition to the foreboding color, there was a large, round bulge in front of the cockpit area. Later they would learn that this was a new supercharger installation.

Just about the time Brown and his crew figured it was all over, the German saluted, rolled over, and was gone. It was an abrupt and curious end to one of the most unusual encounters in the then-short history of heavy bombardment as a major weapon of war.

If there was no other explanation, the gesture was a throwback to the flying knights of World War I, who flew with abandon, valor, and most of all, dignity. It was shades of the Red Baron or Eddie Rickenbacker. And perhaps it proved that the age of chivalry didn't die with the advent of the modern fighting plane.

The crippled B-17 left the enemy coast and headed for home, but it was gradually losing altitude because of problems to three of its four engines.

There was a decision to make. The aircraft was badly damaged, with the number two engine totally inoperable, number three operating at only about 50-percent power, and number four damaged by flak and trying to run away at every whipstitch. The copilot was working frantically to keep number four functional.

The rudder did not respond and the elevators were very, very slow in their reaction. With a large hole in the nose, the aircraft seemed to be swimming through heavy air, grossly overweight for the available power, and sluggish in responding to any control pressure. Attempting to fly a straight and level path was much like trying to guide a log through a raging, rain-swollen river.

Through experimentation, Brown found that by dropping the left wing a few degrees and using trim tabs he could maintain a relatively straight but slightly descending flight path. The question was, could he remain in the air long enough to cross the unyielding North Sea, a distance of approximately 250 miles?

Bailing out over enemy territory, particularly in the freezing cold, was nearly as questionable as staying with the plane. A crash landing was never seriously considered since they were under strict orders to keep the ship aloft if at all possible. They did not want the top-secret Norden bombsight to fall into enemy hands.

Brown gave the men permission to jump if they wished. Not one elected to do so, deciding to ride it out. And what a ride it was to be. Much to their comfort, a pair of P-47s appeared and flew at each wingtip in an attempt to keep Air-Sea Rescue informed of the plane's flight path and position.

The lower the 17 dropped, the more menacing the North Sea appeared in its dull gray mantle interspersed with large whitecaps, indicating strong wind and high waves. As they gradually lost altitude, they began throwing out excess weight, such as movable guns, ammo, ammo cans, and everything else that wasn't absolutely necessary. They dropped to five hundred feet and still no sight of land.

As they approached two hundred feet, Pinky exclaimed, "There it is!" The coast of England was visible, and, even more to their delight, an air base also was in sight. Brown wagged the wings slightly to thank the fighter escort. They wagged back and each of the P-47 pilots gave a thumbs-up signal for a job exceedingly well done.

The crew was able to manually lower the landing gear and to crank in some flaps, just as they started to flare out. They cut the power to three and four, and the landing, essentially without flaps, was completed with the number one engine only.

"Despite the lack of effective brake or rudder control, and by a minor miracle," Brown asserts, "the aircraft remained relatively straight as we stopped, still on the runway."

In addition to the three damaged engines, every major component of their aircraft had suffered severe damage: The plexiglass nose section was almost gone; there were hundreds of flak and bullet holes in the airplane, from the wings and ailerons to the fuselage; one large hole about the size of a bushel basket was apparently from an 88-millimeter antiaircraft shell that had passed through the wing without hitting anything strong enough to explode it; the vertical stabilizer was history; the elevators were badly damaged; the radio compartment was almost totally destroyed; there were sections of the skin missing; and the hydraulic system was completely malfunctional. One military onlooker describe *Ye Olde Pub* as a flying wind tunnel that looked like a piece of Swiss cheese.

After Brown and his crew had a few hours to regain their composure, one big question began to drift through their minds. Brown checked the log: They were hit by flak on the bomb run at 11:41. The bombs were dropped at 11:43, and the first German fighters began their attack at 11:50. The final attack came at 12:03. The only fighters they saw between 11:50 and 12:03 were German.

"There was a thirteen-minute gap," says Brown, "when we didn't see a single American or RAF fighter. We were by ourselves.

"Since that day nearly forty-seven years ago I have tried to find out what happened, and there is nothing. I mean, *nothing* to even show that we did anything at all or that any unusual event happened. There were no medals awarded, except the one for our tail gunner and a Purple Heart for the waist gunner. There was no brass-plated news release heralding the accomplishment, which was common. There simply was *no* fanfare."

The only account of the event was published in one London newspaper, stating that the B-17 was believed to be one of the worst battle-damaged airplanes to return to England. Yet there have been no photos of the plane uncovered. Brown has contacted every source from the Pentagon to the records of the 448th Bomb Group, which are maintained by the National Archives and Office of the Air Force History. Nothing discloses any record of B-17-F No. 42-3167 even having been at Seething Air Corps Base, despite the fact that it landed there and was repaired there during the period between late December 1943 and mid-April 1944.

No matter what the reason for the mystery shrouding the heroism of the ten flyers, retired Colonel Brown was determined to find out more. And two curious postscripts emerged. The first came in the July 1988 issue of the *8th AF News*, published by the Eighth Air Force Historical Society, which contained the following letter (including the writer's home address) in the "Mail Call" segment:

BOMBER CREW SOUGHT. On either 13 or 20 December 1943, my flight of 12 P-47s came upon a badly crippled B-17 being shot up by five or more Me-109s. We had altitude on them, surprising them and destroying all five. Due to our fuel shortage, we had to leave as they exited the coast and returned to Bodney. The press clippings reported that same a/c flew over our field (identified by the heavy damage) and "kinda" waved its wings. Is there anyone who might have been on that plane? George A. Arnold, 352-FG.

Was there anyone who might have been on that plane? An elated Charlie Brown immediately phoned up Arnold and the pair compared notes on the events of that day four decades earlier. Arnold identified the P-47s as being a part of the 487th Squadron of the 352nd Fighter Group.

There *are* records of the destruction of the five German planes, but still nothing about *Ye Olde Pub*. This remains a mystery to Brown and his crew. But on January 18, 1990, an incredible coincidence occurred. Brown's hundreds of letters over the years finally paid off. He received the following letter from Surrey, British Columbia, from a man who was told fourth- or fifth-hand of Brown's efforts to solve the enigma:

Dear Charles,
All this years I wondered what happened to the B-17, did she make it or not. As I am a guest of the American Fighter Aces, I inquired time and again, but without any results. I have been a guest at the 50th anniversary of the B-17, and I would still find any answers, wheter it was worth a court marshal. I am happy now that you made it, and that it was worth it.

I will be in Florida sometimes in June as guest of the Am. Fighter Aces and it sure would be nice to talk about our encounter. By the way after I landet at Bremen Airport, I borrowed the Fieseler Storch from the airport commander to fly out to a B-17 wich I shot down. The field I landet in just was not cooperating and I stood on my head or prop. I just wonted to be sure, that the crew was treated correctly. My landing was not apreciated, I have been told in the Off. Mess, as I was forced to stay overnight to have one of my radiators changed, wich had a 50 cal. bullet stuck in it.

For now,
horrido,
yours,
[signed] Franz Stigler

Needless to say, Brown answered the letter from Stigler within a day of receiving the former German ace's communique. In further correspondence, he learned several facts: Stigler was seventy-five, which would have made him twenty-nine in 1943; he *did* fly on one enemy bomber's wingtip; he was a highly successful pilot, having been shot down seventeen times (he bailed out six times), but he also downed twenty-eight Allied aircraft. He was one of the first jet pilots in history, having flown the infamous Me-262.

Brown flew to Seattle to meet with Stigler and the "old friends" flew the mission again several times. Stigler was able to tell his side of the story:

"The B-17 was the most respected airplane we had to fly against. There was always a wall of bullets; I never came home without holes in my airplane. But I was on the ground when I saw this single bomber coming at a very low altitude. It was apparent that it was damaged, so I rushed to my airplane and went after it.

"When I got near it, I could see that there was much damage to the nose and tail sections. I flew in behind the plane and I could see the gunner lying across his machine guns. There was a huge hole in the side of the fuselage and the rudder was almost blown away. It was in very bad shape."

The former German ace speaks clearly as he remembers that fateful day for Charlie Brown and the crew of *Ye Olde Pub:*

"I could tell the pilot was in bad shape. I didn't have the heart to finish off this wonderful machine and its brave men. I flew beside them for a long time, trying in some way to help; they were trying desperately to get home, so I was going to let them do it.

"The short way to safety was to turn right and fly to Sweden, so when they banked left and headed for England, I thought, You crazy people. I hope you make it."

Stigler's eyes mist slightly. He touches the arm of Charlie Brown, who sits next to him. Both men are silent for a moment. Stigler is the first to break the silence:

"I couldn't have shot at them," he says. "It would have been the same as shooting at a parachute. I shot down eleven B-17s and I always waited to see how many chutes appeared. The more I saw, the happier I was."

Brown smiles slightly at the adopted brother he hadn't seen for forty-six years. "If you made a practice of this," he says to Stigler, "you would have been using a parachute yourself."

"I did," replies the German. "Six times."

• • •

After Pearl Harbor, the thought of striking back at Japan where it would have the most devastating psychological force—Tokyo—was foremost in the minds of everybody from President Roosevelt to the guy at the corner market. But as much as all the military chiefs wanted the fateful blow to happen, it was an unpractical notion at best. There was no way aircraft carriers could get close enough to the mainland to launch bombers toward Tokyo. The strong Imperial Japanese Navy and the advanced airplanes would blow the carriers out of the water and render a second devastating blow perhaps even more debilitating than Pearl Harbor had been.

Still, it was up to the United States Navy, because, after all, they *did* have carriers. How they were going to get into position remained the problem. Someone suggested flying long-range Army planes from the deck of a carrier, thereby not only totally surprising the enemy but protecting the floating airstrip as well. General Hap Arnold turned over the plan to launch B-25 Billy Mitchell bombers from a carrier deck to Lieutenant Colonel Jimmy Doolittle for study. "Study" was the key word. Surely Arnold did not intend to get his key aide directly involved. After all, Doolittle was forty-five years old at the time, which was considered a ripe old age for an active combat pilot.

But Doolittle had ideas of his own. Forty-five years old or not, the former stunt pilot turned racer turned military flyer immediately made plans to lead the raid. He flew to Wright Field in Dayton, Ohio, to help with the necessary modifications to the airplanes. For one thing, they had to be much lighter, and the only conceivable way to accomplish this was by removing most of the guns and armor, which was obviously an unorthodox move in preparing a plane for a vital combat mission.

Doolittle then assembled his crews and explained to the volunteers that theirs was to be a dangerous but important mission. He told them what he had in mind and then gave anyone who desired the opportunity to drop out. Not one chose to stay behind.

Next the feisty Doolittle trained the men in the procedure of getting the B-25s airborne in an extraordinarily short distance, seven hundred feet—the length of the deck on the aircraft carrier *Hornet*. It was roughly half the distance required in the most challenging previous takeoffs.

Doolittle explained matter-of-factly that by jerking back on the control and lifting away in a near-stall attitude, the planes would begin their climb before reaching the end of the deck. Within days the pilots were "in the air" before they got to the painted lines on the runway which indicated the seven-hundred-foot mark, the foreboding line between steel and water at the leading edge of the *Hornet*.

A few weeks later, sixteen modified B-25s sat on the deck of the *Hornet* north of Midway Island, where the floating "bomber field" was joined by the carrier *Enterprise*, four cruisers, eight destroyers, and the support ships to form Task Force 16, fashioning possibly the most daring attack force in naval history.

Plans for the surprise attack went astray when Japanese lookouts spotted Task Force 16, which was more than two-hundred miles short of their launch point. Sentries on the *Hornet* saw the small Japanese craft and then heard frantic radio broadcasts. Although they couldn't make out the messages, there was no doubt that the position and all details about Task Force 16 had been reported to Tokyo.

The B-25s were already in place on the *Hornet's* deck, with Doolittle's lead plane only a little more than 450 feet from the ominous forward end of the carrier; for a man of lesser courage, it could have been the very edge of the earth.

Admiral Halsey, aboard the *Enterprise* and well aware of the fact that Japanese planes likely were being readied to bomb his flattops, ordered the mini-armada to swing around into the wind. Had Doolittle been at his side, he knew what the conversation would have been: "Whatta'ya think, Jimmy?" he would have asked, and Doolittle undoubtedly would have replied, "I think we'd better get on with things." He would have bet on it. And he would have been right, because Doolittle says that he began to "get into my flying gear the minute the *Hornet* began to come about."

"I went down to the flight deck and had another fifty gallons of gasoline put in the planes," remarks Doolittle. "And then I told my boys, 'Let's go get 'em.' "

It was to be the flight of the Gee Bee and all of Doolittle's other intrepid feats wrapped up into one.

"I'll never forget that moment," Doolittle says. "I slipped into the left seat of the Mitchell, checked out my crew of four, and then looked out at the flight deck officer. I could see the worried look on the guy's face, so I smiled at my copilot. He had the same look as the deck officer. I figured I would have to make believers out of them."

Just before 8:30 Doolittle opened the throttles to full power on the B-25, eased off the brakes, and when the airplane started rolling, he wrenched back on the control column with a vengeance. The B-25 fairly leapt into the air with a hundred feet of runway to spare. At that precise moment every man on board the *Hornet* breathed for the first time since the engines had roared to life. The first blow to the Japanese mainland was on its way.

Four hours later Doolittle swept over Tokyo and unloaded his bombs on a factory district; eight planes bombed diverse industrial areas of the city and the rest hit targets around Tokyo, knocking out, among other things, an oil refinery in Yokohama and an aircraft factory in Nagoya.

The raid was a tremendous success, as all sixteen of the bombers were able to elude both Japanese fighters and antiaircraft fire. As smoke crawled toward the sky from the burning factories, Doolittle's air force headed for home. But there was one major problem: There was no home.

A bomber taking off from an aircraft carrier was one thing; landing was another. Even a *light* bomber. The plan was that the planes would get back to friendly Chinese territory and land at an obscure field. It wasn't that great a plan, granted, but it was the only one they had.

A reluctant Hap Arnold had referred to the mission as "nearly suicidal," but the desire to bomb Tokyo was more than even he could resist. Now the moment of truth was upon Doolittle and his men.

As it turned out, only one of the B-25s landed intact. Captain Edward York, dangerously low on fuel, headed for Russia, where he found an airstrip near Vladivostok. The confused Soviets put the crew in jail but not one of the Americans seemed to mind. They were happy to be alive. Even in jail. They later escaped and made their way home.

Doolittle and ten other planes made it back to China, only to find the friendly skies socked in with heavy cloud cover. It would be impossible to find their field. Their fuel tanks were almost dry, so Doolittle gave the command: "Let's bail out, boys. God bless you."

Near Shanghai and some five hundred miles inland, most of the men, including Doolittle, wafted down from the clouds onto Chinese soil. The other four planes crash-landed. When the final tally was in, two men had died in crashes, one from parachuting, and two crews were captured by the Japanese puppet government near Nanchang, where five men were to die in POW camps.

"The Chinese tried to help me find my crew, but we didn't have much luck because they were so scattered. I was sure that most of my men were dead and that all of the planes were destroyed," says Doolittle.

When General Arnold ordered Doolittle to fly out of China and come back to Washington, Doolittle was sure his military career was over. But, instead, a hero returned to America. Jimmy Doolittle and his men had struck the first blow of redemption to an embarrassed nation by bombing Japan's capital city. He was awarded the Congressional Medal of Honor and promoted to the rank of brigadier general.

After Doolittle's raid on the enemy's mainland, the Japanese prepared to retaliate by sending a large portion of their fleet to Midway to strike hard at the important American base. The Imperial Navy had their most important battleships in the center of the flotilla, and had they reached Midway, the island would have been leveled. But Admiral Chester Nimitz's men intercepted radio transmissions and they were ready for the onslaught.

Nimitz had the mighty *Hornet*, *Yorktown*, and *Enterprise* lying in wait, and just as the Japanese got ready for attack, Nimitz put *his* plan in motion. It was perfectly timed. The Navy planes struck with a vengeance. Within six minutes they had sunk three Japanese carriers and shot down three hundred planes. When the smoke had cleared, the Imperial Navy, less a fourth carrier, was rapidly heading home.

Following the battle of the Philippine Sea, U.S. Navy planes shot down 346 more Japanese planes and sank two more carriers, causing it to be called the "Great Marianas Turkey Shoot." But the Hellcat pilots were not able to get back to their floating bases before dark, so Admiral Marc Mitscher broke all Navy rules when he ordered all lights turned on aboard the carriers, so that the men would have bobbing beacons to guide them home. "There was no way I was going to leave those guys out there without any way of finding us," Mitscher said. "They had done one hell of a job and we weren't going to desert them at that point."

The planes did find their way home and Mitscher became legendary. And the carrier had established itself as the most important tool of the South Pacific war and secured its permanent place in warfare.

Davy Jones, one of Doolittle's pilots who was forced to bail out after the raid, was subsequently sent to the European Theater of Operations. On his first mission he was shot down over Africa. He flew two missions in World War II and was forced to bail out both times.

Jones wound up with Jack Moore in Stalag Luft Three.

Chapter Four

A *pilot who doesn't have any fear*
probably isn't flying his plane to its maximum.

— JON MCBRIDE, ASTRONAUT

he pilot of a B-17 Flying Fortress, who was forced to ditch his bomber on a Greenland icecap in blustery weather in the winter of 1943, probably summed up as well as anyone in World War II the spirit and courage of the American airmen. The plane was hopelessly mired in snow, and the crew facing death from the sub-zero temperature awaited rescue. Help first came in the form of parachuted supplies which included cigarettes and whiskey. The cavalier pilot radioed back: "Send us a couple of blondes and leave us alone."

It was with exactly this same fervor that Allied air power overcame great odds and often better Luftwaffe equipment to help turn around the entire course of the European war.

In the Pacific theater another battle was raging—both in the air and on the tally boards back at the American air bases where a record of enemy aircraft destroyed was kept. The chronology showed that Captain Richard Bong was steadfastly becoming America's top ace, followed by Neel Kearby, Thomas Lynch, and Thomas McGuire.

It was McGuire who had the most burning desire to take the title of "Top Ace." So intense was his lust for top honors that he lay sleepless at night, planning his strategy for the next day, just so he could "catch Bong" in their own personal war.

Bong was not to be denied. Despite the fact that he was a notoriously poor marksman, his kills continued to climb. To compensate for what he lacked in the gunnery department, Bong developed an unmatchable style of diving in from above and blasting the Japanese planes out of the air at almost point-blank range. Knowing full well that Bong couldn't miss at that range, the equally determined McGuire kept trying.

Try as he might, McGuire could not catch Bong. Week after week, mission after mission, McGuire remained eight kills behind Bong. Surely McGuire must have felt that when the war was over he still would be eight behind Bong.

The gap was to be narrowed, although McGuire would never catch the spirited and bold Bong. With forty Japanese planes to his credit, Bong became America's greatest aerial ace of any war. But General George Kennedy, fearful of his hero's intrepid tactics, ordered Bong back to the States to "help with the war-bond effort and to test new planes." General Douglas MacArthur presented him with the Congressional Medal of Honor, and the collective chest of an entire nation swelled with pride as he toured the country.

With Bong out of combat and contention, McGuire became almost as daring, shooting down six Japanese Zeros in the next several days to up his number of kills to thirty-eight. But Kennedy once more stepped in. He was sure McGuire was trying much too hard, so he decided to give him a rest. He grounded McGuire "for his own good."

That didn't stop him; McGuire took to the air on his own and led a sweep by four P-38 Lightnings over an island to the west of Leyte. When the Zeros appeared, McGuire was sure this would be "his day." Instead, fueled by a fanatical ache to be Number One, he committed an error far too basic for the meritorious service he had logged, a miscue he had often warned new pilots to avoid.

He attacked a Zero much too near the ground, and when he missed he attempted a tight turn to jump on the tail of another Japanese fighter. His speed was too slow and the P-38 shook violently for a few seconds, stalled, and plunged to the ground, where it burst into flames. He, too, was awarded the Medal of Honor. Posthumously.

When Kearby with twenty-four kills and Lynch with twenty also died in combat, it appeared that Bong surely would wind up the war as the lone spokesman for the stellar quartet of aces, but while testing a new P-80 Shooting Star jet on the very day the atomic bomb fell on Hiroshima, Bong crashed. American's greatest ace died on friendly soil. He had logged but four hours of test time in the airplane that might have carried him to even greater victories.

The North American P-51 Mustang may well have been the consummate fighter plane of World War II. The plane was rapidly designed in 1940, although not for the Army Air Corps; the Royal Air Force had requested North American to build the planes for their use against the Luftwaffe.

Despite its quick development, the Mustang was to become the greatest all-around combat airplane of the war. The long-range fighter immediately began to fly escort for raids over Germany and other central European targets and, along with the British Spitfire, proved to be equal to if not greater than either the Focke-Wulf 190s or the Messerschmitt 109s.

The cooling duct, located under the fuselage, gave the airplane greatly reduced drag. The efficient structure and laminar-flow wing section enabled its designers to build in a fuel capacity that gave the Mustang three times the range of its rivals.

The single weakness of the P-51 lay in its performance at high altitude, which was a result of the 1,150-horsepower Allison engine. Later installation of British Rolls-Royce Merlin engines, built in America by Packard, gave the plane the high-altitude performance it deserved. The new water-cooled engine also increased the plane's low-altitude speed to 440 miles per hour, making it one of the prime performers in both the Battle of Britain and the bombing of Germany. It joined with the RAF and the Army Air Corps to begin their control of the air war.

With heavy armament, the Mustang became the terror of European skies and the most dreaded sight of Luftwaffe pilots. Unlike its earlier cousin, the P-40 Warhawk of Flying Tiger fame, it needed no shark teeth to raise our enemy pilot's blood pressure.

P-51 fighter pilot Jack Sims, who is now retired and living in Houston, Texas, had this to say: "The 51 had the speed and the range to fly with B-17s right into the Reich and, once there, it could kick the hell out of the 190s and the 109s, or any damn thing the Luftwaffe had.

"You can feel it in the pit of your stomach when you first begin your takeoff—that awesome power," he exclaims. "Jesus, you're slammed back into the seat as if a truck was pushing on your chest. Everything about that plane was what the fighter pilot had wanted. After the 51 you never heard the usual gripe: 'Why the shit can't we keep up with the Krauts?' Hell, no, it was 'Goddamn, I can't *wait* to get up there and kick some ass.'

"The P-51 had it all—range, durability, maneuverability, and, most of all, it was easy to fly. As fighter planes went in those days. We felt confident, and why not? We could stay up there eight hours if we had to. It made our jobs easier; the 17s would lumber off at six in the morning and we'd leave a couple hours later and still catch them before they even got close to the target."

The fighter pilots in those great silver birds were dazzling figures, the knights of old, jousting with fiery mounts among the clouds. But aerial combat was not always like in the *Knights of the Round Table*. Or *High Noon*. On the contrary, it was usually the surprise tactic that worked best. Strike and run like hell. If you could shoot a guy in the back you were a hero; if you couldn't, you were dead.

"One second you couldn't see anybody. You were up there having the time of your life," says Sims, "and then like out of nowhere there's this 109 on your tail. And two more at twelve o'clock. Right then and there you know damn well that within seconds, somebody is going to die. But you're damn sure it's not going to be you.

"Within seconds you know just how good your opponent is, and you know how tough your job is going to be," Sims states. "I remember all too well how I felt the first time I got a German pilot in my sights. We were at very close range. I took a deep breath, put my finger on the trigger; I couldn't pull it. After what seemed an eternity, I squeezed it off. Then the guy did a sort of slow roll and the plane plunged toward the earth.

"There was a second there when I could see the guy's face; he looked shocked that it was all over for him, and then the plane burst into flames and the face was gone. But for a millisecond before his face was consumed, there was the faintest trace of a smile. I watched as the fiery plane disappeared through the clouds. When the airplane had disappeared, a feeling of excitement came over me. I had done exactly what I had been trained so long to do. And I thought of that night in the officers club. I knew *I* would be one of the ones standing up and moving my open hands back and forth, telling all my buddies exactly how I had done it.

"It's exactly what I did. I bought beers for everybody and I laughed and had a hell of a time. But when I laid there in my bed that night in the dark, I could still see the German's face. That look of shock was still on his face and then the faint smile. When I tried to squeeze my eyes tight to make it go away, the face lingered, but this time it was *my* face. I felt tears roll down my cheeks.

"The second kill didn't bother me at all. But there are still times when I see that shocked face of the first man I ever killed," Sims says. There is a look of faraway pain on his own face, a pain not bleached much by time.

General Robin Olds (USAF retired), an ace himself, says of the whole concept of combat: "The fighter pilot is an attitude. It is aggressiveness—cockiness, if you like. Take self-confidence and add a big measure of rebelliousness. Add competitiveness to this and you've got a fighter pilot.

"There is a huge spark that drives him to be good, to be better than anybody ever was. And, you probably wouldn't believe it, but he is filled with discipline. He's full of it.

"You can't fully understand how this great vault of blue sky is your *home* unless you've been a fighter pilot," declares Olds with a passive but convincing voice. "I mean, if you're flying from point A to point B and simply winging around up there in the clouds, you're merely passing through the bargain basement of the great blue vault.

"For one thing, a fighter pilot has an uncontrollable urge to fly; hell, he doesn't see clouds above him or the ground below; he sees his environment. He *lives* in the sky. It's a heavenly stretch of tumbling, rolling waves. It's the valleys and mountains of his life. Below him, the green fields don't even relate to his environment. It's something he doesn't even belong to.

"There are a couple of other things about the fighter pilot," Olds says. "He is happy-go-lucky, he is filled to the brim with light-heartedness, and he's usually a pretty good drinker. They're convinced—every damn one of them—nothing on the face of the earth can defeat them.

"A good fighter pilot has to be willing to take risks. It must be inborn; you can't teach it. And independence is one of his main traits.

A lot of good fighter pilots could fly a 747, but they wouldn't like it. They're independent thinkers and have to react to individual situations.

"You have to have the basic skills; it is situational awareness coupled with personal characteristics—a mind that can grasp a situation or an event that is rapidly occurring, with an almost instinctive reaction to it. Some of the personal attributes have to be integrity and courage—military, I'm speaking of. In this case you have to be very fast-reacting and quick-thinking, with a sense of teamwork.

"I know, discipline is a strange word to use in connection with fighter pilots, because I've already said he has to be an independent thinker, but it's necessary. There are pilots and there are pilots, and they run the whole gamut of skill and capability, from one end of the spectrum to the other. Chuck Yeager and I could fly a 747 and do it well, but neither of us would like it a damn bit."

Glamorous Glen was the name given to the P-51 Mustang that Yeager flew in Europe to become an ace. "She always looked beautiful as I went out to the flight line," ponders Yeager. "And she was beautiful in the air. Hell, with a two thousand-mile range, the P-51 turned around the air war in Europe.

"But I'll tell you this," says the retired general, "she was a tricky airplane to fly when she was loaded with all that fuel and ammo. And here's something that most aircraft historians—the Americans, at least—don't talk about. She was vulnerable. I mean, you got hit in the radiator and you were going down. It was as simple as that.

"The flights were almost always the same. I'd crawl into the cockpit and look up at the sky, which you could have bet would be overcast. It gave me some confidence in knowing that there was a thick piece of armor plate protecting my back. But that was a shallow assumption because right behind that armor plate was a tank with eighty-five gallons of high-octane aviation gasoline.

"The cloud cover didn't bother us much," says Yeager, "because we flew at about thirty thousand feet most of the time, so we usually climbed out of it real quick. Sure, there were butterflies—there always are before a mission—but the one thing that ran through my mind was I hope to hell the sky is filled with German fighter planes and that my buddies and I shoot them all out of the sky. The urge was so strong that it pushed the butterflies right out of my stomach by the time the engine was started.

"Don't get me wrong," he adds quickly, as if one might think he had been frightened. "I wasn't scared. Hell, I was at my *peak*. And when I got up, there wasn't anything going through my mind except what I was up there to do—trying to shoot down airplanes and stay alive. There isn't any use worrying about the outcome because you have no control over it.

"But I do remember one thing: On my first mission, I remember thinking, Jesus, that's occupied territory down there. Damn, it looked evil as the flak rose to meet us. I could hear the drone of German radio on my own VHF radio, and I was sure they were zooming right in on *Glamorous Glen*. But we didn't encounter any German fighters that day, and I don't think any of us were too disappointed. It gave us sort of a trial run over the target. But that was unusual and never happened again."

Yeager credits eyesight as one of the things that enabled him to down thirteen German planes. "You have to have a baseline," he remarks, "such as outstanding eyesight and hand-to-eye coordination, not to mention stamina. One of the things that came out of World War Two, especially in Europe, was that eleven percent of the pilots involved in combat shot down ninety percent of the airplanes destroyed.

"And listen, they did some research and found out that every single one of the eleven percent was a rural kid," Yeager says with a knowing grin, because almost everyone knows he came from a rural area of West Virginia. "You know why these rural guys were better?" he asks, not waiting for an answer. "It's because they understood deflection shooting—you know, the lead—and they had excellent eyesight. Also, they were aggressive and self-sufficient. And that makes a damn good airplane driver.

"Nationality or color or sex doesn't have a damn thing to do with the capability of a pilot: it all boils down to what I just said. And experience. It teaches us all to stay alert, because complacency is the one thing that will kill you quickest if you're a fighter pilot."

Yeager is proud of his legendary eyesight. "It's as good at sixty-seven as it was when I was a kid," he says. "I still do stuff at Edwards [Air Force Base] that requires almost perfect vision. And, you know,

I got to fly a P-51 again a couple of years ago. It was the first time I had flown one in forty-four years. Damn, it gave me the feel of combat again. And, obviously, combat flying is the ultimate type of flying. There's nothing like it.

"I don't recommend combat flying to everybody because it tends to be fatal," he remarks, with the same dry wit that has characterizeed him as one of the last American heroes, a cowboy. A cowboy *gunfighter*, if you please.

But as in the Wild West, the good guy doesn't always win. As auto race driver and pilot Johnny Rutherford put it, "Some days you eat the bear, and some days the bear eats you."

Yeager's eighth mission was one of the times when the bear ate him, this time in the form of a Focke-Wulf 190. He recounts what happened after he bailed out of *Glamorous Glen*:

"I knew that if I opened the chute too soon the Krauts would strafe me going down, so I waited. I was free-falling from sixteen thousand feet and doubling my velocity every second. The worst part of it was that I knew I was coming down in France—occupied territory.

"My fingers inched toward the chute ring. Hold off! I told myself. Just a few seconds more. I could *smell* the fields below. It was time. I jerked the ripcord and I felt the heavy snap as the chute opened. As I rocked back and forth I could actually see the German soldiers below. I also could see the black smoke from the wreckage of my airplane.

"The dogfights were still raging above me and I could hear the screaming of the planes and the blasts of the gunfire. But there wasn't time to think about it; the trees were coming up fast at me, so I reached out and grabbed the top of a pine tree. I held on and the tree began to bend toward the ground. You won't believe it but I remembered doing the same thing as a kid in West Virginia, riding trees through the woods."

Yeager was officially "missing in action." It all had come about as a result of the 20-millimeter cannons of the Focke-Wulf. He was flying tail-end Charlie when the 190s attacked. Three of them dove on him and all he had time to say on the radio was "Cement Green leader, three bogies [enemy fighters] at five o'clock. Break right." And as he turned, the first 190 hammered him.

He had ducked when the explosion occurred and when he straightened up again, the engine was on fire and there was a huge hole in his wingtip. It all happened so fast that he didn't have much time to reflect on the situation at hand, so he unsnapped his safety harness, released the canopy and crawled to the edge of the cockpit. When the plane did a snap roll, Yeager fell out.

After tending to his shrapnel wounds, Yeager began to plan an escape route out of the Pyrenees and into Spain. He was confident because he knew how to trap and hunt and live off the land if necessary. He could survive in those woods for as long as it took. Yeager foraged French gardens at night for parsnips and potatoes and eventually was led to freedom by sympathetic Frenchmen.

"I was ordered back to the States," says Yeager, "but that's the last thing I wanted to do. I wanted to get back up there and get that bastard that had shot me down, but now I was going home. I appealed to the powers that be, and I'll be damned if a bomber pilot—who also didn't want to go home—and I didn't get an audience with General Eisenhower. As I stood there in front of him, I was so in awe, I could scarcely talk."

Eisenhower was the first to speak: "I just wanted to get a look at the two guys who think getting sent home is a raw deal," he said. The two pilots immediately began to plead their cases and the Supreme Allied Commander finally agreed to take up the matter with the War Department. It goes without saying that Ike was able to convince the guys in Washington that the two pilots should return to their units.

With Yeager back in the saddle, his gunfighter image returned quickly, and was most properly displayed on October 12, 1944. It was the day Yeager became the first "ace in a day" of the war.

"I credit a lot of it to luck," Yeager says, in a rare moment of humility. "We were headed for Bremen, and we had picked up two boxes of B-24s over Holland, so I sent two squadrons to escort them and I took my squadron a hundred miles ahead to look for bogies.

"We were over Steinhuder Lake when I spotted some tiny specks about fifty miles ahead of us. We called it combat vision. You focus out to infinity and back, searching one section of the sky at a time. I'll have to admit, not everybody has it; it's a gift that's hard to explain, and in our squadron only Andy [Bud Anderson, Yeager's closest friend] and I had it.

"The guys on the ground got so they simply took our word for it. 'If Yeager and Anderson say they're out there, they're out there,' they'd say. We were at twenty-eight thousand feet and I just kept leading our group toward the specks. We were closing fast so it didn't take long to turn the specks into twenty-two Messerschmitts. They were just sitting there, waiting for our bombers.

"I guess you could say they had become complacent, because they didn't see us coming out of the sun. We closed to about a thousand yards, and even if their leader did see us he must have thought we were some more 109s because they didn't even try to scramble out of our way. Damn! It was what I had dreamed of.

"I was the lead plane so I was the only one in firing range. I swept in behind their tail-end Charlie and let loose. The pilot suddenly broke left and slammed right into his wingman. I guess I scared the living hell out of him, and he just overreacted. I suppose there was a shortage not only of airplanes at that stage of the war but of good pilots as well. But damned if I didn't get two planes without hardly firing a shot.

"You know," Yeager says, "I wondered as I watched the two parachutes open what really was happening to all of the great German pilots. Had we gotten all of them? I mean, at that point we had a ten-to-one kill ratio. I later learned that some of their top aces had flown more than one thousand combat missions and had bailed out as many as twenty times. You talk about heroes.

"I didn't have any time to dwell on it, though, because the sky was full of diving, twisting airplanes. It was the damnedest dogfight you had ever seen. I blasted a 109 from not much more than five hundred yards, and I looked back and saw another one coming in on my tail, so, man, I pulled back on the throttle so damned hard I almost stalled it, and then I rolled over and came in behind and under him. I kicked the right rudder and fired. Simultaneously."

Yeager continues the account of that notable day with the same calmness as he surely had when he sat in the cockpit of the fierce Mustang, intent on fulfilling the dream of his buddies and him shooting them "all out of the sky":

"I was only about fifty feet from him when I started firing and I opened up the 109 just like it was a can of Spam. That was four. It was only a minute or so later when I got on a guy's tail in a steep dive and I blasted his tail; I pulled up at about one thousand feet, and he took it straight into the ground. We got eight of them before they hightailed it for home.

"That night in the officers club the other squadron leaders were madder'n hell because I didn't invite them in for the party that afternoon. They had to sit back there guarding the bombers and listen to the battle on the radio: 'Watch your tail. He's going down in flames.' And so on.

"I told them there just weren't enough Krauts to go around, but that didn't make it any better. Then they started ragging me about the two kills I got without putting a bullet in either one.

"Don Bochkay was the old man of the squadron [he was twenty-five], and on rare nights out in London, he carried a supply of silk panties and nylons, which he had his dad send him from California. He always hoped to trade them for, well, you know . . . So that night he presented me with a pair of silk panties; across the back was written: HILLBILLY PARACHUTE. DROP THESE WHEN YEAGER GETS ON YOUR TAIL."

The *Stars and Stripes* was kinder to Yeager. Their front-page headline read: FIVE KILLS VINDICATE IKE'S DECISION. And Yeager was recommended for a Silver Star. All in all, it had been the kind of day Chuck Yeager had prayed for.

In the Battle of Britain, the Mustangs and the Spitfires were the major weapons against the ravaging Luftwaffe. It was almost singularly up to them to stop the blitz. One of the RAF luminaries was Wing Commander Douglas Robert Stewart Bader. Bader had lost both legs in a crash, but he had gotten wooden ones, so he pestered the Air Ministry until, simply to get him off their backs, they agreed to let him go into combat again.

Bader and his squadron accumulated an outstanding record of kills, but the gutsy "Wooden Wonder" was finally shot down and captured by the Germans, who treated him with dignity because of his uncommon valor. They even got him new legs, which he promptly used to escape.

All sorts of tales drifted in from the Pacific Theater of Operations toward the end of the war. Airmen and airplanes were tired; morale was low because the war droned on. One such tale came out of New Guinea and concerned the use of P-47s to lift spirits. In more ways than one.

Harsh landings had begun to take a toll on the P-47 Thunderbolts, so pilots ferried them to Brisbane, Australia, for fresh ones. While they were there, they loaded up with a goodly supply of Foster's beer. The beer did wonders for the squadrons' morale, and would have done more if they hadn't had to drink it warm. *Hot*, in fact.

Then one enterprising pilot got an idea: "It's cooler than hell up there," he said as he pointed skyward. "If you get just the right altitude, you know, where it's below zero . . ." Enough said. The ground crew members already had a case packed in the wing slot where the cartridge belt normally was located, and off went the pilot. It goes without saying that that night in the officers club was one of the most festive in weeks. There was mile-high beer, cold and frothy.

After that, there was a plane or two in the air at all times, "frosting the Foster's" as they called it. They had to be careful, of course, because there was no armament on the P-47, and an attack by a Japanese fighter would have resulted in, at best, a foamy mess and a lot of broken glass. The pilots were not as concerned for their hides as they were for their suds.

And it put an end to drop-it-in landings. It was easy to tell a beer-laden plane by the way it sat down, as if it were an English sparrow landing on a tight wire. Most of the pilots could land the big combat aircraft with all the finesse of a ballerina.

But for every sort of zany antic, there were hundreds of deadly serious missions. Navy Captain David McCampbell flew his Hellcat with such skill that he became the Navy's top ace. McCampbell and his men would act as decoys, flying in low to draw flak so that the dive bombers could sneak in and deliver their single bomb loads. It became the modern-day equivalent of "running the gauntlet."

By the time the bombing raids were completed, the Japanese fighters had scrambled, so they attacked the Hellcats. "It made for a very long day," McCampbell remembers.

"Carrier pilots were a combination of responsibility, independence, and courage," says Tommy Burns, who flew an F4U Corsair from the deck of the *Hornet* in the late stages of the war in the South Pacific. "The landings were always on the brink of disaster—really, they were controlled crashes—but the guys who were flying those planes were ones who could think well on their feet.

"We all had enough little boy in us that we couldn't wait to get out there and blast someone; hell, it was the ultimate game of cowboys and Indians. But I'll have to admit that I wasn't all that gung ho when I got ready for my first carrier landing. I didn't sleep a damn wink the night before, and when I got up at five I got sweaty palms and my heart was pounding. By the time I got to the airplane, my stomach was in knots.

"Unless you've done it, you have no idea how small that damn carrier looks the first time you spot it—hell, *every* time. But all of a sudden I was about to touch down. You have to realize that a carrier landing is not like most other landings; for one thing, your runway— the deck—is bobbing and weaving like a good welterweight; for another, you're at full power and in a stall. You have to be at power, otherwise if you miss the hook, you need the power to get that thing back in the air. Quick.

"As it turned out, I *needed* the power. I missed the hook. I missed all four hooks. So I went around again, and this time when it caught, it felt like I had hit the superstructure. I mean, that damn plane stopped so fast that it felt like the whole rear of the fuselage must have been ripped off. It wasn't, of course, but that's what it felt like. I had gone from one hundred knots to zero in a hundred yards."

As World War II drew to a close, the Luftwaffe had one surprise left in its tattered bag of tricks—the Messerschmitt 262, the first jet fighter.

The air-war seesaw had balanced back and forth: First the 109s and 190s ruled the air, then along came the Mustang and tipped the board back toward the Allied side. But when the 262 appeared, it left them all standing with their collective mouths agape, as one might imagine. But there were problems, as there are with most new concepts.

Simply finding a position from which to shoot at the Mustangs was difficult because of the tremendous speed of the new craft. It was difficult to fly the 262 at slower speed, so half the time they zinged right on by the slower Mustangs without firing a shot. At least, without firing accurately.

The engines, which had been hastily thrown together in an attempt to save a badly sagging cause, had a scrap life of about twenty-five hours, but the Germans, who had lost the superiority of the air by then and had taken a dispassionate view of the entire war, probably felt "Why should we worry about the life of the engine when the pilot probably won't last any longer than that anyway?"

Several of the 262s were captured after the war and tested, because Allied and Axis powers alike knew full well that the curtain had risen on a new concept of aviation—the jet-propelled airplane. Although somewhat rudimentary, the Messerschmitt 262 led the way for future generations of aircraft designers. And pilots.

"Anyone who transitions from reciprocal engines to jets is in for a big surprise," says Jack Moore, who did just that in the days following World War II. "The airplane was way ahead of me for the first two or three hours. Things were happening so damn much faster and I was porpoising the airplane because the controls are so sensitive.

"It was ready to land and my mind was still on the downwind leg. Hell, I could have read a book coming in on final in the C-47s I had been flying right after the war. But once you catch on and once you get used to the sensitivity of the controls, it's wonderful. It's so smooth and responsive. The B-17 was like flying a truck; you came back from a mission and you were dog-tired. I mean, your ass was dragging. The mission usually lasted from five to ten hours, and you were flying in formation almost all the way and, I'll tell you, I was whipped."

The days of manhandling a fighter plane were gone. And, after the Korean conflict in particular, there would never again be the nose-to-nose and wing-to-wing dogfights of yesterwars. The knights of the air faded into the past. Their ranks were replenished with a new crop of pilots, and the new kids on the tarmac began to learn as much about electronics as they did about ailerons and vertical stabilizers.

One of the most important jobs within the aviation fraternity was created—the test pilot. With the greatly increased speeds came even greater dangers, not just pilot reaction times, but airframe integrity and a host of other newfound problems.

One of the first heroes in the test ranks was Chuck Yeager, who was not only to test the Bell X-1, but was expected to fly it supersonic. What would happen when a plane flew through the sound barrier? Would it disintegrate or melt from the intense heat? It was as if Magellan were sailing toward the end of the earth.

"We didn't consider ourselves heroes," says Yeager. "Hell, if I didn't do it, somebody else would have. But on the day it all happened,

I shouldn't even have been flying. I had had a horse accident the day before and I was beat all to hell; I had some broken ribs and a shoulder that felt like it had been transplanted, but everything was all set so I went on over there and said, 'Okay, y'all, let's go.' "

The date was October 14, 1947. Because of its small fuel load, the X-1 had been transported aloft below the bomb bay of a B-29. At last, the goal was the sound barrier.

"We were in a vast gray area where there was no test data, no wind tunnel test. Nothing," comments Yeager. "But the damn sound barrier had restricted us to no end, so it had to be done. Once we broke it, we all knew that it would open up the universe for everyone. I just wish I had been more sure what would happen when we went through that previously unknown curtain.

"I climbed down through the bomb bay and dropped into the plane. I buckled up, closed the door and I waited, not having any idea what was going to happen next because there had been so many screwups; there had been fires, and igniters that didn't work, you name it. I waited. Then I heard the countdown: 'Five, four, three, two, one.' I flipped the switch, the plane dropped down out of the bomb bay, and then it blasted off. The airplane buffeted and bucked and then when the needle got close to Mach One, it smoothed out."

Yeager smiles faintly and continues: "All of a sudden it was there. The needle pointed to Mach One. I was supersonic. After all the worry about what was going to happen, it was sort of a letdown that the damn thing *didn't* disintegrate. And, hell, I was ready. My combat experience had made me a very disciplined pilot and I had learned to control my emotions, so it didn't make any difference to me if the X-1 blew into a million pieces, because I really didn't have any control over it. You learn that in combat."

Scott Crossfield, who in later years did most of the tests on the X-15, characterized the offhand attitude of the test pilot when asked how he felt about the prospects of going Mach Seven. "Well," he said, "the guys on the ground are the smart ones; you get into the airplane, and they get into a blockhouse. They really know how to build up your confidence."

Test pilots such as Yeager and Crossfield and scores of others blazed yet another aerial path for those who would follow. Unknowingly they were heading aviation literally toward the stars.

"With jets came the accurate, precision, light-as-a-feather-touch flying," says Robin Olds, who would, about twenty years later, fight in the skies over Vietnam. "The heavy-handed flying of old was gone. Chuck Yeager, for example, was the best because he had the best eyes in his squadron, but with the new technology, it's possible that he would have been defeated even before he *saw* his enemy."

It was a whole new ball game.

A lot of World War II pilots stayed in the service after the war, and when they first flew the jets, they were concerned with the greatly accelerated speeds. They remembered the 262 and how those early jets whizzed past their opponents, often without a chance to fire a shot at their plodding prey. But not Olds. "I looked on it as another challenge," he says. "After all, what the hell's the difference if you're going six hundred and the other guy is going six hundred? Zero. It's all relative.

"At first they flew the F-86s in Nam and I'll be damned if they weren't as good in dogfights as the Mustang, and I didn't think I would ever see a plane that good. And then our squadron got the first thirty-five F-86a-ls. I'll tell you right now, the plane wasn't built well. We had all sorts of problems with it—rudder control, you name it. Parts fell off the damn things all the time and nearly every landing was a crisis.

"We crashed twenty of the first thirty-five. But they did improve it and once more we could outfly the MiGs. When the 86 was right again it was a good airplane; it would maneuver like hell. And then we got the F-4 and it was even better. How's this for a record: Between the 86s and the 4s, we shot down more than eight hundred of theirs and they only got seventy-eight of ours.

"It got more exciting with each war," the former ace mentions. "I mean, the planes were going faster than hell when I was flying a Mustang, but by the time I got to Nam, it scared the piss out of a lot of guys just to fly the damn jets at full speed. Let alone do it in combat.

"For one thing, they were so fast that decisions almost had to be instinctive. There simply wasn't time to *think* about what to do. You did it and then hoped to hell it was right.

"I had always wanted to be a wing commander and with Vietnam I got the chance," says Olds. "When I first took over my wing, the big talk wasn't about the MiGs, but about the SAMs—the surface-to-air missiles. I'd seen enemy planes before, but those damn SAMs were something else. When I saw my first one, there were a few seconds there of sheer panic, because that's a most impressive sight to see that thing coming at you. You feel like a fish about to be harpooned. There's something terribly personal about the SAM; it means to kill you, and I'll tell you right now, it rearranges your priorities."

There were many times when the missiles altered a mission. After a pilot had dodged a couple dozen of them, he might find himself right down on the deck, which is definitely nowhere to be over Vietnam.

"We had been told to keep our eyes on them and not to make any evasive move too soon, because they were heat-seeking and they, too, would correct, so I waited until it was almost on me and then I rolled to the right and it went on by," Olds reflects. "It was awe-inspiring.

"I'd wake up in the middle of the night, down at the foot of the bed, fighting the covers to get away from the SAMs I was dreaming about," he says. "Then I found out that Scotch was the only way to get a good night's sleep. You do a lot of drinking. If you didn't, you couldn't sleep at all, because all these things were going through your head. Whether they were aggressive thoughts or not, they were so strong you couldn't sleep. So about three belts of Scotch, sleep like a baby, and then up in six hours and ready to go again. It worked wonders."

The Air Force had sent Olds to Vietnam primarily to build up the morale in a wing that was having serious problems in the *esprit de corps* department. "You know what to do," he was told. "Perk those guys up."

As it turned out, Robin Olds *did* know what to do. On one of the first missions, Olds was in the pilot's seat of a tandem-mounted fighter jet assigned to a strafing mission. A less than gung ho lieutenant was in the seat behind him. As Olds deftly guided the fighter over a railyard, dodging antiaircraft fire on the way in and out, he sang a spirited song into the intercom. On the way back around, he out-maneuvered a SAM and got set up to go in again. The flak was particularly heavy this time, and the jet bobbed and weaved in the air like Sugar Ray Robinson setting up an opponent for the kill. It was like flying directly into the hub of hell. Suspecting that the young, white-knuckled pilot would much rather have been back at the base, and thinking of his prime objective, Olds spoke into the intercom:

"Can you believe they're *paying* us for this?" he asked. There was no answer from his bewildered companion. But that evening as Olds walked into the officers club for his sleeping potion, he saw the young pilot standing at the end of the bar. He was surrounded by half a dozen other pilots of the wing to which Olds had been assigned, and the flat-handed, swooping gestures indicated he was recreating the day's happenings to the others. As Olds neared the group he overheard the young pilot as he said, ". . . and do you know what that son of a bitch said when we got to the railyard?"

His plan was working.

"The truth is," Olds declares, "you never do get used to the SAMs; I had about two hundred fifty shot at me and the last one was as inspiring as the first. Sure, I got cagey, and I was able to wait longer and longer, but I never got overconfident. I mean, if you're one or two seconds too slow, you've had the schnitzel.

"In Nam I did the same thing I did in World War Two, I lived one day at a time. But back then I was very young, tremendously eager, and I knew I was a good pilot. There were times when I was very excited—times when I might have a momentary tightening of the stomach muscles, constriction of the throat, or whatever. But things happened so quickly and I was so damn busy coping that I really didn't have time to sit there and be afraid. Fear came at night, when I was alone and dropping off to sleep, and that takes on a more— to use a word I'm not sure of—*mordant*—anyway, a deeper thing of dread. And, if you let it, this builds and builds and builds.

"I had a roommate who was that way and sure enough, it happened: He was killed. So I was determined not to let myself think things like that. I was shot at and missed and shot at and hit quite a bit in World War Two. There were wild times; like getting hit very, very solidly strafing an airfield. Pieces of my plane were flying off and I was knocked upside down right above the ground, going like the hammers of hell, and I managed to extricate myself and roll out to try to get away and damned if I wasn't slammed again. I knew what was going on—I didn't have time to be frightened right then— but by God, they certainly got my attention.

"Anybody who doesn't have fear is an idiot," Olds says, in an easy, convincing voice. "It's just that you must make the fear work for you. Hell, when somebody shot at me, it made me madder than hell, and all I wanted to do was shoot back."

Lieutenant General Frank Petersen retired from the Marine Corps in 1988, the thirty-sixth man in history to become the Gray Eagle, the active-duty naval aviator with the longest term of service, longer than any other pilot in either the Navy or the Marine Corps.

When Petersen went into the Corps in 1950, he couldn't even ride in the front of the bus from the Pensacola Naval Air Base into town. As a black man he couldn't drink from the same water fountain as whites. But when he learned that the U.S. armed forces had been desegregated, he decided to give the Marines a try. Flying an airplane was the farthest thing from his mind. In fact, the death of a pilot he didn't even know inspired him into climbing into a cockpit.

Ensign Jesse Brown had been the Navy's first black aviator and had won great praise, but his luck ran out in the skies over Korea when a North Korean fighter filled Brown's F4U Corsair with bullets. His plane crashed but Brown survived, although he was trapped inside. So well-liked was the black aviator that his wingman actually landed his own Corsair and tried valiantly to free him. It was futile.

Petersen, who had chosen a career as an electronics technician in the Navy, immediately decided he would pick up the mantle flung down by Brown. When he found out there had never been a black aviator in the history of the Marine Corps, he was sure this was for him.

And he proved it. He went on to win the Distinguished Flying Cross, the Air Medal, the Navy Commendation Medal, and the Purple Heart.

The Purple Heart came when his F-4 Phantom was hit over North Vietnam in 1968. He was a lieutenant colonel at the time and had been leading a squadron. With one engine shot away while over enemy territory, Petersen was "concerned," as he puts it. But he managed to get the airplane back over safe territory before he and his backseat man bailed out.

"Anybody who says he isn't afraid at times in combat is an idiot," he exclaims. "Braggadocio and swagger just do not exist in a true combat outfit."

Asked what his worst combat mission was, Petersen once replied: "The last one and the next one."

Jon McBride was an astronaut, but, as did most of the NASA pilots, he reached that lofty pinnacle through the school of hard knocks as a Navy pilot. Twenty years after the fact, he wonders "what the hell we were doing there."

"During the whole time we were over Nam, I never saw so many air-to-air missiles and air-to-air artillery," he says. "The sky was lit up. On my first mission, I thought, Damn, this is a great way to break a guy in.

"Back then I was willing to give my life for my country, and I saw a lot of my buddies do it. Now I have my doubts, because I believe my air wing alone [two fighter and two attack squadrons aboard the USS *Saratoga*], if given the opportunity, could have gone in there and defeated the North Vietnamese. Instead, we had to fly around Haiphong Harbor and watch the ships offload the missiles that eventually were going to be shot at us."

Visible indignation begins to well up within McBride's sturdy frame. He pokes holes in the air with his finger as he talks: "Those were the rules. Hell, we couldn't hit their air fields; we couldn't shoot down their MiGs except at certain points; we had to go down and play around in the air and hope they came over to where we could shoot at them.

"I've had as many as six or seven MiGs on my screen at one time, and I couldn't shoot at a damn one of them," he asserts. "We avoided the ships and dams and just about everything that would have hurt them—the strategic targets. Hell, no, we went out and bombed a wooden bridge instead, something they could build back in two days.

"We were ready to give our lives, but we were bombing wooden bridges."

Despite the frustration McBride and his fellow pilots experienced, the action was just as great as men had faced in any previous wars. And so were the concerns. "A pilot who says he doesn't have a little fear probably isn't flying his plane to its maximum," McBride says, "because a good pilot is made up of a little bit of fear, a little bit of exhilaration, a little bit of determination, and a lot of guts and God-given talent. And, you know, it really pisses you off when you get up every morning thinking this could be it; I might not be coming back to the ship, and then you go out and let people shoot at you. Sure, there's fear.

"By the time they get your plane refueled and you go through all of the preparations, the fear is gone; it has become secondary, and the foremost thing in your mind is going out there and getting the job done. Such as it is. I just loved flying that plane and it wasn't until I got back to the ship each time that I realized I had made it through one more. So it becomes a series of situations that begin with anxiety and end with exhilaration.

"Combat is a mix of emotions—fear, euphoria, and satisfaction—one of the few professions where you get a mix of everything," McBride declares. "It's hours and hours of anticipation, culminated by a few minutes of exhilaration—a rush.

"Usually our missions were about an hour and a half; we launched one group and then when we were ready to come back, another group was launched. This went on around the clock. Flight crews generally live right below flight deck, so there's always slamming and banging. It's a very intense existence, one you never get far away from. You never really get relaxed."

McBride flew sixty-four missions before the war ended.

With the advent of jet air speeds came another problem that not too many pilots had ever had to face—G forces. It was an invisible nemesis that often rendered them unconscious and left the plane to fly itself, usually into the ground. The very nature of the phenomenon led to its name, with the "G" appropriately coming from gravity.

If there is no air resistance, a coin dropped from the top of the World Trade Center in New York City (the tallest being 1,710 feet at the top of the antenna) would fall thirty-two feet per second faster than it had one second before. Its acceleration, in other words, would be thirty-two feet per second per second. This represents one G, or the extent of velocity produced by the earth's gravity.

The weight experienced by a pilot in a sudden change of direction can also be felt by the airplane. Additional Gs mean that the airframe feels more weight, and if the wings are overloaded, they break off. Fortunately, air resistance slows the airplane in a turn and causes the Gs to drop. By the same token, pilots can level off to reduce Gs. But, if not properly combatted, these forces can be fatal.

G-induced loss of consciousness, called G-LOC by the military, is combatted in such planes as the F-16 by a computerized "G inhibitor," which keeps the airplane from exceeding nine Gs in any maneuver.

Acceleration forces defy the cardiovascular system and increase pressure against the blood traveling from the heart to the eyes and brain. The weight of blood is increased by every G, so the heart has to work harder to circulate it.

"A pilot can help keep the blood in his brain by performing a sort of 'grunt' maneuver," says former astronaut Jon McBride. "By exhaling heavily without letting any air escape and tensing the stomach muscles as if you were going to the bathroom, you can nearly double your tolerance to G forces. This, combined with anti-G suits, which squeeze the legs and stomach in a corset-like effect, prevents the blood from pooling and thereby further increases resistance to G forces."

The man singularly most associated with G loads is Colonel John Paul Stapp (USAF Retired), who rode the G-force vehicle, the Air Force rocket-powered sled, some thirty times in the mid-1950s and, along the way, suffered several cracked and broken bones, as well as retinal hemorrhages. Undaunted, Stapp, on December 10, 1954, reached maximum velocity as the sled, powered by nine rockets with a combined thrust of forty thousand pounds, was catapulted 2,800 feet in less than five seconds. He reached 632 miles per hour; the extraordinary force propelled him along at nineteen Gs. In four-plus seconds Stapp became the fastest man on earth. He had worn only a protective helmet and a rubber block in his mouth to prevent the force from knocking out his teeth. In comparing Stapp's rocket ride with more common forces inducing Gs, a roller-coaster ride produces between three and four Gs in its most violent maneuvers, and a race-car driver experiences less than one G in turns.

"In the first second everything quickly blurred," emphasizes Stapp. "And then I couldn't see anything and it felt as if my eyes were being pulled out of my head. My vision went through a series of color changes, from yellows through reds. The pain in my eyes and head was almost unbearable. When it was over, I couldn't see anything for a several minutes."

Doctors quickly examined Stapp and found that his eyes were filled with blood and tiny hemorrhages; blood blisters were spread across his face and shoulders from the tremendous velocity and from the blasting of the sand. After three days in the hospital, Stapp was released with little more than two black eyes for his heroic efforts. And a profound respect for speed.

There is another side of flying in combat; one where speedy jets and maneuverability and dogfights never enter the conversation—the helicopter pilot.

Of these daring men who fly into combat zones with a lot of faith and even more skill—not to mention a ton of courage—perhaps the most fearless were the Medevac pilots, who flew directly through enemy gunfire of all types, for all practical purposes unarmed, landing in a small clearing to pick up the wounded and then hightailing it out of there.

Robert Brady, who is now a lawyer in Washington, Pennsylvania, became a Medevac pilot before his nineteenth birthday. Why did he chose such a bold profession? "Truthfully, I didn't have an education, so I couldn't fly in the Navy or the Air Force," he says. "It's that simple."

"I started taking flight lessons when I was fifteen and I wanted to fly in combat from the first day, so it was a matter of *where* I could do that in the Vietnam era. The *only* place I could go was to the Army, and the only thing I could fly was a helicopter. You see, the big thing that made a helicopter pilot different then was that we were much younger. I was eighteen."

Brady had never been in a helicopter in his life, so he took his first ride in one after he entered flight school in 1968. At that time it was a one-year program; the students went through five or six months of primary training. They were taught how to fly the aircraft, and then they went into advanced tactical, in which they worked on instrument flying. For the next six months, they learned the tactics they would later use in the jungle battlefields.

Virtually all of the pilots at that point were on direct orders to Nam, so Brady was sent directly from flight school to Vietnam.

The Medevac training was different from the other types of flight instruction because they didn't do any type of formation flying or multi-ship operations. They were always alone. But the big difference was that they had to learn landings. Anywhere. If there wasn't a place to land, they were told to "make a place."

Brady survived more than seven hundred missions, retrieving three thousand patients, so the training must have worked.

"On my third mission," says Brady, "things began to happen. Fast. We were on our way to make a pickup and I saw a whole line of 'black pajamas' in the trees as we were going in. Hell, I had no idea who they were. It never occurred to me for a second that they might be North Vietnamese.

"I didn't bother telling anybody else in the helicopter what I had seen; I don't know why, it just didn't occur to me, but when we came out of there, they shot the hell out of our ship. There were bullets flying everywhere; we were all covered with shrapnel from the sheet metal of the fuselage where the small arms fire hit it. That was my indoctrination, and I remember coming out of there thinking this is going to be a long year.

"You were called a 'cherry' until you were hit, so it didn't take me long to 'lose my cherry,'" Brady says, with an elfish grin.

Another thing that differentiated Medevac flying from the rest, even the other helicopters, was the conditions in which it was done— mostly at night or in extremely bad weather.

"Troops usually adjusted mentally to war very quickly," Brady explains. "But not helicopter pilots, at least not in Medevac. The conditions took care of that; it's extremely difficult to adjust to terrible weather and flying at night with no lights to guide you. It was some- thing I never adjusted to. I was always scared. *Always*.

"We were flying five or six feet off the tops of trees in pouring- down rain, knowing that a mountain may appear in front of us in any second. That keeps your mind on what you're doing."

Finding the destination at night was not as difficult as one might imagine. "Vietnam was so dark; it's not like flying in the States, where you see lights everyplace you look out. When you flew out of the compounds of Nam," Brady says, "it was absolutely black. We went out in an area we were familiar with—the northernmost portion of Nam, right up next to the DMZ and down through Danang—and it's a good thing we knew something about it, because you couldn't see your hand in front of your face.

"We got coordinates from the troops when they called for Medevac, so we had a general idea where we were going, but still we had to pinpoint the location. It usually was easy. When they heard us coming, one of the ground troops took a helmet, turned it upside down, and held a lighted match inside it. It was like a beacon. You'd be surprised how far you could see it in the total darkness.

"We made our approach into the matchlight, which, of course, didn't show out to the side. They did it that way so that if there were enemy troops around, they couldn't see it."

But at times they *did* see it. During his year in the jungle, Brady had several helicopters shot out from under him. When that happened he got an extra day off.

The most dangerous missions they faced were when there was no place to land, as in the midst of the jungle. In such cases, they dropped what was called a "jungle penetrator," which is a hoist with a little bullet chair that drops down through the trees, breaking the branches at it goes. The troops on the ground strapped the patient on the bullet chair and he was hoisted up to the helicopter.

"It was extremely dangerous," Brady pointed out, "because here we were, hovering up there about a hundred feet above the ground, not being able to move, so if we started taking fire, we had to *sit* there. I lost a couple of helicopters that way. They shot our tail rotor off on one occasion; when that happens there is no recovery. You have to crash.

"I guess I was lucky, but I was always able to walk out of the jungle to freedom. On one flight, I was running low level down a river stream in Laos, picking up for special forces; of course, we didn't have troops in Laos at that time," he says in a way that makes it clear he knew otherwise. "But we went in low and they had antiaircraft set up on both sides of the river and they literally blew us out of the air. We spent a few days out in the woods on that one."

The Medevacs had no assault or defensive capability at all, with the inadequate exception of one M-16 and some side arms. The best tool they had was their ability to get in and get out.

"We had several tactical approaches; at times we flew in as low as we possibly could, hiding behind trees or anything we could put between us and the enemy. At other times we came in at three thousand feet so that we were out of small arms range. The trick then was to get the helicopter to the ground as quickly as it would fly. We literally *dropped* it out of the sky."

The Medevac helicopters usually flew a thirty- to forty-minute roundtrip flight, mostly back to field hospitals or M.A.S.H. units.

"The doctors were truly out in jungle compounds. It wasn't the best of jobs for a doctor," Brady says understatedly. "They didn't even have nurses there. Or golf courses.

"It wasn't at all like what you see on television."

As for the Vietnam protest so many people take cover in, Brady has a thought on that, too: "I'll bet if you took a poll of the helicopter pilots who were there, very few would have any complaints at all."

Chapter Five

*There was little laughter aboard the presidental airplane
after Watergate.*

— RALPH ALBERTAZZIE, PILOT, AIR FORCE ONE

ollowing a war, a goodly amount of vaudevillian traits
routinely surface as the combatants return to mundane life
back home. In World War I, dogfights spurred aviators to
postwar displays of courage and craziness, with wrong-
way flights and barnstorming and cow pasture thrill shows. Carrier
pilots and drivers of other superfast airplanes in World War II and
literally thousands of intrepid warriors took to airstrips everywhere,
rigorously looking for more excitement. There were no more Messerschmitts or Zeros at which to shoot; there were no railyards to
strafe, and assuredly no more playing mother hen to droves of bombers. As their predecessors of two decades before had done, the pilot
veterans of World War II strove for the bizarre. Only planes change;
pilots don't.

Stunt pilots emerged from the woodwork after the second war. Air
shows were more popular because of the faster planes and daring men
who flew them. The spectators had never seen anything like it. But
the pilots—being pilots—felt that the shows leaned toward the hum-
drum. It was a long step down from the aerial battles they had encountered in Europe and the South Pacific. So they became even more

inventive and more plucky. To the horror of thousands, many of these pilots crashed to their deaths in their futile effort to resume life on the brink of disaster.

The motion picture industry was a magnet for many of the former military pilots, as film after film about the glorious victory over Axis powers rolled from the cameras of Hollywood. Movies gave an opportunity to relive the glorious days of battle, even though it was a screenwriter's impression and the bullets weren't real. Still, once more they were heroes.

Other daring pilots, who hadn't seen combat, or hadn't even been in the military, watched in awe at the aerial feats, and then the ones with true grit and talent took to the air and emulated the skillful and zany antics. Probably the best of this group of make-believe aces was Art Scholl.

When Scholl performed in his Pennzoil Chipmunk, a tiny experimental plane he designed himself, he was a star. He became an accomplished competition aerobatic pilot who represented the United States all over the world. And the word in Hollywood whenever an aerial stunt was to be choreographed for a film production or a TV commercial was "Get Art Scholl."

At one time or another Scholl had been a trumpet player, a successful Ph.D candidate, and a powerboat racer. In his familiar role aloft, he had been pilot-in-command of 182 different types of craft, from a 1908 Curtiss Pusher to a modern fighter jet, with time logged in helicopters, gliders, ultralights, balloons, and jumbo jets. Altogether he logged fourteen thousand hours in more than thirty years of flight, dating back to high school days when he washed planes and gassed them to earn enough money to take flying lessons.

Scholl didn't start out to be a stunt pilot, but it might have been surprising if he hadn't ended up that way. Graduating from high school in Brown Deer, Wisconsin, he moved to California to enroll in engineering at Northrop Institute. During a free day of roaming on his motorcycle, Scholl rode out to Mount San Antonio College in Walnut, just as the school chimes were echoing off the hillsides surrounding the campus. The setting was too captivating for a boy from the rolling country of Wisconsin to resist—he dropped out of Northrop and enrolled at Mount SAC.

There Scholl earned his degree in aeronautics to add to his pilot's license that already rated him to fly commercially and to teach flying. His first job out of college was at the China Lake Naval Ordnance Test Center. But a desk job was not for a guy who was happiest when doing a Cuban Eight or a Hammerhead Stall. He left China Lake and enrolled at San Jose State College where he obtained a B.S. degree in aeronautics, following that with an M.S. and a Ph.D.

"At that point, Art apparently decided he had enough time in the classroom and wanted more time in the cockpit," says longtime friend and publicist Deke Houlgate. "He participated in his first air show, flying an 85-horsepower Swift in a series of schoolboy maneuvers."

"I think I did a roll, a loop, and a Cuban Eight," Scholl recalled one time. "I thought nobody did all of that. I was wrong, of course, but it did get my blood pumping."

Scholl began performing aerial acts for spectators in the early 1960s, but he saw career possibilities when Hollywood's most respected stunt pilots at the time, Frank Tallman and Paul Mantz, employed him to do some movie work. By the time Mantz and Tallman died, Scholl had built a track record for filmmaking gags that vaulted him into the top spot.

For example, an early film stunt called for him to chase an automobile with his airplane, bouncing a wheel on the top of the car until it stuck in the roof. Well, not really. The caved-in roof with a wheel stuck in it was to be shown by camera trickery. But when Scholl crashed through the roof for real, his wheel really did get stuck, and there he was, pasted to the car as it sped down an Arizona highway, not completely under control.

"The stunt driver was trying to hold his course, straight down the highway, and I was trying to get loose," Scholl said. "There were wires on both sides of the road and I didn't know whether I was going to get loose or not. Or where I was going to go if I *did* get loose."

But he did rock the plane loose and was able to pull up over the wires, and another movie gag tragedy was avoided. It didn't phase him. Art Scholl moved on to the next movie.

For "Spencer's Pilots," a television series, Scholl was to land on a mesa to rescue a dying man for a trip to the hospital. On takeoff he was to crash through a set of trees made of balsa wood, dive down a five hundred-foot cliff, and just barely clear the ground below, making it appear that he struggled to keep the damaged plane in the air.

"Duck soup," Scholl told the director.

There were cameras above (in a helicopter), to the side, and down below at the bottom of the cliff. What Scholl didn't know was that the director had ordered the main cameramen not to start their cameras until he gave the word. Then he promptly forgot to give the word.

Scholl's takeoff was perfect. He sliced through the fake forest, feathered one engine, and dived down the cliff for a beautiful pullout. Dirt, leaves, and branches hung on his fuselage. It would have made great footage.

But the camera jammed in the helicopter, there was too much dust to see anything from the side, and the crew down the cliff was still awaiting the order to start shooting. With the spirit of the true stunt pilot, Scholl flew around a while and watched the special effects people begin to build another set of trees.

"All in a day's work," he said later. "And besides, they had to pay me double." But, as it turned out, he had to work for his money. The special effects people, short on balsa wood, built the trees out of two-by-fours, so when Scholl hit them, they really did knock the engine out. The other engine was damaged and only operating at 80-percent efficiency. "But I did what I was supposed to and then headed for Van Nuys, where I was supposed to land. I called Burbank approach control to tell them the problem. A week before, a DC-7 had landed on the golf course next to Van Nuys Airport, so I guess everybody panicked. When I touched down, I didn't know Los Angeles had that many firemen."

But Scholl was not without logic. Once he drew the line when a director proposed that he land a DC-3 on the roof of a speeding truck for an episode in a TV series. He persuaded the director to change the script to make the stunt feasible. Instead, he landed a Piper Cub on a moving eighteen-wheel truck. It was just as spectacular and a whole lot safer.

Spectacular as some of these stunts were, they weren't Scholl's biggest concern. "Weather is a pilot's biggest worry," he said. "One time while I was flying to Rockingham, North Carolina, the weather closed in before I could select an airport to land, so I started following an expressway to the next town.

"There was no traffic so I decided the safest thing to do was land," Scholl said. "I throttled back and began to glide in when suddenly out of the fog came a clear view of traffic lights. I wasn't on the expressway anymore, I was right downtown.

"I climbed to seven hundred feet and called the center. Every place in the area was zero-zero [no visibility or ceiling]. They took me to Charlotte where I could make a precision instrument landing. It was getting very dark when approach control positioned me for a radar approach.

"All the way down they asked me if I could see the runway yet. I kept saying, 'Negative.' There was not enough fuel for a missed approach. They told me I was at fifty feet, then twenty-five. I was still telling them, 'I can't see the runway,' and then I felt my wheels touch down. It was a good feeling," Scholl said in a classic but typical display of understatement.

Scholl would often tell young fliers that even though the skies were clear it was important to be vigilant, because fog sometimes sneaks up behind an airplane. One day, while flying between Pensacola, Florida, and Mobile, Alabama, it happened. A trailing fog bank suddenly engulfed Scholl's craft. He couldn't land on the interstate right below, because it was the five o'clock traffic hour.

There was another problem. Solar panels that were supposed to be charging the batteries weren't working because of the overcast conditions, and the batteries were being drained. He called the nearest control tower, but he wasn't able to tell them where he was. "See if you can find a landmark," the air controller said. Scholl, who was right over a town, banked the airplane and looked at a building. He read the name on its side to the tower.

"Simple," the guy said. "Just go down two more traffic lights, make a right, and it'll bring you right to the airport." Scholl did as he was told and within minutes, he saw the taxiway. "I could have stopped for a hamburger along the way," he said, "because I was so low I could see every store."

Even when flying is a familiar routine, it has its inherent dangers, Art Scholl advised. He always admonished his students to "stay calm, but be alert."

It was advice he always followed. But there are "unpredictable" things that can happen, even to a pilot of the stature of Art Scholl.

Top Gun was to be a box office smash for young actor Tom Cruise. It also was to be one of Art Scholl's greatest challenges—not that he hadn't had many, because the list and intensity of his aerial gags was unsurpassed. To the producers and director and camera crews it was a tough act; to Scholl it was another bowl of duck soup.

Scholl was vigilant. As always. The Pitts Special he was flying, with the camera mounted in the front cockpit so that it could simulate some of the footage of a modern dogfight, had always been a reliable plane. That day, for reasons that nobody ever will know, it was not responsive.

"Art radioed shortly after he had begun a dive that he 'had a problem,' in his usual calm voice," says Deke Houlgate. "At fifteen hundred feet, he said 'I've got a real problem.' It was just what those of us who knew him would have expected. His last words were as calm as if he were taxiing into the terminal and requesting a place to park his plane."

He had been calm and he had been alert, the two things he had always told his students.

Scholl's plane, with the unknown problem, dove straight into the ocean at terminal velocity. There was nothing left but a small oily splotch on the sea, which slowly vanished. The business of stunt flying had lost its most spectacular star.

Art Scholl had no time to talk with the observer plane to describe the problem; he had no time to relive his life as the screenwriters on the ground would have had him do had it been a film version of the incident. Assuredly he was doing everything he could to correct it. Right to the very end.

And when the end came, Art Scholl more than likely realized that the odds had caught up with him, as they had with so many of his predecessors in stunt flying. And just as surely he accepted his fate with the same sanguine attitude he had every other time there had been a problem.

It's one of the characteristics of pilots who do daring things.

One of the airplane's most perilous if rewarding uses was developed by the bush pilots. It all began in the early days of flying, as prospectors and fur trappers and hunters began to settle in the most remote areas of the world, where they could best practice their chosen professions.

But man cannot live by moose alone, so food supplies, not to mention medicine and other "necessities," which had taken dogsled teams weeks to get to them, could be flown in within a matter of hours. Merely "getting around" in those remote areas had been a highly difficult task. The airplane could replace a trip that might have consisted of a narrow-gauge railroad ride, transferring to a mule and then a canoe, and finishing on foot. So the flying machine provided a transportation service that was unexcelled.

But it was an arduous task to drop down from above a ring of menacing ranges into a tiny clearing or a placid mountain lake. Arduous? It was next to impossible.

It was just the ticket for the pilot with moxie to spare.

To the pilot, it meant a meager income, but, more importantly, it also meant that he was doing something that few had the courage or even the desire even to try. To the mountaineer hermit in Alaska's Brooks Range or the hunter in Australia's outback, the bush pilot was the only link with the outside world. He also was a larger-than-life folk hero. And rightfully so.

Jack Jefford became the pride of Alaskan bush pilots following World War II. His career had begun when he moved to Alaska and taught himself to fly blind by installing a gyroscopic compass and an artificial horizon in his plane. Then he covered the cockpit with a hood and took off. "It's like learning to swim," Jefford once said. "You just jump in the deepest part of the water and there's nothing else to do *but* swim." Simple logic, but effective. Assuming you have the fortitude that Jefford had.

Fog and sleet usually produced a flying blind effect so Jefford's cockpit cover was exactly what he needed to master the art of flying into one remote airstrip after another without the benefit of vision. It prompted locals to look skyward when they heard a plane droning through a thick cloud or fog cover and say, "There goes Jefford."

It was mostly through Jefford's ability and desire to "broaden the scope of Alaska" that new airfields were opened throughout the territory, thereby blazing a foggy trail for others to follow. Waiting in the wings was the heir apparent to Jefford's crown—Don Sheldon. Sheldon had come to Alaska as a youth to seek adventure in America's last frontier. Finding little to excite him, other than seeing the bush pilots flying over from time to time, he took the small savings he had picked up from odd jobs and applied them toward a pilot's license.

With license in hand and hope in his heart, Sheldon went from one small bush pilot operation to another. There was no work, so he returned to the Lower Forty-Eight and enlisted in the Army Air Corps. He saved every cent he could so that he could buy a Piper Cub after the war, but when he got out he found that the waiting list was so long that it was unlikely he would ever be able to buy one.

But Sheldon got lucky. He found a surplus auction sale and was able to buy a Taylorcraft Cub L2M for $1,200. Off he went to Alaska, where he set up his *own* bush pilot operation.

Sheldon was an outstanding pilot to begin with, but the next few years' experience, flying in "every kind of bad weather God ever created" and landing on postage stamp–sized lakes and dirt strips barely long enough to fly a model plane into, made him a legend.

His skill accounted for scores of daring and frightening recoveries, the most notable of which may have been the rescue of eight Army Search and Rescue personnel. Sheldon had learned of their plans to chart the fierce Susitna River, which necessitated navigating their small yellow boat through a five-mile stretch of one of the most treacherous white-water rapids in the world.

The Army wouldn't listen, of course, when he tried to talk them out of it, but Sheldon had flown over those rapids and he knew they couldn't make it. When they pushed off down river, Sheldon kept a vigil on their progress until, on the second day, he saw dozens of small pieces of yellow floating in the river. It came as no surprise.

But what *would* have surprised even the most foolhardy adventurer was Sheldon's next decision. He had spotted seven of the men clinging to a rock. The canyon at that point was two hundred feet across at the top but only about fifty feet at the bottom. Even the bold Sheldon elected not to try to land his plane in the ferocious water. If the current didn't sweep him downstream, the jagged rocks would have ripped the pontoons apart and then finished off the plane.

There was a quieter pool of water about a quarter of a mile upstream so down Sheldon went, with the floats of his plane pointing into the current and the tail toward the swift water. The thirty-mile-per-hour current immediately began to carry the plane toward the rapids, so Sheldon pushed the throttle far enough forward to create a prop wash strong enough to give the rudder a bite into the wind and keep the plane straight with the current.

For Sheldon it must have felt like he was riding a roller coaster.

The plane was bobbing up and down like a cork, but he knew he could make it. If he hadn't possessed that positive attitude, he wouldn't have been there in the first place.

He was floating backwards at twenty-five miles per hour when he came up beside the surprised men. They must have thought they were hallucinating to see an airplane floating backward toward them. The water was beating up over the struts of the plane but Sheldon advanced the throttle even more, hoping to slow down its rearward movement and enable the plane to get close enough that one of the men could grab hold of the float. Of course, the huge rocks on either side were treacherous, so the maneuver had to be one administered with the skill of Admiral Farragut and Jimmy Doolittle combined.

To Sheldon's surprise, it worked. One of the men lunged toward the float and clung on for dear life while Sheldon forced the throttle forward and ferried the man to the calm section of water. He eased the plane to the river bank, dropped the man off, and then, in true bush pilot fashion, he went back for the others.

Carrying them out two at a time, he saved them all. Before the day was over, he had found the eighth man and had flown him to safety. It was all in a day's work.

To acknowledge one of the most miraculous feats of skill and bravery with an airplane, the Army awarded him a special citation: "Seeking neither claim nor rewards, Don Sheldon willingly and voluntarily pitted his skill and aircraft against great odds. His intrepid feat adds lustre to the memory of those stalwart pilots whose rare courage and indomitable spirit have conquered the vastness of the Alaskan Territory."

But to Sheldon it was no big deal. The guys needed help and he was there to give it. After all, he was performing in the true fashion of the bush pilot.

His feats continued for several years until he succumbed to cancer in 1975 at the age of fifty-three.

Mickey Rupp's ranch is at the end of a sandy road near Stuart, Florida. A high chain-link fence and a security gate isolate him from the outside world. But inside the fence—just to let his friends know where his place is—is a sign that says simply: NAKED LADY AIRPORT.

It's just offbeat enough to tell anyone who knows Rupp that this is "Mickey's Place." The rest of the world can stay out.

Actually there is an airport there; a small grass landing strip accommodates Rupp and several other friends who collect and fly some rather unusual aircraft. Rupp's personal favorite is his P-51 Mustang. Or maybe the T-34. It depends on how fast he wants to go on any given day.

"My dad bought a [Beechcraft] Bonanza in 1947—hell, it had serial number eleven—and I learned to fly the thing by the time I was twelve years old," Rupp says. "But my real ambition was to fly a Mustang. One of the guys at the airport in Ohio, close to where we lived, had one, and I figured this was the ultimate thing to do.

"I took some lessons just so I could get my license, and by the time I was eighteen I was flying about anything that people would let me fly. Except a P-51. But I found one I could afford in 1966. I bought it for $12,500, and I'll tell you, I wouldn't have taken a million bucks for it at that point.

"I had never flown a tail-dragger like that but a guy named Dean Ordner at Wakeman, Ohio, gave me six hours of instruction, and I thought I was hot shit," Rupp declares. "The truth is I was pretty safe for the first twenty-five hours or so, and then for the next fifty hours I tried to kill myself.

"The Mustang is a little different than most planes; it's pretty easy to fly in a certain sense, but they can do some nasty tricks, and if the airplane gets ahead of you, it can scare the shit out of you. At first. Then I realized that I could throw it around and do just about anything with it. But you have to get the feel for it first."

Rupp leans back on the stool near the workbench in his massive hangar, which is attached to his impressive Florida-modern house, and looks lovingly toward his current Mustang, which, even though it didn't actually see any action, is painted just like that of Bud Anderson's World War II fighter. *Old Crow* is painted in bold letters on each side of the fuselage.

Mustang pilots aren't much different from Piper Cub pilots or 747 pilots. They're all long on reminiscing. Rupp is like the rest:

"In the last Rockford-to-Reno Air Race in 1969, there were eleven of us flying P-51s," he says, with a disconsolate look on his face. "In 1978 Jack Sliker, who was one of the eleven, and I happened to run into each other and we got to talking about that race. In fact, we got shit-faced, if you want to know the truth, because we were the only two left out of the eleven Mustang air racers of '69. The rest had all wiped out at one time or another.

"About two years later, Jack's wife called me and said, 'Mickey, you're the only one left. Jack just bought it.' "

Rupp once more looks toward the Mustang sitting near the open hangar doors. The look in his eyes is one of wonderment. "Is this friend or foe?" he seems to be asking himself. The look fades as quickly as it had appeared.

"I thought a lot after that," he recalls. "And I realized that in the first hundred hours that I flew a Mustang, I almost killed myself a dozen times. But somehow I got through it and each time it made me a better pilot. But I also realized that those ten other buddies of mine hadn't been so lucky.

"I lost another friend just last week; he was doing loops down near the deck [ground] and something happened; I don't know what. But I do know from experience that it's not a good practice to do stunts at a low level. Even in a Mustang."

A great deal of love and respect for the P-51 is shared by most who fly World War II aircraft—warbirds, as they call them. "The Spitfire performs better at low altitude," Rupp says, speaking as an air racer. "The Bearcat climbs faster; the Corsair will outturn you down low. But the Mustang is a good strong 'nine' right across the board; most of the ones with 'tens' in some areas have 'sixes' in a lot of others. This is the plane that turned the war around."

Rupp is no newcomer to speed. A former race driver, Rupp finished sixth in the 1964 Indianapolis 500, so he knows what he's talking about when people compare fighter pilots to race drivers.

"On a race car you have to be right on the ragged edge if you expect to win. In an airplane you have to manage more systems, you have to keep thinking much farther out than in a race car. There's a big difference between racing cars and racing planes," he says. "For one thing, an auto racetrack has walls around it, but at Reno, for instance, if you go into a turn too fast you can go out to the mountain and turn around. All you've lost is time."

But there is also a similarity between car racing and air racing. Racers are racers, it turns out. Rupp tells how quickly one can get caught up in it: "One day I was sitting on the pit wall at Indy. The press had just interviewed me as a promising rookie. When they left, Parnelli Jones walked over and sat down beside me. Now keep in mind, here's one of the all-time Indy greats about to give advice to some green-ass kid. 'Don't let those bastards ruin you, kid,' he said. When I asked what he meant, he said, 'They'll write about how great you are and you'll get to believing it. You'll read what they write, and one day you won't feel as good as you do on the others; things just won't be clicking, but you'll be determined to go out there and live up to your press clippings and look as great as they say you are. And if you don't really *feel* like looking that great, you're going to get in serious trouble.'

"I never forgot what Parnelli told me and, you know, I've noticed a lot of air racers are just like he said: The only reason they're out there is so they can read about themselves. It's why a lot of them aren't with us anymore.

"One day a bunch of the guys were talking about how air racing requires so much skill, and I told them, 'If you guys want to put some skill factor in this, put some walls around it. You miss a turn then, buddy, and it's *splat!*"

What is it that makes a good air racer? "You have to have good discipline and very good hand-to-eye coordination. You have to have *instinct*; at times you only have a fraction of a second to make the right move, so you have to be real confident. It's very important to know yourself and your airplane," advises Rupp.

"You don't just push a plane like the Mustang to the edge like you do a race car. The edge on these things is really rough, and you usually don't return from it. But if you're going to do some serious playing around, you'd better go to ten thousand feet and do it. It gives you more room to get things sorted out if you screw up."

As for the air races, Rupp feels that most pilots come there just to get together with other air racers. "Most of them aren't necessarily bad pilots; it's just that they aren't real *good* pilots. At Reno you don't have to be good at aerobatics, but to get in and fly close, you have to be brave. And the winners are those who are brave *and* good.

"And you have to enjoy it because there isn't that much money in it. Hell, if you went to Reno and cleaned house, you'd barely make expenses. You know, sometimes when I look at what I have invested and what it costs to maintain the airplane and to race it, I think that maybe if I had any sense at all, I'd sell all this shit and fly something like everybody else flies. You know, a Bonanza or a Cherokee or something like that."

But Rupp doesn't believe that any more than the people he says it to. Particularly his wife. "I get to thinking like that," he says, "and I take the T-34 out. It will do almost everything the 51 will do, but it just won't do it as fast. I come back feeling like I've just kissed my sister.

"There's nothing close to flying a Mustang," he says proudly. "There are days when I have troubles at the shop or the day isn't going well, so I just take the 51 up and wring it out and I feel great again. At times my wife says, 'Mickey, why don't you go fly your Mustang.' When she says that I know I must be a bear that day."

With that, Rupp heads for the P-51. All of the talk has gotten his adrenaline pumping. "Let's go," he says.

The first thing I noticed when I climbed into the cockpit of the 51 was the starkness. There are aluminum airframe members running all around the cockpit, and there is a simple, hard seat. Up front are amazingly few gauges and controls. Somehow I expected more from such a celebrated war hero.

There was a cloud of dense blue smoke when the mighty Rolls-Royce engine came to life and then it settled down to a hearty, rough idle, rumbling like distant thunder. The thunder got closer as the P-51 began to roll. After taxiing from the back of his rambling ranch house, Rupp used the radio to contact the nearest control tower, just to let them know he and the Mustang would be going up.

The 51 was in the air in an amazingly short time. Rupp pulled back on the stick and the airplane climbed nearly straight up at an amazing rate. He leveled off above the low cloud cover and did a couple of rolls. Then he pushed the throttle and stick forward and *Old Crow* dove. The entire cockpit was blasted with heat from the engine. The plane shuddered as it accelerated, and I wondered how the relic fighter withstood this tremendous force for so many years. It was a thought I immediately dismissed from my mind. The feeling in the pit of my stomach was enough to think about.

As Rupp pulled the airplane out of the dive, the airspeed indicator was pointing to 450 miles an hour, 700 feet per second.

Most of the noise was blocked out by the earphones, but once I moved away from the ears, even slightly, the decibel level was unbelievable. With the large earphones snugly back in place, Rupp spoke over the intercom: "We're going down on the deck," he mentioned casually. "Go for it," I replied.

He called the tower again: "This is Mustang, we're going to be out over the beach for a while at five-oh." The guy in the tower answered, "Okay, Mickey, you're cleared for five hundred feet. Have a nice day."

"Guess he doesn't understand," he said on the intercom. "We're not going to be at five-oh-oh, we're going to be at five-oh. What the hell."

He leveled off at what seemed to be the tops of the white caps, heading north with the beach immediately to our left. We were doing a little over four hundred and the posh beach places were blurring past like a very expensive kaleidoscope. It was a rush like few other things I've done—including driving race cars; it doesn't take long to understand why a lot of people worship the P-51. It is a very fast and very responsive way of life.

Ralph Albertazzie grew up with his grandparents in a West Virginia coal camp near the state university. Despite the fact that he was to become one of the world's most renowned aviators, his interest in airplanes began with a car. When he was a youngster he used to see a gleaming red Auburn Speedster zip down the dirt road past his house. He made up his mind right then and there that he would someday own such a car.

He found out the car belonged to the airport operator at Star City, so he hitchhiked to the Cheat River, took a ferryboat across, and started to hang out with guys with names like Jelly Belly Boone, Weyman Howe, and Skyland Scotty. They were all barnstormers.

"Jelly Belly actually let me run errands," says Albertazzie. "I was their runner and I'll tell you, I did everything I could just to be around those guys. It was sort of like a point system: Once I ran enough errands, Jelly Belly would take me up in his C2 Aeronca. I remember that first flight so well. I was excited, there's no denying that, but not as excited as you might imagine. I mean, I wasn't jumping up and down like some damn fool kid.

"It was just what I expected it to be. I could see a lot more from up there than I could see from the top of the hill behind my house in Cassville. But the feeling was almost commonplace. Flying was exactly what I had thought it would be.

"I could see the river and the old Mountaineer Field at the university. I could see them all from one location," he recalls. Albertazzie was thirteen.

As the next few years passed, Jelly Belly increased Albertazzie's pay scale; instead of free rides, he gave the youth flying lessons. And when Albertazzie got a football scholarship to West Virginia University, he continued flying with Jelly Belly. Football became the second most important thing in Ralph's life, but when he showed up for practice in the fall of his sophomore year in 1942, he was dismayed to learn that more than half of the team had been drafted.

He got on a bus headed for the state capital, where he took the Army Air Corps Examining Board test. He passed with flying colors and two months later he was in flight school.

Albertazzie's goal was combat flying, but his skill at the controls of a B-17 kept him from it. The air corps made him an instructor and that's where he stayed for the duration of the war.

"Hell, I was still instructing months after the war was over," he says. "The classes continued to pour in because nobody had turned off the spigot at the other end. The military wasn't ready for the war to be over."

But Albertazzie was. Since there no longer was even a chance to fly combat, he got out of the service and returned to college. He also returned to Jelly Belly's flying school, where he instructed part-time. But all of this was far too prosaic for the young man who had such high hopes for his flying career. He accepted a job with a company called Air Export-Import. "We flew C-46s and DC-4s between Puerto Rico and New York City," Albertazzie says. "There was such an exodus of military pilots, and all of the planes were left scattered everywhere. We'd pick up Navy planes and ferry them somewhere else, and then maybe we'd pick up Stearman trainers and fly them to another central location until the War Department could figure out how to dispose of them.

"I did everything I could to keep some excitement in my life," Albertazzie reflects, "so I signed a contract with a major exporter named Charlie Babb who sold a lot of these planes to what we call

Third World countries today. Babb bought them at surplus sales, and four or five of us flew them to New York, where they were dismantled, put into crates, and loaded onto ships bound for South America or Africa or whatever."

Albertazzie made enough money in the ferry service that he could buy Jelly Belly's old flying school back home. But he didn't have much of a chance to relive the days of his youth. In May of 1951 he received his orders to return to active duty.

"I really didn't want to go," he says, "because I wanted to make something out of my own school instead of teaching a lot of Air Force guys how to fly, but they decided my job wasn't essential and there was a national emergency and all, so off I went. But it wasn't as bad as I expected. They took my transport background into consideration and put me in the Transport Squadron. I ended up flying USO trips and it was great. I mean, I flew the Bob Hopes to Southeast Asia or wherever and then returned five or six days later. The next day I might be on my way to Germany.

"I did this for several months, until I got a call one day from the guy who was in charge of the Special Air Missions outfit in D.C. He said, 'Your reputation for flying VIPs is excellent, and we're going to put your name on the list.' It was fine with me because I knew it was an important job, but he had told me the only way you get on the SAM list is by attrition, so I figured I might never make it.

"In the meantime I was residing in Brazil on a mission to support downrange activities of the Cape Canaveral operation, and I'll be damned if I didn't get a call about a year later at my hotel in Rio to report to D.C. if I was still interested in the SAM job. I left immediately."

Albertazzie's first mission was to fly Secretary of State John Foster Dulles to the NATO conference in Paris. From then on he personally flew Dulles to most of his conferences.

"The Secretary told me one day," says Albertazzie, "that he was getting damned tired of arriving at these conferences in propeller-driven aircraft when all the other diplomats were showing up in jets. 'I'm going to talk to Ike [President Eisenhower],' he said, and sure enough, the President told General Curtis LeMay, who was vice chief of staff, to 'handle it.'

"Damned if he didn't. He worked out a deal with Continental

Airlines to get three of the six 707s they had on order. I was sent to Boeing for transition training to the 707 and we were in business. Then Curtis LeMay decided to step up the program; they needed one guy to fly the President and that guy turned out to be me. I began flying President Eisenhower everywhere in the *Columbine*, which, of course, was the predecessor to *Air Force One*."

But Albertazzie was to take a brief respite from presidential flying. When John F. Kennedy was elected, Jim Swindell, who was the detachment commander for Albertazzie's group, volunteered himself for the job.

"A four-star general asked me to fly him to Wiesbaden for a conference. On the way back he came forward and chatted with me. 'Ralph,' he said, 'you're never going to amount to a goddamn thing if you don't go into combat; you're never going to make general.' I told him, 'I don't want to be a general, General.' But I'll be damned if he didn't send me to Nam anyway. And then *he* retired.

"General McConnell was Chief of Staff of the Air Force and he wanted me to come back and be chief pilot of SAM. I jumped on it, and when I got back to the Pentagon, he said, 'If the White House accepts, I want you to be the presidential pilot, Ralph. Nixon wants a new crew and you're going to be the chief pilot of *Air Force One*."

Albertazzie picked up the president-elect the next day in New York City and flew him to Key Biscayne, Florida. He had accepted a job with probably the most responsibility of any pilot in the world.

"I didn't feel there was any particular anxiety that came with flying the President," he maintains. "I didn't feel it was any different than flying any other VIP. I don't know, maybe that's why they select certain people to do jobs like that. I just know that I don't get that emotional or concerned over things like that, and I suppose they knew that."

Perhaps it is another fiber shared by pilots who do singular things. "I felt that if I hadn't had the sense of responsibility, they wouldn't have offered me the job in the first place.

"But there were many times when we faced some pretty unusual things. Once I broke out of the clouds over Manilla to find two F-5s on my wingtips. They had the markings of the Philippine Air Force. It scared the hell out of me because nobody told me they were there— the tower, nobody.

"We had been in the clouds all the way from Guam, and I had no idea how long they had been there. It pissed me off so much that I took it on myself to go straight to the Chief of Staff for the Philippine Air Force and say, 'Don't ever, ever try that again.' I knew it might step on some political toes, but I didn't give a damn. I told him we didn't require an escort and if we wanted one we would ask for it. 'So don't ever put the President's life or my life in jeopardy.'

"Those kinds of things, you know, where you have to worry about the politics or whose toes you were going to step on were my biggest concerns—who I was going to piss off—not flying the President," says Albertazzie. "Here's something you won't believe: I had established a reputation for getting the President there on time, and the press had begun to pick up on it. They made reference to the fact that I always got the President there right on the dot, and Bob Haldeman didn't like the ink I was getting. He didn't want some substandard cabinet guy to develop that kind of reputation.

"General James Hughes was the military assistant at the time and he called me and said, 'Bob Haldeman wants you to bust the block time; he wants you to arrive fifteen or twenty minutes late.' I told General Hughes, 'You tell Mr. Haldeman if he doesn't like my style of flying to get himself another pilot.' It's the last I ever heard of it.

"There were always little nit-picking things like that. Larry Higby, who was Haldeman's assistant—in fact, we called him Haldeman's Haldeman—used to annoy the hell out of all of the department heads. He talked to them like they were kids, because he loved the power and influence that being connected directly to the White House gave him.

"One Thanksgiving Day we were going to Key Biscayne after the dinner at the White House. But we had the usual turkey and all the trimmings on the airplane for all of the people who went with us, including pumpkin pie. It so happens I prefer pecan pie, and the wife of one of the President's staff knew that, so she sent me over a piece. After we had flown a couple of hours, the steward was given this piece of pecan pie to bring to me.

"I was sitting there with the tray on my lap when Larry Higby came into the flight deck. 'Where did you get that?' he asked. 'I *prefer* pecan pie,' is all I told him. You have no idea how much paperwork was generated between him and the military office by my remark.

Most of it centered around 'Why does a pilot think he can have pecan pie when the rest of us get pumpkin?'

"Nixon heard about it, because a couple of trips later, he asked me, 'Did you and Higby ever get over the pecan pie incident?' But fortunately I was left alone with the flight crew most of the time. In fact, there were times when I only got up and walked around a couple of times in a six-hour flight, so as glamorous as it sounds, it also was tedious as hell a lot of the time. When I did get up, I'd go back and see if everything was all right with my VIP passengers. Of course, there were times when I didn't go back at all because it was big, big business back there and I didn't want to interrupt.

"Contact between the President and me was usually pretty formal. Nixon seldom came forward, unless it was to introduce Brezhnev or Pete Rozelle or whoever might be on the airplane. He'd say, 'Ralph, I'd like you to meet General Secretary Brezhnev,' and that was it.

"But he would always stop before he deplaned and say, 'Thank you, Ralph. It was a good flight.' Oh, he did *call* me a few times to inquire about the weather; he was doing it for Pat, just to see what she should wear. 'What's the temperature going to be in Anchorage when we get there?' he'd ask, or 'Is it going to rain tomorrow in Paris?' He could have called any number of sources, but he'd pick up the phone and say, 'Get me the pilot.'

"Ford was different," Albertazzie states. "He would come up and tell stories and talk about golf. So would Lyndon Johnson. But Eisenhower was the only one who was genuinely interested in what was going on up there. Of course, he flew, so he really could identify with all of it."

Maintenance was a matter of vital importance on *Air Force One*. All major components that have a time change were replaced at half the recommended time; say, a generator that was supposed to be changed at four hundred hours would be changed at two hundred. "We eliminated as many possibilities of problems as we could," says Albertazzie. "But there's one thing we had no control over—bomb threats. I got calls at home in the middle of the night, the guys at Andrews [Air Force Base] got calls, everybody did. And, as much security as there was, the airplane was rolled out and gone over thoroughly each time.

"On one particular flight, we left D.C. at eleven A.M. We had only been in the air a few minutes; in fact, we were climbing through twenty-five thousand feet near Lancaster, Pennsylvania, when I got a call from the White House, telling me we had a bomb on board that was set to go off at eleven-fifteen.

"I looked at my watch. It was eleven-twelve; there was no place we were going to go in three minutes. I didn't feel there was any need for concern, because I was sure there was no way a bomb could be there as a result of anything the crew had done, since everything had been checked from stem to stern—all the baggage, including crew and passengers. The only possible way could have been in the President's or First Lady's luggage.

"I got on the phone to Bob Taylor, who was the Secret Service agent in charge of the presidential detail, and said, 'Bob, don't say anything to the President, but is there any way a bomb could be in his luggage?' 'There's no way in the world,' he said. And then paused. 'Why?' he asked. I told him and he said, 'I'll be right up.' "

What is the next step in a case where the life of the President is in jeopardy? There's nothing to do but wait and see. "There was no other choice," Albertazzie contends. "Bob and I sat on the flight deck and stared first at our watches and then at each other."

Eleven-fifteen came and went and neither man said a word. Finally, at about 11:18, Albertazzie broke the silence. "Want some coffee, Bob?" he asked. "No thanks, Ralph, I think I'll have a drink," he responded.

Nixon made more dramatic trips with *Air Force One* than any other President, particularly to China and the Soviet Union. But it was the trip to China that gained more worldwide attention than any other. Few people realize how long the trip was in the making, and even fewer knew the secret flights that were required to set it up.

"In July of 1969 I got a call from the White House to come down for a meeting," says Albertazzie. "They told me not to wear my uniform because they wanted it to look casual. When I got there Ron Ziegler took me into the Roosevelt room. It was about eleven A.M. when Henry Kissinger and Al Haig came in with Don [General James] Hughes."

Albertazzie had no idea what was up, but he figured it must be important. Hughes addressed the group: "The President wants us to move Dr. Kissinger into Paris for some conferences with the Chinese and North Vietnamese. We have to do it clandestinely," he said, "and the President doesn't want anybody to know about it. Not even Congress. Not even the Secretary of Defense or the rest of the Cabinet. Ralph, you have to provide the transportation. We'll do all the rest."

"Trips to Europe were often training flights to shake down new equipment, so nobody asked any questions when I filed a flight plan from Andrews to Frankfurt," says the President's pilot. But he built a thirty-minute pad into the flight plan. And once he got into the Oceanic Control area of Shannon, nobody in the United States followed the airplane anymore, so he planned to refile for another destination, France. Plans were made for French President Georges Pompidou's plane to meet them at an obscure airport and whisk Kissinger back to Paris while *Air Force One* headed for Frankfurt—on time. It was a fully orchestrated plan of international intrigue.

"We always went to some remote area of the airport. The French would escort Henry to their plane and we would take off immediately, with the French Falcon quickly heading in the other direction," Albertazzie explains. "Even the French air force didn't know what the hell was going on.

"After about eighteen hours, we would repeat the whole thing, with the same flight plan filing and refiling. The only tricky part was fuel. We had to *buy* fuel in France because we didn't want any official documents showing they had absorbed the cost, no matter how minor. There wasn't anything left to chance."

Albertazzie made fourteen such trips in the next three years, then in September 1971 Nixon routinely announced that he had decided to go to China the following year.

"One of the most difficult parts of the secret rendezvous was getting Henry out of the country without anybody missing him," Albertazzie says, grinning as if he were about to reveal another secret maneuver. "As it turned out, the fact that Henry was so visible made the plan all that much easier. They simply set the meetings for a Saturday, so they would send Henry out to a big Washington gala on Friday night with someone who was even more visible than he—like Jill St. John. This was before he was married, of course, so all of the papers and weekend news shows shot pictures and footage of Henry and Jill— or whoever it happened to be—establishing the fact that he was out on the town.

"About ten-thirty the Secret Service guys would sneak Henry and his date out the back to a limousine that was waiting. They would take the girl back to her hotel and then whisk Henry to the helipad at the Pentagon, where a chopper took him right to Andrews. When I saw the helicopter coming, I had engines three and four already running, and when he came up the steps, they closed the door and I started one and two. And we were off."

Not even the press people at the White House knew that Kissinger was gone. But when he came into the office on Monday morning, looking a little the worse for wear, everybody figured he had a wild weekend with the girl who was pictured with him in the Sunday paper. Little did they know he had been in Paris at a highly important international summit.

"When time came for the trip to China, I almost had Henry talked into sitting in the left seat as my copilot, Frank Hughes, taxied the airplane up to the tarmac. I told him, 'Just think what it would do for your image; I mean, they'll think this guy does *everything* for Nixon, even fly the plane.'

"I think he wanted to do it, but he finally declined. 'If this administration had any sense of humor,' he said, 'I would do it in a minute.' "

"One time we were to fly to Syria," Albertazzie recalls, "so I called our guy in Damascus and said, 'How's everything going?' 'Fine,' he said, 'the Syrians are not even going to let an airplane fly.' I told him I didn't think it was necessary to let it go that far, but he assured me that was the way they wanted to do it; they didn't want the plane in jeopardy in any way.

"It's only ninety miles from the Jordan border to Damascus, so we were already in descent when we crossed into Syria. Everything was fine until I looked out and saw two MiGs coming up fast. They could have been Iraqi or anything, we had no idea.

"The Syrians had said there wouldn't be any planes up there, so I could only assume they weren't theirs," Albertazzie says, speaking in a soft, unruffled manner. "There were puffy clouds with tops at about twenty thousand feet, so I popped the air brake, pulled back the power, dumped the airplane, and got underneath the cloud cover. I slowed down as rapidly as I could—to about one hundred and eighty knots—and the MiGs went right on by because they had been accelerating to catch us. As soon as they went over the top of us, I could look through breaks in the clouds and I saw them break off to see where we went, so I slowed down even more.

"At that point, the door to the cabin burst open and Henry Kissinger and Ron Ziegler came rushing in. 'What the hell's going on?' they asked in unison. 'Beats the hell out of me,' I said. 'We've got a couple of MiGs out there.' While we were talking, my copilot, Frank Hughes, was on the radio to Damascus control. In less than a minute it was established that the two planes were piloted by a couple of Syrian student pilots who just wanted to see the President's airplane.

"They're probably still student pilots," Albertazzie adds.

The tranquil days aboard *Air Force One* were about to come to an end. As was the entire Nixon administration.

During Watergate, things changed. There was little laughter.

"You began to notice a lot of mistrust between the players," Albertazzie reflects. "There began to be a lot of dissension. The conviviality of the whole party began to shrink into a small group of people like Haldeman and Ehrlichman and the President. Even Ziegler wasn't in on a lot of it.

"Normally, when we got back to Andrews, the President was anxious to get off the plane, but now he would just sit back there in the conference room or in his private stateroom. The First Lady would come forward to talk to me, and she would say things like, 'Ralph, isn't it terrible what they're doing to Dick?'

"I don't think she realized the significance of the obstruction of justice charge. But I had heard from some of the people around the President that they thought McGovern was getting a lot of money from foreign sources, particularly Castro. They thought there was a big influx of capital into his campaign from the Caribbean. I heard these things," Albertazzie confides. "I could flip a switch and listen to conversations between anybody on the plane and anybody on the ground. I was sure that they felt there was evidence in the Democratic National Headquarters."

As time wore on, this small group of people even began to distrust each other. "You could feel it. But I don't think Pat or even Julie or Tricia ever had the sense of importance of it. I tried to rationalize the whole thing; I guess that's why I wanted to learn as much as I could, because, knowing how much the President thought of his family—especially Julie, who was in Puerto Rico at the time, making an appearance—I don't think he would have let her go out and do those things if he thought he was guilty."

It was just past three in the afternoon of August 8, 1974, when the White House phone rang in Albertazzie's office. It was General Lawson, who said in a hoarse voice, "You have a ten A.M. departure for El Toro tomorrow."

"How long are we staying?" Albertazzie asked, out of habit.

"You're *not* staying," Lawson said. "You're making a drop. The President is announcing his resignation on television tonight."

End of conversation.

Albertazzie knew the flight was delayed until the next morning because the President didn't like to fly at night. He also knew that the next day's flight—one of the most historic of all time—had been summed up in a telephone conversation that lasted only seconds. Somehow, he felt, it should have taken longer.

Even though Albertazzie, along with the rest of the world, knew the announcement was imminent, it still came as a shock. The next day he would be flying the only President of the United States ever to resign from office. He would be flying home the man he respected so much.

Albertazzie automatically began the process of executing the notification checklist. He had done it hundreds of times in his five and a half years as chief presidential pilot for Nixon, but this time it seemed somehow as if someone else was doing it. It was almost surrealistic, as if another person was saying the words for him.

On the morning of August 9, the President's pilot sat in the cockpit of *Air Force One* and scanned the western horizon for a glimpse of the President's helicopter, *Army One*.

Finally it was in sight. It was the beginning of the end.

The huge olive green Sikorsky came to a stop a few feet from the nose of *Air Force One*. Albertazzie could see Nixon in the large window of the helicopter. When the blade stopped, the door was flung open and an Army sergeant popped out and froze in a salute. Mrs. Nixon was the first one out, followed by Tricia.

It was several minutes before the President emerged. He was somber as he routinely shook hands with those on the tarmac. Usually he nodded to Albertazzie before boarding the airplane, but this morning there was no sign of recognition. It was going to be a long flight.

Master Sergeant Earl Van Valkenburg usually was entrusted to carry the "black box," which contained the top-secret files that went everywhere with the President. There always was a ceremonial transfer of it to the safe within the airplane. This morning there was no black box. This morning there was no *need* for a black box.

The second the President's foot touched the boarding stairs, Albertazzie gave the command to copilot Lester McClelland to "Start three." When Albertazzie heard the rush of air through the engine and heard McClelland reply, "Rotation," he said, "Start four."

He heard the cabin door close and he glanced out the window. The stairs were being removed. "Start one and two," he said calmly.

It was McClelland who spoke to ground control on his microphone: "*Air Force One* taxiing," he said.

"Roger, *Air Force One*," replied the voice in the tower.

It was 10:15 A.M. One minute had passed since the President had departed the helicopter. The final flight for "President" Nixon was underway.

"We usually chatted away in the cockpit," says Albertazzie, "but that day there was very little conversation. It was limited to commands and reports of the progress of the flight. Nobody felt like saying anything. Or knew *what* to say."

Albertazzie spent most of the time remembering the events of the past five and a half years. He knew that he had the best job in the Air Force, despite some of the politics of the past. Even the pecan pie incident was by now a pleasant memory.

During his tenure in office, it seemed that Nixon was in the air more than he was on the ground. On one trip alone, he had visited more countries—twenty-eight—and traveled more miles outside the boundaries of his own nation—137,500—than any President in history.

Albertazzie had selected the best route between Washington and San Clemente early in his *Air Force One* command. That day would be no different: It was Mercator Projection, a straight line that took him over central West Virginia, Cincinnati, St. Louis, Wichita, Gallup, and Palm Springs, right into El Toro Marine Corps Air Station near Santa Ana. It was the swiftest route.

At thirty-five thousand feet and about one hour into the trip, Albertazzie decided to see what was going on behind the cockpit. He would check on lunch, who was on the telephone, and what the cabin temperature was. Busy work. But mostly he was concerned about the President.

Nixon was in his private compartment with the door closed. Mrs. Nixon was in hers with Tricia. Albertazzie returned to the cockpit, where he sat in silence for a long time, thinking of the rare despondent mood in the cabin behind him.

"There was some small talk in the cockpit," Albertazzie recalls, "but it was just to break the awkward silence. Les McClelland, whose earphones were tuned to a radio channel, turned to me and said, 'I think you'd better listen to this, Ralph.' It was the swearing-in ceremony for Gerald Ford, my new boss.

"As Ford finished the oath, Les punched the button to determine the exact position of the airplane. *Air Force One* was thirty-nine thousand feet over a point thirteen miles southwest of Jefferson City, Missouri. It was three minutes past noon. The plane was no longer *Air Force One*; officially it was now only SAM 27000."

Lunch was being served in the back, so Albertazzie slipped on his jacket and went back. The meal consisted of shrimp cocktail, prime rib, baked potato, green beans, tossed salad, rolls, coffee, tea, or milk, and cheesecake. To Albertazzie it seemed like the Last Supper.

As he continued his stroll, he saw the door to the President's compartment open. Nixon looked strained, but there was a smile on his face. He was wringing his hands softly.

"Well," he exclaimed, "is everyone enjoying the trip?"

No one replied.

He looked at Albertazzie and said, "Ralph, when we get to El Toro, I'd like some pictures of the crew and me, and some of Mrs. Nixon and me. And one of just you and me."

"Of course, Mr. President," Albertazzie replied.

And then the President said, "Ralph, you know, before we went to China, I told you that I was going to make you a general. I really meant to do that, but, you know, so many things got in the way . . ." His voice trailed off, as if he was speaking to someone who wasn't even there. He added, "It's one of the things I'll have to leave undone. I'm sorry."

"I understand, Mr. President," Albertazzie said.

"He went back to the VIP lounge and I went back to the cockpit," says Albertazzie. "It was a very emotional moment for me. I wanted to blot the whole thing out of my mind. But I couldn't."

On the final approach to El Toro, the airplane swung out over the Pacific and took dead aim on El Toro, approaching at 160 miles per hour. The plane touched down at 125 miles per hour. It was a smooth landing. Richard Nixon was on the ground in his native California.

Unlike the departure, which had been made with no fanfare whatsoever, there were about five thousand people on hand to greet Nixon. They cheered and applauded. A lot of them wept. To a person, they were loyal supporters. As he stood on the top step he paused, smiled broadly, and raised both arms high with each of his hands forming the familiar V-for-victory greeting.

"I watched it from the cockpit window," says Albertazzie, "and then I got up, put on my jacket, and got ready for the photographs. It was going to be difficult to smile."

Richard Nixon was home. It was time to get President Ford's airplane back to Washington.

"I was very close to them," he says, with a tinge of sadness in his voice. "We still correspond. And, you know, I've wondered so many times why the same thoroughness and thought wasn't used in Watergate as was in the Kissinger flights to Paris. If that had been the case, I'll guarantee you, there wouldn't have been a Watergate."

Chapter Six

From the beginning, men have built a chauvinistic barrier around flying.

Private pilots feel the rapture of flight just as surely as fighter pilots or test pilots. They fly on weekends and a few evenings each week, but they very well could be what aviation is all about; they *are* the millions of people who fly strictly as an avocation. On the surface, at least, they appear to be a different breed from the crop duster or the top gun, but underneath, their fears and delights of flying are exactly the same as those of their illustrious counterparts.

"Sure, the problems you had before you took off come back when you land, but not with such intensity; you've found a serenity that carries over. And it makes them bearable. Hell, you can *solve* them," says Frank Stankiewicz, who sells Buicks in Fort Myers, Florida.

"I'll never forget my first flight," he says. "As the ground began to drop away, so did my ability to breathe. It came in short gasps and there was a heavy pressure on my chest. But as I gained altitude, my chest stopped heaving and a calmness swept over me like waves at a beach. I was a bird; I could personally control my destiny. At that particular moment, I was king of all I surveyed. I eased back in the seat and let my grip on the controls relax." Once more the voice of the pilot speaks.

"But, you know, after thirty years of flying, it's still a puzzle to me: You have to put your faith in something you don't fully understand or can't even see—the principle of flight. Oh, I know what makes an airplane fly, but that's stuff out of a textbook.

"None of that makes a damn bit of difference—you know, the fact that I accept it but don't fully understand it. The only thing that does matter," says Stankiewicz, "is the fact that I'm in a special world up there, a world where there are no boundaries. The clouds are fences and walls you can dart through and come up through, and on the other side of them, you have yet another world, perhaps one of sunshine when you've just left rain below."

There are no walls, no desks, no worries. No Buicks to peddle. Back at the office maybe the worst thing that could happen is the computer going down, but up there in the sky, there are a lot more things that *could* happen, and the pilots who survive are the ones who constantly remind themselves of that fact. But they consider the rewards to be far greater than the risks. It's why people pound pitons into sheer rock cliffs and pull themselves from one level to another; it's why they drive race cars and a host of other things where the outcome is more than slightly on the nebulous side. And just as sure as there are clouds above, it is why most people fly. Riding a bicycle could never do it for them. Even if they were pedaling across the top of the Tioga Pass at Yosemite Park.

The major difference between private pilots and the daring aviators of battle and of high adventure is that hardly any of them have ever even *been* in a life-threatening situation. They read about aircraft failures and hijackings, and surely they can identify better with them than a guy who races a car as a hobby can, but still it is a somewhat detached association. They understand the terms, but they certainly don't understand the circumstances.

The truth of the matter is, private pilots—not to mention commercial and military pilots at times—face one peril that is seldom discussed: boredom. "Once you get up there, all leveled off and on course, it can be tedious as hell," says Richard Sammis, who, as one of the fly-for-fun pilots of America using a single-engine plane to get him from place to place quickly, speaks for a lot of pilots. Most of them, in fact, who don't look to the airplane merely as a weekend diversion.

"There are times when I play the same games I did when I was a kid. I try to name all the capitals of all the states," he remarks. "Or the Presidents. In order. I do anything I can to keep awake. Hell, there's nothing going on. You're sort of trapped in this tiny capsule and you have to make the most of it.

"I think fighting the boredom is the greatest obstacle a pilot can have," says Sammis, "because ninety percent of the time, there is absolutely nothing to do but look at a bunch of clouds. And, after all, you can only play child's games for so long. I mean, you have no idea how many times I feel like saying, 'Are we there yet, Daddy?' "

Private pilots represent the vast majority of the men and women who take to the air. And even though the percentage of those who have ominous problems is infinitesimal, the ones who do have problems usually come through with the same skill and courage as those who have placed themselves in hostile surroundings in combat or stunts.

Private pilots, like fighter pilots, are mostly loners. They enjoy being "up there" by themselves. Of this group, probably the loneliest ones are those who build experimental planes. They build them alone and, since most of them are single-seat craft, they *fly* them alone.

"When the moment comes that you install that last instrument," explains Fred Wichlep, who built his own kit plane, "when you know you're going to fly it, to test it, your palms sweat and your heart pounds. But you have to have confidence in what you create.

"When I went down the runway that first time and pulled back on the stick, and the thing I'd created out of fiberglass and aluminum and nuts and bolts took off, there was no feeling I ever had that equaled it. There were tears streaming down my cheeks, and my heart was pounding a mile a minute. I thought to myself, 'I just want to keep going and never come down.' "

It's not always sweethearts and flowers, even with people who fly strictly for fun. "I'd been flying for fifteen years," says Stankiewicz, "without anything other than an occasional instrument that went out, and then one day it happened: I was flying over Ligonier, Pennsylvania, enjoying the beautiful rolling foothills of the Alleghenies. The sun was shining and my Swift was purring along like a kitten. And then the propeller came off. I kid you not, the damn prop came right off. I looked at the nose of the plane and it looked like a jet. I said, very quietly to myself, the only thing there was to say: 'Oh, shit.' "

So much for the purring like a kitten.

"I don't remember being particularly scared, but I do recall feeling that I was in some trouble," Stankiewicz states stoicly. "I had to get that plane down, so I immediately started looking for a place to land. I never realized it before, but there isn't a whole lot of flat country around here. I mean, nothing without wires and fences and hills and you name it. I decided the Pennsylvania Turnpike was my only answer. The Swift was in a pretty good glide pattern and I was sure I could make it. Fortunately there wasn't much traffic, so I figured that if I picked as long a straight stretch as I could and got close enough to the highway where the cars could see me, they would figure out what I was trying to do and stop.

"I picked the lanes going in the direction of my glide, and I got the plane down to about twenty-five feet. Traffic stopped. On *both* sides of the turnpike. I don't mind telling you, it was as good a landing as I ever made. Dead stick or not.

"I've heard this bullshit about people kissing the ground when they got out of tight places and landed airplanes, and it's what I would have done if my knees hadn't been shaking so much. So I just sat down and *patted* the pavement."

It was only a matter of time until the Pennsylvania Highway Patrol was on hand, writing Stankiewicz a ticket for blocking traffic and a couple of other charges the cop even had to look up. "I was never so glad to pay a ticket in my life," he said.

They pushed the plane off to the side of the highway so that only one lane was blocked, and called a guy who came out, took the wings off, and hauled it away.

"I flew that plane again the following week," he says, "and you know, I never had any more prop problems with it again. But I sure as hell checked the prop a lot. I still do on every plane I ever fly."

Thomas L. Root was a Washington lawyer who everybody, including his family, felt was well on his way to success. But on July 20, 1989, Root took off on a routine flight in his Cessna 210 and wound up spreading his name across the front pages of every newspaper in the nation and on all the evening news shows.

His bizarre six-hour flight was tracked by nineteen airplanes from the Air Force, Coast Guard, Navy, and Marine Corps. It initially drew the attention of radio listeners when reports came in of a light plane at ten thousand feet and headed out into the Atlantic Ocean—with the pilot unconscious.

The curious flight came to a watery end a dozen miles off Eleuthera Island in the Bahamas. Root survived, although there were a number of mysteries unresolved at the conclusion of his flight. For example, Root said from his hospital bed that the .32-caliber Smith & Wesson revolver he kept in the glove compartment of the Cessna apparently discharged when the plane impacted the water.

"Nonsense," said Smith & Wesson officials. "It is impossible for such a gun to discharge without pulling the trigger."

The Coast Guard surgeon who examined him said the wound was made several hours before the crash, and police officials reported that powder burns indicated the wound had to be made from a gun at close range, probably self-inflicted.

Here's how the peculiar flight began: Root took off from the Butler Aviation terminal at Washington's National Airport for a 155-mile flight to Rocky Mount, North Carolina. It was 6:26 in the morning. He had nothing on board but his briefcase and a compact disc player. And the revolver, which he told friends he carried "in case I land in a remote area."

As he neared Rocky Mount he radioed the FAA's radio control center at Leesburg, Virginia. "I'm having trouble breathing," he said. And then he asked, "How far am I from Rocky Mount?" Then, at 8:24 A.M., Root's radio went silent.

The FAA immediately called the Coast Guard because already the plane was on its way to the North Carolina coast on a heading that would take it out over the Atlantic. The Coast Guard assembled a search-and-rescue mission in hopes of intercepting the airplane. And, sure enough, they did. In fact, they followed the plane for two hours. The man inside was slumped over and motionless.

They radioed the information back to their bases, who in turn informed the news media. Television and radio bulletins went out. Coast Guard planes were sent from up and down the East Coast. The terse message from Root, along with the silence of the radio, made everyone immediately feel that the man had succumbed to a heart attack and was unconscious. The planes "escorting" him judged from his airspeed, the tailwind, and the fuel capacity that the Cessna would run out of fuel about two hundred miles east of Cape Canaveral, so they dispatched para-rescuers to an area where they assumed the plane would crash at sea. The transport plane with three Air Force reserve parachute rescuers joined the other rescue planes.

Finally, at 12:19 P.M., Root's plane began to spiral toward the ocean, with the host of rescue and observer planes close at hand. It was within a few miles of their original estimate. They were right on the spot. Again the news media sent out bulletins.

The plane dove from ten thousand feet and when it hit the water it skipped across the surface like a stone skimmed across a country pond. The aircraft sank within minutes.

The para-rescuers jumped from three thousand feet. They found nothing. But a Navy plane spotted the wreckage just before it slipped beneath the surface, and dropped a life raft that drifted toward the body near the plane. Root grabbed hold of the raft, pulled himself aboard, and waited. When the Air Force rescuers reached him, he said, "Boy, am I glad to see you." And then he held his stomach, where the bullet had entered, and collapsed.

Later Root told reporters, "The first conscious thought I had was that water was pouring in the windshield. The water was very blue. I reached over and turned off the master switch." And then he added: "Can you believe a useless gesture like that; turning off the master switch so the plane won't catch on fire when you're in the ocean?"

The press marveled at his spirit and wit.

Before word of the rescue hit the radio airwaves, Root's father listened in horror at the news on his automobile radio. Twenty-three years earlier another son had disappeared in an airplane in a thunderstorm, and the father had brought him home in a body bag. Was history going to repeat itself? When he reached his son's home, his daughter-in-law gleefully informed him that Thomas had survived.

"Tom had a shaky law practice, a personal life that was far from blissful, escalating financial woes, and a passel of troubles with the FCC, which stemmed from his representation of scores of companies in radio station deals. He had been repeatedly reprimanded by the

FCC for missing appointments and filing deadlines and was being forsaken by many of his clients," says a former associate who prefers not to be named.

So the story that began as the newsbreaker of the day took a sudden twist at the end. The airplane may have been little more than a vehicle to carry him totally away from his problems.

Most female pilots agree—especially the pioneers—that it was a man who coined the terms "aileron" and "vertical stabilizer." Men were the ones who *invented* the airplane, after all. But they also are quick to point out that men, from the very beginning, have built a sexist barrier around the pastime of flying. To a degree, it still exists today.

But aeronautically educated observers feel very much to the contrary; they are certain that women can fly every bit as well as men and, in some cases, *better*. General Tallman, president of Embry-Riddle Aeronautical University, says that women have a "lighter touch," which, with today's more sophisticated aircraft, is very important. There are other aviation educators who feel the same way.

Women are not new to aviation. Sure, we've all heard the story of Amelia Earhart, and of Jacqueline Cochran, who was not only a pioneer, but ferried airplanes to Europe during World War II, so that *men* could fight in them. But there are literally hundreds of stories about other pioneer women pilots that seldom, if ever, got into print.

In an article in Embry-Riddle's publication *Update*, Peggy Baty, a pilot who is associate dean of academics, reports that women were piloting aircraft as early as 1798, when Jeanne Labrosse made a solo balloon flight over France. Granted, it wasn't exactly an Aero Commander, but it *was* flying. And she *was* one of the very first pilots.

Margaret Graham of England dedicated a thirty-year career to the sport of balloon flying by charging a fee for carrying passengers for a ride, surely becoming the first female charter pilot. Mary Myers set altitude records in balloons, including one to twenty-one thousand feet over Pennsylvania in 1886. And she did it without the aid of oxygen.

As much as we know about the Wright brothers' historic flight of 1903, few are aware that Wilbur rejected all female applicants on the grounds that they were merely notoriety-seekers. Glenn Curtiss, the Wrights' early nemesis, accepted a female flight student, but only when coaxed by public sentiment. Nevertheless, Curtiss is said to have fixed the airplane so that it could not actually develop enough power to fly. Needless to say, it restricted his "student," Blanche Stuart Scott, to ground school class instruction and taxi tests.

But Scott would not accept that fate. With help from a mechanic at the field, she was able to make her first solo flight in 1910. Ms. Scott flew in many exhibitiions after that. She was known as "the first American woman to solo in an airplane." Since licenses were not required by law then, she never bothered to apply for one, assuming, naturally, that some restriction would prevent her from obtaining one.

American women were not alone in their battle for the right to fly. In 1911, Germany's first aviatrix, Melli Besse, found that her male colleagues had tampered with her plane's steering mechanism and had drained gas from the fuel tank. When she was unable to fly that day, and when the monkey business was discovered, one of them replied, "For a woman to fly would take the glory away from us." Nice guys.

In the twenties, thirties, and forties, women aviators faced the same problems as other women wishing to enter a male-dominated career or hobby. Would a "real lady" fly around in an airplane? seemed to be the prevalent comment.

The question of physical ability also became an issue for those women who wished to fly. In fact, many women were forced to fly only as passengers before they were allowed to attempt flying themselves. Then the fledgling airlines promptly promoted air travel and safety by advertising that flying was safe enough "even for women."

Following World War I, many women found an opportunity in barnstorming. It was not only a chance to earn money, but one to prove their mettle as pilots. Many began as wing-walkers and parachutists, working their way up the ladder to the controls of the airplane.

Women in general found it difficult to break into aviation, but it was an even greater struggle if you were female and black. Such was the case for Bessie Coleman, who went from flying school to flying school throughout America to try to get her license. Finally, in desperation, she went to France to take her flying lessons, and in 1921 became the first licensed black female pilot.

To make sure that other black women would not have to go through what she had to endure, she immediately began plans to open a flying school and to encourage other blacks to fly. To raise the money, she began a barnstorming career. She drew large crowds everywhere she went, but in 1926, when she had almost enough money to open her school, she was thrown from her plane when it inverted in a nosedive, plunging her to her death.

It was not unusual in the late 1920s for women pilots to go into business for themselves. Anita Snook is credited with being the first woman to give flight instruction, when she opened her flying school at Kinner Airport in Los Angeles.

Women established passenger-carrying operations in several cities, but these kinds of ventures did precious little to promote women in the field of aviation. If they were to receive national recognition, they would have to compete, as male pilots already were doing, in the record-breaking arenas—distance, altitude, and speed.

Viola Gentry is credited with one of the first attempts by a woman to set an endurance record. On December 20, 1928, she stayed aloft for eight hours and six minutes. Two weeks later, her record was broken by Bobbi Trout, who managed to stay in flight for more than twelve hours. The following spring, Elinor Smith astounded flyers everywhere by staying in the air for twenty-six hours.

But women still had a long way to go, because the men's record at that time was sixty hours.

In 1929 the National Women's Air Derby was held. It was a cross-country race which included such pilots as Amelia Earhart, Ruth Elder, and Bobbi Trout. The winner of that first race, which began in Santa Monica, California, and ended in Cleveland, was Louise Thaden.

This first race did more than show women's ability to compete as pilots; it allowed these women to realize they were not alone in their chosen career or hobby.

When World War II began, it looked like American women pilots would be grounded or forced to fly only in civilian capacities. But thanks to people like Jackie Cochran, women did have an opportunity to fly *and* help with the war effort. Many went to England to join with the Air Transport Auxiliary to ferry airplanes to the fighting men.

These women flew with great valor because of the many obstacles they faced; they were denied the use of radios for security reasons and were forced to navigate by sketchy maps and hearsay information.

In 1942, a similar group of women pilots was formed in the United States, known as the WAFS, the Women's Auxiliary Ferrying Squadron, but due to their lack of military status, these women were ineligible for insurance, hospitalization, death or veteran's benefits. In fact, it was not until 1977 that these women were retroactively militarized and became eligible for benefits.

That same year, American Airlines and Eastern Airlines hired females as flight crew members, but it was not to be an easy trip. The first female pilot for Eastern was arrested twice for "impersonating a flight crew member." To prevent this from happening at almost every airport, Eastern began to telegraph ahead to airport managers, telling them that a female pilot would be on a particular flight.

Early female pilots were not allowed to wear makeup, have pockets in their flight jackets (so they couldn't sneak in cosmetics), or make announcements over the airplane's public address system. They were required either to have their hair cut very short or tucked up under their hats in an apparent attempt to hide from the passengers the fact that there was indeed a woman in the cockpit.

But, in the privacy of the cockpit, with no makeup or pockets, these women took off, flew, and landed many commercial airplanes. Although far from auspicious, it *was* a step forward for women in the air.

Pilot Peggy Baty, looking back over the early years of women in aviation and ahead to their future, says, "You are limited only by your dreams and willingness to see them through." It could well be the motto for women flyers in the decades since "man" first flew at Kitty Hawk, North Carolina.

Some of the women who began flying in the 1920s are still at it. Edna Gardner White is one of them. At eighty-eight years of age, she still teaches and performs aerobatics. At least, she did until recently.

"The darn FAA grounded me about a month ago. You see, I didn't take care of my diet and my cholesterol got out of hand, so I had to have a cardiac bypass. I can't see why they took my license," she says, with fire in her eye. "Just because I had the bypass, they figured I wasn't able to fly. But I didn't die, did I?"

Before the operation, Ms. White still got up there and did snap rolls and loops. At eighty-eight. "It's good for your veins," she exclaims. "Knocks the cholesterol off the walls."

But she hasn't given up the thought of flying. "Right now I'm convalescing," she says, "but I'm going to try to get my license back one of these days." Most people who know Edna Gardner White assume she'll do just that. Nothing has ever stopped her before in her quest for the wild blue.

It began in 1912 when she read in the newspaper that President Woodrow Wilson had asked Catherine Stinson and her sister, Marjorie, to go to Dayton, Ohio, to teach pilots for the war.

"I couldn't understand how two women could teach men how to fly when men thought women didn't have enough sense to vote," she declares. "That did something to my mind and I decided right then and there that I was going to pursue a man's profession. Actually there were two professions a woman wasn't considered able to do back then, flying airplanes and being a doctor. So I did both.

"I took my premed courses at Madison, Wisconsin, and then went to Seattle for my flight instruction. I guess the flying stuck better because I've been teaching it for sixty-four years. I've got men and women in the airlines and in the services," she says proudly.

The first time White flew was in a Curtiss Jenny. A friend had offered her a ride and assumed that, being a girl, she would refuse. Little did he know that she had been counting the days until she had the opportunity.

"He let me fly the plane," she recalls, "and I got such a thrill out of it. I'd push the stick forward and the plane would go down, then I'd push it sideways and the airplane went sideways. It was wonderful.

"When I tried to land it, the Jenny bounced so high and then it hit the ground again. Slam! I thought this must be the way airplanes land; I figured they had to hit the ground. You know, he was a lot more scared than I was."

White was in the Navy nurse corps for a stint, but she was making more money flying students than she was nursing, so she elected to give up the military and head south. "I packed up all of my belongings in a red DeSoto roadster and headed for New Orleans to start a flying school," she says. "But I only got to Norfolk, Virginia. I stopped to look at the airport there, and the mayor, who also ran the airport, asked me to stick around for a few weeks until he could find a permanent instructor.

"He had a Fairchild and a Great Lakes and a Ryan and some other airplanes I had been drooling over for a long time but which no damn man would let me fly, so I figured that was the place to be. I would get a chance to fly those special airplanes.

"Every day that I didn't have students in the afternoon, I took the Ryan out along Roanoke Rapids or Suffolk and all those peanut-patch towns, and I landed along a fence beside the highway somewhere. The Ryan had great big wheels and you could do that," she comments. "So, I'd get a kid to collect the money and I'd take people for rides.

"We'd have a crowd in no time. In fact, one day I sold so many rides I didn't think I was going to have enough gas, so I had to make them short. When I took off, I'd throw my left wing all the way down and then as soon as I cleared the ground, I was in a left turn. I would go all the way around, side-slipping with my wing down, and land just as I got it straight again. That way I could take four people up in about five minutes.

"But the kid finally came to me and said, 'Ma'am, you gotta stop that. These people want their money back. They say you can't keep your wings straight.' "

Of course, it was only a matter of time until she decided to try her hand at aerobatics. "One of the guys at the air base told me that a loop was simple. He said, 'All you do is dive for the ground until you get a lot of speed and then you pull it up and keep it up until you get right side up again.' I tried it and it was terrible; I would fall off at the top and do all the things wrong that I know better now. But I didn't give up; I kept at it until I could do it.

"And I'm gonna keep after those FAA guys until I get my license back," she adds.

Dorothy Hester Stenzel also began her flying career in the twenties and is still flying. After she gave up parachuting at air shows, she flew in them, billed as "Miss Kick-a-Hole-in-the-Sky." Her specialty was the loop, the wide, circular forward roll, which was beautiful to watch but hard on the airplane because of the constant rhythmic G-forces.

But on May 15, 1931, with twenty thousand people looking skyward from Omaha, Nebraska, Stenzel performed sixty-nine consecutive outside loops, tracing them again and again for more than two hours.

As she hung upside down, she worked the stick with one hand and the wobble pump with the other, so that the fuel would keep flowing. Her record stood for fifty-eight years.

On July 13, 1989, petite Joann Osterund stirred up the skies over North Bend, Oregon, to break Stenzel's record. Among those in the audience was Dorothy Hester Stenzel, who watched her record fall and then cheered Osterund on through the new record she was setting.

Ironically it was Stenzel who recruited Osterund to break the record. "I had seen her at air shows," Stenzel says, "and I was impressed. It was well past the time for the record to be broken anyhow, so I talked her into it. She was a smooth flyer, so I didn't think she would rip her wings off. And, you know, I still have the inverted snap roll record."

She's right. Her record, set in 1931, two days after the outside loop mark, still is intact. "You know," she says as she taps one of her bright pink fingernails on the table, "that's not an easy maneuver to do." That, of course, is an understatement. The pilot flies inverted, then does a sudden 360-degree spin, which has been known to rip off the wings.

"Jimmy Doolittle was the Army's stunt pilot back then," Stenzel says, "but he lost his tail during a snap roll and never would do it again."

With that, Joann Osterund added, firmly, "The inverted snap roll is a very difficult, violent maneuver. I wouldn't ever try it."

Betty Skelton is remembered for her automobile speed records on the sand at Daytona Beach. But when she was eight years old naval aviators who did aerobatics over her backyard instilled in her the desire for adventure. She "unofficially" soloed at twelve and simply "stayed in the sky for the next several years."

"I started flying air shows when I was eighteen," she says, "so it was only natural that I would wind up in the International Aerobatic Championship for Women."

As it turned out, she more than wound up in it. She won it in 1948, 1949, and 1950. After she had exhausted all of the things a woman could do in the forties and fifties in aviation, she turned to automobiles. And then she went into advertising and became a vice president in an ad agency. But she didn't give up flying.

"It never gets out of your blood," she advises. "I mean, if you're a dedicated pilot. Besides, flying was my first love. Automobiles were exciting, but flying takes a lot more planning and coordination. Just being aware of your equipment and taking care of it is challenging enough. I don't mean to say that you can ignore your race car," she adds. "It's just that you're usually not allowed a *second* crash in an airplane."

How does she feel about women in aviation today? "I still have one pet peeve, so far as discrimination against women in aviation," she says. "And that is that NASA still has failed to select a woman because she is a *pilot*. It's simple. They needed a woman to satisfy public sentiment. They haven't even had a crew member selected just because she was a pilot. I'm hoping that they will have a woman as a command pilot. Until they do, they're still discriminating."

But the tide is beginning to turn. Scores of women sit in the left and right hand seats of commercial airliners today, and their number is growing. They can wear makeup and they even have pockets in their jackets.

"I fell in love with flying very quickly," says Stephanie Wallach, who is a first officer for Alaska Airlines, based in Seattle. "But, as much as I loved it, I was hesitant, almost embarrassed, to express this to anyone for fear of being ridiculed. At that time there were few opportunities."

But opportunity knocked for Wallach; she obtained her pilot and flight engineer ratings, and by the mid-seventies she had made her way into the ranks of the professional pilots.

"I was among the first ten women in the United States hired as airline pilots, and I may have been the first to fly in the right seat of the Boeing 727.

"Things are much better now," she thinks, "but still I hear through the grapevine that some male pilots think women can't cope under stress. I've been doing it for ten years, and I *know* women can deal very effectively with the stresses of the job."

As much change as there has been for women, many have come back to where a lot of them were half a century ago—the air show. Cheryl Sterns became the first female member of the Army's elite parachute team, the Golden Knights, before becoming a commercial airline pilot. But it is jumping out of airplanes that thrills her more than flying. Flying she does for a living, skydiving for fun. She has earned more than two dozen national and international skydiving championships. She also holds a world record for style and accuracy.

One impressive feat involved jumping from an airplane from 2,500 feet and landing dead center on a four-inch disk—not just once but an incredible forty-three times.

A number of race car drivers fly; it's natural for them. For one thing, it gets them back and forth to races quickly, but probably more important, it provides them with another vehicle in which to play. Such is the case with the legendary Cale Yarborough.

"I was flying back and forth to most of the races in my Bonanza," Yarborough says, "and I'll tell you, the trips home were long. Can you imagine racing for five hundred miles and then spending another two or three hours flying home? There were times when I was so tired after a race that I had trouble even getting into the airplane, and my ears were ringing so much that I had to turn up the radio as loud as it would go, just to hear what the guy in the control tower was telling me.

"There were times when I dozed off while I was flying. But I wasn't alone; many of the other drivers were doing the same thing.

"I took my wife, Betty Jo, and our daughter, Julie, along with me to Rockingham, North Carolina, for one race, and it got rained out, so I went over to the driver's lounge to see if Lee Roy [Yarbrough] or any of the other guys had called the airport for the weather. They had. Lee Roy said, 'It looks okay for us, Cale. I checked Florence [South Carolina]. The storm is moving away from us, so we're all right.' It would have been all right if we had left then, but you know us—we stayed there for another hour, talking racing.

"When I took off, I expected to climb out of the weather by the time I got to five thousand feet, but instead, I climbed right into the worst rainstorm I had ever been in. The weather had changed drastically in the hour we had been shooting the bull. I kept climbing, trying to get out of it, but there seemed to be no ceiling to it.

"I had turned south because the weather there had been better, according to the Florence tower. But the higher I got, the harder it rained. It was raining so hard, I couldn't see the prop. I was at thirteen thousand feet, and the lightning was flashing all around us. I hadn't said a word. I looked at Betty Jo, and she was holding Julie tight. She hadn't said a word either.

"The engine started missing," says Yarborough. "It was being drowned out. I leveled off and cut back on the power. I knew that it would miss more if I pushed it too hard. I knew I was in real trouble. It was by far the worst weather I had ever flown in. I put the landing gear down because I was afraid I would be too busy later. And because I was sure we were going down.

"The engine finally quit completely. We were at 13,500 feet. I banked the plane and turned it around, keeping as level a glide path as I could. I didn't want to go south anymore because I knew we were headed for the Great Pee Dee River Swamp. I knew if we went down in there, they would never find us.

"The turbulence was so bad that at times we were going straight up and at other times we were going straight down. All of the needles were locked on the instruments. I kept pulling back on the stick when we were heading straight down, trying to save it, but it didn't help. It didn't help to work the stick when we were going straight up either.

"The plane was in someone else's hands.

"It would fly straight up until it finally stalled out, and then it would fall, sometimes backward, for a couple thousand feet. Then I was upside down. With no power.

"There wasn't a thing I hadn't tried to do to save the plane, but it was useless at that point. I looked over at Betty Jo and Julie. I didn't give a damn how bad it was, I *had* to save that plane. If I had been there by myself, I think I would have given up, but I couldn't let them die."

Yarborough stops momentarily. Race drivers are a hearty lot and they don't scare easily. But when the danger involves a loved one— or, in this case, loved *ones*—it's an entirely different situation.

"Sweat was popping out all over me, he says. "I don't even know what I did, but the plane turned right side up. It was still being tossed around like a toy. I looked at Betty Jo again, and she put her hand on my arm. She didn't say a word, but she was telling me she had faith in me.

"I held on and did everything I could think if. I still couldn't see the prop. And it was stopped.

"But, wait! What was that? Through the rain and lightning I thought I saw a yellow streak down there. But it went away. I was able to get the plane headed for whatever it was I had seen. I leveled up, and the lightning lit up the sky again. There it was! I had come out of the clouds right over an old country dirt road. It looked like it had been cut out of the thick, piney woods, probably by loggers. And I was right over it, not ten feet over the treetops. It looked like Kennedy Airport to me. I made a perfect dead-stick landing; it was as perfect as it could be under the circumstances," he says with a smile that still showed relief, as well as disbelief.

"The mud and water were flying as we bumped down the road. The plane finally sank to a stop in the mud. We were safe.

"We sat there in silence for a long time. I know we were both thanking the Lord. Finally I said. 'I've gotta go find help. Y'all stay here and I'll be back soon.'

"When I got out of the plane, my knees were so weak that I almost dropped to the mud. Betty Jo handed me an umbrella. 'I don't need it,' I said. 'I just want to stand here in this beautiful rain and in this beautiful mud.'

"I started walking. It *was* a logging road, so there were no houses anywhere. I walked for miles. Then I turned around and went back to the plane. 'I'm going the other way,' I told Betty Jo.

"There was nothing the other way," he remembers, "so I went back and told her we would have to spend the night in the plane. 'I'll get help when it gets daylight,' I said. 'I'm not going to leave you alone in the dark anymore.'

" 'I'm not afraid, Cale,' she said.

" 'Neither am I,' said Julie.

"I had some family! We covered up with a couple of blankets I had in the back of the plane. Just after daylight I was awakened by somebody pounding on the door of the plane. I jumped up and opened the door. It was three Marines who were out on maneuvers in a Jeep. They had been coming down the logging road when they suddenly saw the airplane in the middle of the road. They told me it was a ten-square-mile wooded area and we were in the only clearing in all of it.

"The plane had broken out of the clouds right over the road, just at treetop level, and all I had to do was drop it in. The good Lord had put us there. I didn't have a thing to do with it."

Yarborough is composed as he relates the rest of the story: "The Marines took us in to a country store where I made a phone call. I knew where James Garner and Dickie Smothers were staying in Rockingham. They had come from Hollywood for the race, and they were the only ones I knew who had stayed over in Rockingham. They came after us and took us home.

"I called a fellow at Pinehurst, which was near where the plane was, and I asked him if he could go get it and fly it out of there. It was going to have to be dug out of the mud and it was going to take more flying than I knew to get it out of that tiny clearing.

"They had to wait until the weather cleared and the road dried up, and they dug it out. They had to cut the tops out of the pine trees before they could fly it out. And even then they had to get a crop duster to fly it. Nobody else could.

"When I went to look at the airplane, every bit of paint was off the wings. They looked like polished aluminum. In fact, they were."

Did Yarborough "get back on the horse"? In one sense, he didn't. "I sold it and bought a *twin*-engined plane," he says. "I never took my family along in the airplane after that because, if you must know, it scared the hell out of me. I've never been afraid to do anything— race cars, skydiving, everything I've ever tried. Oh, there have been butterflies a lot and there have been times when I'm scared for a second when the race car is spinning through the air and about to crash big-time—but the airplane incident was something completely different. It didn't just involve me, it involved my family, and I'll tell you, that's a whole 'nother ball game."

If the pilots who fly the X-15 fly the fastest planes in the world, Pat Henry leads a group of pilots who fly the *slowest*—the Goodyear blimps.

"I started my blimp career in the Navy," says Henry. "I didn't really want to go into lighter-than-air; I had been an instructor on T-34s and T-28s, but you know the Navy. That's exactly where they sent me. I'll never forget the day I arrived at Brunswick, Georgia, and walked into the hangar where the airships were. They were towering over me, and I thought to myself, What the hell have you gotten yourself into?

"The first flight was a full enlightenment. I learned a different sense of 'feeling' an aircraft. And, I'll tell you, there's a big difference. The biggest contrast is that in any other aircraft you have three accesses of control—pitch, yaw, and roll. With a blimp you only have pitch and yaw.

"You have to learn to anticipate the turns, and you make them entirely differently than you do in an airplane. With the Goodyear blimp—which is a lot lighter than the old Navy blimps—you begin to learn that it is buoyed up and you're actually riding 'on' the air," Henry points out. "Of course, that makes it the most susceptible of any craft to all disturbances of air—thermal, wind shear, or whatever. You pick up more of the natural influence. That's why they call it an air*ship*, because it operates something like a boat.

"It takes longer to make some corrections [in a blimp] because it's much slower, so you learn an entirely different sense of feel, a sort of a seat-of-the-pants impression of what the ship is doing. You have to develop a sense of over-control and then correct for it to get the response you want."

One of the most dreaded aspects of flying a blimp obviously is weather, but it is not the total bugaboo one would imagine. "You have to fly around all thunderstorms," Henry says, "but an airship is a very durable craft, so once you learn that you can take care of yourself, you begin to relax a little. Probably the worst thing about the weather and blimps is that it's more likely to change on you in an airship than it is in a fixed-wing craft. We move so slowly that it gives the weather much longer to change its mind. We're only traveling at thirty or forty knots, so a lot of things can happen weatherwise between, say, Chicago and Des Moines.

"And if the weather guys miss the wind velocity by five or ten knots, it's no big thing to an airplane. But the difference between, say, twenty-five and thirty-five knots is pretty dramatic in a blimp," he explains. "We make very little headway in strong winds and we burn a lot more fuel, which, in itself, can be a problem because we've already planned our fuel stops. You can't just fly another hundred miles over here and pick it up."

"If the ship didn't keep you busy all the time, it would be as boring as hell on most flights, because we're moving so slowly and there's usually not that much to see," says Henry. "But you have to pay attention. There's no autopilot. You have to keep pumping the rudder pedals and cranking the elevator to keep it going where you want it to go. I mean, very seldom do you run into a situation where you can trim it up and take your hands off and let it fly itself. The airship really doesn't do that."

The Goodyear blimp is an institution at important American sporting events, but as glamorous as covering the World Series or the Super Bowl might seem, it is perhaps the most "boring" aspect of flying to a blimp pilot. Granted, they have the best seat in the house, but the demand on their time is at its peak.

"Sports events," Henry asserts, "are very tedious for us, because we have to hover most of the time. And keeping that big thing stationary is not exactly like dropping anchor. Also you're sort of keyed-up all the time because you know how important your job is to the network. At any second the director could want to use the particular shot you're in, and it could come just when you're in a turn to get a better position. So you have to stop and keep the ship as stationary as possible.

"If the director has to wait for even one minute, he's probably already thought of six other shots he wants, and that particular one he had in mind thirty seconds ago is history. He's not going to use your shot, and I'm enough of a 'company man' to know that Goodyear is there to get as much ink as possible, so it's up to us to deliver. So you have to pay attention all the time.

"In our particular situation," says Henry, "we use a split headset; we listen to our radio for air-traffic control and tower and approach control, not to mention our company frequency that allows our guys on the ground to keep in touch. On the other side you're hearing the director or maybe the production people, so there may be three or four conversations going on at the same time. You have to be able to pick out the pertinent one or two and respond accordingly."

Airships are designed for maximum altitudes of ten thousand feet and even that pushes it. "It's not operationally feasible to fly even close to the max," Henry feels, "because to do that, you would have to valve off so much helium that there wouldn't be any life at all in it when you came back down. And we're either carrying night sign equipment or camera equipment or passengers, so we need all the lift we can get.

"Since the air bags expand as you go higher, it means you have to release enough of the gas to compensate, so we usually restrict our altitude to three thousand feet. That means that we have to fly great distances to get around even simple mountain chains. And it means that there are a lot of places we don't go to at all. Like Denver."

"You get used to the problems, though," Henry says buoyantly. "And with the experience comes a level of maturity as a pilot so that it becomes almost routine—all of the thunderstorms and air traffic and temperamental directors. Everything becomes 'part of the job.'

John Creighton, pilot of the Goodyear blimp *Columbia*, based in California, says, "Most airplanes fly the same; the instruments work the same, you put in the numbers and fly it. Not with the blimp. You're not flying with aerodynamic lift, you're flying with buoyancy. After three thousand hours of flying fixed-wing aircraft, I had to get used to the sluggishness of controls compared to an airplane.

"In an airplane you're afraid to put in a lot of rudder, even if you feel you *need* a lot of rudder. But with the airship, the speed factors and the attitudes are so different. One of the hardest things to get used to is that when the ship is light, you have to physically fly it into the ground. Otherwise it won't go down.

"When you're on final, you have to roll the nose over twenty or thirty degrees and apply full power. With nose down. You'd never think of that in a fixed-wing craft. Other than that, there isn't a great deal of excitement in flying it. It's routine after you get used to it.

"Actually, it takes more getting used to by the tower than it does us," says Creighton. "They give us things like a quarter-mile visibility and we get down to two hundred feet and still can't see the damn runway, and you say, 'Shit, what am I doing here?' I mean, we don't have time to go around again and there's no telling what else is out there, waiting to come in.

"We try to stay out of the way of the air traffic, but most of these guys don't realize we're only flying thirty miles an hour. They're not used to speeds like that. And we ask for weird altitudes and that rattles their cage. They say 'Climb to fifteen thousand,' and I come back with 'How about five hundred?' And they usually call in a supervisor to talk with us.

"I always get the impression that there's a great sigh of relief in the tower when we finally get moored. It's not as exciting to us as it is to them."

But, as in all types of flying, there are days when the excitement nearly defies description. October 17, 1989, in the skies over San Francisco was one of those days. And nobody had a better vantage point of the colossal happenings below than Creighton.

Most San Franciscans remember the day, not because of the World Series—the much talked-about Bay Bridge Series between the Oakland Athletics and the San Francisco Giants—but a monumental trick of nature.

"We were flying the game for ABC," says Creighton, "so I was directly over Candlestick Park, just three miles south of San Francisco International Airport. Departures that day were north/south, with a right turn over Candlestick and then they were on their way.

"We were doing pregame setup shots and a rehearsal of what opening shots ABC needed. I had cleared everything with SFO [Airport] tower, so we were running back and forth over the stadium, about five hundred feet above home plate. Just about that time a 747 flew right over the top of us and I got a lot of wake turbulence. There was a lot of vibration. And then we lost our picture. I figured somebody had screwed up and it went to black, which, of course, is something you never want to do on live television. I thought, Oh, shit, somebody's ass is going to be grass.

"Just then I noticed a landslide on the hill north of Candlestick. And then we got the audio back and the first word I heard was 'Earthquake!'

"It all started to make sense.

"I looked around and I saw several flashes of transformers going up," Creighton exclaims, "and I saw smoke and dust rising around the city. In the Berkeley area I saw clouds of smoke. I knew it was something major.

"San Fran tower called me and asked me to get in touch with Oakland tower immediately. I thought it was weird for me to be in their air space and them wanting me to talk with someone ten miles away. But when I got to them, they were having people check the runway for damage."

They were diverting all traffic from San Francisco International, a move that usually isn't done unless there's a real problem, such as an aircraft that's upside down on the runway.

"The coordination of air-traffic controllers was terrific," says Creighton. "But it looked like everything else was going to hell down there. Our TV coordinator on the ground told us there was a fire in Berkeley and asked us to go look at it. All of a sudden I was flying the only live news broadcast of the earthquake—probably to the whole world.

"As we went by the Bay Bridge, I noticed there was a section down. I held the blimp over it while the cameraman zoomed in on it. Then I noticed that the Nimitz [Freeway] had collapsed. I had gotten clearance from the Coast Guard to stay in the bridge area, as long as I stayed out of their way, but then I saw the fires in the Marina area, so we moved over there."

When the sun began to set, Creighton and the men on board the blimp *Columbia* started to realize the immensity of the earthquake. The entire downtown section was blacked out, and the fire in the Marina section was intensifying.

"We did the best we could to get good coverage for the network," Creighton contends. "We were the first there, so I knew we had a scoop."

Not only were they there first, but they had the only power at that point. They had the mobile power units at Candlestick, so they were transmitting back to there and, in turn, sending coverage out to New York. "We were doing a live network feed when most of the local stations were unable to get anything to their networks because their emergency power generators hadn't come on yet." There were a lot of stations that didn't get back on the air for forty-five minutes, and when they finally did they used the blimp footage, which, by then, had been put together in an ABC show.

While the local stations were doing mostly traffic and emergency information, telling people where the shelters were and giving reports of missing people that had turned up, ABC was sending out a world-wide news show.

"Ours was an overall global operation. We had a cameraman and a technician from Akron on board; all of us stayed up there for more than eight hours. It was a long, long night. But, other than the hel-icopters, we were the only ones who didn't have any trouble landing.

We don't need a prepared runway; we can land out in a field if we have to, so in a disaster situation, the blimp is ready to go."

Every experienced blimp pilot has at least one good weather-related blimp story. Here is John Creighton's.

"I had been flying a blimp about four years," says Creighton, "but I had never flown from Spokane to Portland in a blimp. I had done it in an airplane many times and it was no different than flying from Miami to Tampa, so far as effort was concerned. It was anything but that in the blimp.

"We had to fly up through the Columbia Gorge, with the wind whistling through there like a wind tunnel. The trip to Pasco wasn't too bad. That's where we made our turn to head up the river through the gorge. And that's where it got interesting."

The *Columbia* left Spokane about eight in the morning but the ground speed kept deteriorating. By afternoon, they were down to about ten miles an hour and fuel was becoming a problem. By the time they got to the airport at the east end of the gorge, the winds were so strong on the ground that they couldn't keep the ship stationary enough to fuel it normally; they had to add fuel from five-gallon cans, sloshing it in as best they could while the wind rocked it like a child's toy.

"I had to run the engines at full power," explains Creighton, "just to try to stay put, and we were still moving from right to left and then back again because of the wind shear. We finally got one hundred gallons on board and took off again, although I wasn't exactly excited about it."

Forty-five minutes later, the blimp passed the west boundary of the airport. Three and a half hours after that, they had reached the Hood River, for a total of ten miles. All in all, it was beginning to rival the flight of the Wright brothers.

"I looked everywhere in the gorge for areas of less wind." At one point it took twelve minutes to travel approximately twenty feet. The blimp was bobbing up and down and all over the place, but they finally made the Hood River Airport, which sits in a little canyon off to the side of the gorge.

"We put in more fuel, and then we struggled on to Cascade Locks, which was another five miles. I know it doesn't sound like much, but the adrenaline was pumping by the time we got there because we were low on fuel again."

Finally, most of the wind subsided. The worst part of the trip was behind them. They arrived in Portland about eight hours later than planned. They chalked the whole thing up to "experience"—an experience that few modern-day flyers will ever have.

Flying a blimp is a lot like flying the mail in the early days. With wind whipping you around a rocky canyon, it is not at all hard to imagine what a World War I fighter pilot must have felt like.

If the sun is just right and if you squint your eyes, you can almost see the Red Baron closing in on you.

Chapter Seven

There wasn't much light in the DC-9 cockpit, but I could see the revolver in his hand.

— HIJACKED EASTERN AIRLINES PILOT

*A*re commercial airliners safe? "No," says nearly every seasoned pilot I talked with. But, despite all of the information that leads them to this answer, there are more young pilots with their eyes on the left seat of a major air carrier than on any other place in flying. It is what most aspire to—more than the military, more than instructing, and certainly more than merely flying for fun. The thought of "getting paid for something I love to do" is the dream of many young pilots.

But if our aging fleets of airliners are basically unsafe—as everyone except the carriers themselves says—why do pilots still fly them? "Ego," says Jack Albrecht, who flies for Pan Am. "I think all of us have the idea that one, nothing is going to happen on this flight, and two, we're good enough to fly that bastard out of any problem if it *does* happen. If I didn't believe that, I'd be bagging groceries or something."

Perhaps pilots *are* slightly outsized.

But, as glamorous as it might seem to be paid for doing something one truly enjoys, the life of a commercial pilot is not all fun and games. There are "anxious" moments, but more often there are many more cases of fighting off extreme boredom or tenseness.

What goes through the mind of a pilot who has a hijacker's gun to his head? Or when the airplane is showing serious mechanical problems? The answers are fairly simple: They deal with the problem at hand. Maybe they are a special breed of people, with a common fiber of courage and spirit of adventure running through them.

Luckily some threatening situations have comic endings. A few years ago a C-142 with an unusual cargo—a water buffalo that was being transported to a zoo in the Midwest—droned along routinely over the flat prairie below. Suddenly the huge beast broke loose from its crate. Not totally pleased with flying in the first place, the water buffalo tore through the cargo bay like a bull at Pamplona, rocking the plane from side to side as it frantically sought an escape route.

Finally, the pilot, who was fighting to control the airplane and fearing what the worst scenario could be, shouted into the intercom, "Kill the son of a bitch before it kills *us*." To the delight of the Society for the Prevention of Cruelty to Animals, the keeper who had been sent along to watch over the animal had a tranquilizer gun, and he sedated the angry creature before it literally tore through the side of the air transport.

It was anything but a routine flight. And surely more memorable than the one with the load of lobsters the pilot had flown the day before.

Conversely, some flights, no matter how sensational they may appear in the newspaper, are, in reality, little more than milk runs to the people inside. Astronaut Jon McBride, who piloted one of the early flights of the shuttle *Challenger*, feels "The first lift-off was an anticlimax. We had spent so much time in simulators, practicing lift-offs, that I knew exactly what the real thing was going to feel like; it was exactly what I expected.

"The actual lift-off was so routine that by the time we got into orbit—which was about eight and one-half minutes—I turned to look at the crew and they were looking out the windows. Sally Ride looked like she was in a bus, for Christ's sake."

A veteran airlines pilot, who wishes not to be identified because he would like to stick around with Noname Airlines until his retirement, says there is a lot more pilot error than you ever hear about.

"Take the Avianca crash on January 25, 1989, for instance," he relates. "Here are three guys who may not be the hottest pilots in the world, but they can fly a damn airplane. The 707 got held down over

South Carolina somewhere and then again somewhere around D.C. They were low on fuel and all of them should have known it. Shit, all you have to do is check your gauges.

"But apparently they thought these guys on the ground had some way of knowing how much fuel they had, and they assumed everything was all right. Wrong. They didn't say a damn word when the aircraft got down to 10,000 pounds of fuel (it carries 51,500 pounds). Since kerosene weighs about 7.5 pounds per gallon, this means these guys have got less than 1,300 gallons, and they're still at full power with four engines porking away. All they had to do was make a simple declaration of emergency and the plane would have been put on fast track for landing. Instead they kept quiet and were kept in the holding pattern for thirty-eight minutes more."

The absence of fire or explosion on impact and the lack of fumes afterward were an indication that the twenty-three-year-old 707 had completely run out of fuel shortly before it was to land at Kennedy.

"In a situation like that, you can look at the gauges and just watch them unwind," pilot X admonishes. "It's unbelievable how much fuel you suck down at low altitudes. All of a sudden these guys find out that all four engines are out of fuel. At any point the captain could have said, 'Hey, we're in deep shit.'

"I suppose on a plane as old as that 707 it *is* possible that the gauges were reading wrong—that happens too damn often. I mean, you've got a plane that's twenty years old and it's been started and started and bounced and jiggled all over hell, so gauges can be off as much as twenty percent. I can't begin to tell you how many times that's happened to me, but damn, I still have a feel for how much fuel I have, even if the gauge says something else.

"But here's where a lot of problems begin. And end. There's a point where a pilot can declare an emergency, but if you do and you get the plane on the ground, the paperwork will be up to your ass. It's unbelievable how much you have to go through, so an awful lot of guys on a near miss or a somewhat minor mechanical problem don't even declare it because they don't want to have to go through the tons of paperwork. Also, a lot of them don't declare an emergency out of pride. Can you imagine that?"

Our pilot speaks calmly but firmly: "When I hear of some stupid mistake like this, I always study every aspect of it. I read the FAA reports, the newspapers. I ask questions. I do everything I can to find out all the facts available because it concerns me when I think how old this fleet of airplanes is that we're all flying."

Most airlines put such a crash as the Avianca one on their flight simulators and recreate the circumstances, just to see how it might have happened. "Sometimes it helps, but most of the time they give up, just like the FAA, and say, 'It was this or it was that.' Hell, most of the time they don't have the foggiest idea what caused it," says our confidant.

"Listen to this: A few years ago Eastern's Flight 401, a Lockheed 1011, an airplane that was state-of-the-art at the time and had never had an accident, was on the New York to Miami run. They had been cleared for approach, so they went through the final checklist and everything was going according to plan. Then they put the gear down. The light that told them the gear was down and locked in place didn't come on.

"They acknowledged to the tower that they had a problem and aborted the approach. They went out over the Everglades to try and sort it out, which was smart. They retracted and lowered the gear a couple of times. Still no light. So now they've got three guys looking at one light bulb. Of course, the airplane is on autopilot, but it's common practice to look around every once in a while to see how things are going out there.

"They couldn't get the light bulb out to see if it was faulty, so the captain told the flight engineer to go down in the lower hold and visually check the gear; there's a place down there where you can actually tell if the gear is down and locked. That's apparently when it happened: In leaning over one time to check the bulb, the pilot apparently bumped the yoke and disengaged the autopilot.

"The airplane was slowly descending while in its holding pattern. Nobody was looking at the altimeter; nobody was looking at their radar scans like they're supposed to, because they're all working on a light bulb or climbing around in the hold. There were no altitude-responding transponders, which meant that nobody was reporting to them that they were getting into trouble.

"When the autopilot was accidentally disengaged, the airplane was so well trimmed that it just started to descend very slowly, not sharply enough for any of them to tell. So, while they were working on a light bulb, the plane was headed for the ground.

"When they finally looked out the windows, they were less than fifty feet from the ground. It was too late then. They drilled it right into the Everglades. Some of the passengers and the flight attendants survived, but the crew was killed."

Why have there been so many recent survivors in recent major crashes? "I'm not real sure," replies pilot Christian Allison. "Maybe it's the fire-retardant measures they've taken; but more than likely, it's the point of training. It's getting so intense that the airlines are actually putting guys into these very same situations and letting them work it out.

"Recurrent training is a bitch; they're putting you into one emergency situation after another. And it's not like being a doctor. Hell no, what you're doing is putting your license on the line.

"Oh, it's not quite that drastic," admits Allison. "I mean they've got FAA inspectors who are working for your company and if you bust one of the emergency situations, they're not going to send you out the door with an apple and a 'thanks.' The company has too much invested in you. But you're sure as hell going into a lot more training."

Most pilots, including Allison, feel that recurrent training is important, as much of a pain as it is. "It's gotten a lot more crowded up there," he says. "But with the new state-of-the-art equipment, it makes it a little easier. I know when I started flying we used high-level routing almost exclusively—and we still use it at times—but if you can go from point A to point B direct, using all this jazzy new equipment, it saves the company money and leaves the high air space for the guys to use that are flying across the country.

"It hasn't been that long since I started flying, but my first ship was a DC-6," he recalls. "You know, now that I look back at it, I'm glad I had that brief time in some of the old prop planes; I feel like a pioneer, for Chrissakes."

The new jets have glass cockpits where there really aren't any instruments. They are computerized screens, with heading indicators and everything that tells you where to fly your airplane. When the flight crew walks into the cockpit and all of the power is off, there is nothing but blank, black glass panels. But once all of the information has been programmed into it, all the flight crew has to do is sit back and watch the glass screen. Not all agree with this new procedure.

"You just fly the little airplane on the screen up into the bars and the screen tells you the rest—when it's time to make a heading change, exactly where to put the airplane at all times. For the younger guys coming in, it's super," Allison says. "But for a lot of the old-timers who are used to gauges, it's a little confusing. And, in some ways, it's harder.

"On the old systems all you had to do was learn the position of the gauges and where the needles should be pointing, and your hands were free to fly the airplane. Now you have to hit this button and that one and maybe a couple more before it tells you what to do.

"If you put in one wrong number, you can end up a hell of a long way from where you want to be. But it's not really a bad system; it's just that you've got a lot of older pilots who hate that shit and their hearts and confidence aren't into it.

"It bores the hell out of me," explains our recalcitrant pilot. "I find my mind wandering, just because there's less to do, so I guess I subconsciously figure, let the fucking computer fly the plane. But then I'm jolted back to reality and I realize it's really up to me. Deep down I know the glass screens are better, just like automobiles built by robots are better, but I still agree that 'the human mind is a terrible thing to waste.'

"Jesus, I can hardly wait until they get robots for flight attendants. Instead of carrying a condom, I guess I'll have to carry an oil can," he says.

"I do know one thing," he continues. "The airline never lets you get bored. Part of the time I'm flying the 'bagel run'—New York to Miami—and another month I may be flying the European route. And then, just to break the monotony, they might give me an air-cargo flight, flying pigs to Florida. I prefer the Florida flights—even if it's flying pigs. In fact, I think I'd *rather* fly pigs.

"Think about it: There are no people to bitch if you're late taking off or if the weather is rough. Or if the roast beef is tough. There is no pressure at all. And there's always this thought in the back of your mind: Hey, if I fuck this thing up, everybody can handle it. All we've got is a bunch of dead pigs. And all the airline has to do is pay some guy the market price for pigs. Hell, it wouldn't even make page one of the daily paper."

Another pilot, who insists on remaining anonymous, sits in the right seat—the place reserved for the copilot. And instead of showing the proper respect many captains demand, he shows a certain amount of resentment. "I hope someday the airlines break this business of the guy in the left seat being a god," he declares. "You know, technically, if you're the captain and I'm the first officer, and I say something you don't like, you can write me up. Then I have to go to the supervisor or the chief pilot and explain what's going on. I only have three stripes and he has four, but that extra stripe gives him the power to be a dictator. And not all of them are benevolent.

"Some captains get the whole crew together and say, 'All right, this is the way things are going to work: *Everything* reverts back to me and I'll delegate the duties. I'll also make all the decisions.' That includes when we eat, when we take a piss. Everything.

"Some other guys say, 'Here's how I'd like to do things; if you have any suggestions, I'll be glad to listen to them.'

"You have to know who you're flying with," says one copilot, "and I have a system that helps break down even the toughest captain. I make notes the first time I fly with a new captain—how he takes his coffee, what sports team he likes, whether or not he appreciates a well-turned ankle. Then the next time I fly with him—even if it's three months—I'll haul out my notes and say to him, 'You want some coffee, Bill? Still take it black?' Or 'Damn, your Yankees looked good last week.' He thinks I'm a goddamn genius. What a memory! So he usually ends up saying, 'Why don't you fly the leg over to London and I'll fly it back.'

"I not only make a lot of points, but I also gain a lot of experience. Experience that will get me in the left seat a lot sooner than waiting around for a bunch of guys to retire."

It should come as no surprise that it's not all work up there in the cockpit. There *is* play.

"We heard that we had a brand-new flight attendant joining us in Miami one flight," says an unnamed flight engineer, "so the captain, the first officer, and I went down to Walgreen's and bought some thick glasses off the rack. You can imagine the kind; they were so thick they looked like the bottoms of Coke bottles.

"We told the other three gals what we were going to do, so when we got in the air and everything was working smoothly, we called back to have some coffee brought up. They sent the new gal.

"When she came in," the flight engineer admits, "all she could see were eyeballs. Hell, these things were magnifying glasses. I was holding a chart up close enough to my face that my nose was touching it. I said, 'Yeah, I think this says Atlanta. Or maybe it's Augusta. Hell, I don't know. It doesn't matter, they're both in Georgia.'

"The first officer said, with his nose right on one of the gauges, 'Does this say full or empty?' The captain answered, 'How the hell do I know, I can't even see the damn altimeter.'

"She sat the coffee tray down very carefully, made sure our fingers were tightly clasping each cup and she returned to the cabin. White as a sheet. She was leaning against the bulkhead, lifeless, when one of the other flight attendants came up to her. She had a glazed look in her eyes. 'All three of those guys up there are *blind*,' she said.

"But you have to do things like that from time to time to keep from being bored shitless," he says.

Commercial flying has become so much more sophisticated today that a lot of pilots feel that it has taken a lot of the fun out of flying and has replaced it with a yard of monotony.

Not *all* flights are lethargic. Some that have all the earmarks of being prosaic can turn out surprisingly. On June 10, 1990, a British Airways BAC 1-11 was on its customary flight from Birmingham, England, to the resort town of Malaga, Spain. They were at twenty-four thousand feet. Captain Tim Lancaster, forty-one, had just put down his tea and had turned to hand the empty cup to flight attendant Susan Prince. He had momentarily unfastened his shoulder harness as he finished the tea and handed back the cup.

Without any warning, the left windshield on the eighteen-year-old airliner blew out. The instant decompression literally sucked Lancaster from his seat. His body smashed against the windshield frame. He tried to hold on but, little by little, his grip was weakening. Ms. Prince grabbed his legs. Purser Nigel Ogden, who was preparing tea in the forward galley, dropped everything when he heard the commotion and rushed to the cabin. He, too, clutched Lancaster's legs.

Steward Simon Rogers rushed to the cockpit, strapped himself into the pilot's seat, and also held onto the pilot as the enormous force dashed Lancaster's body against the side of the aircraft. Most of his clothing had been torn away. Ogden was bleeding profusely from a gash caused by broken glass. Twenty-degree-below-zero winds blasted through the airplane as other crew members tried to calm passengers and gave Ogden first aid.

Copilot Alistair Atchinson donned an oxygen mask so that he could remain as alert as possible and slammed the jet into a steep dive to get below ten thousand feet where the pressure would drop to normal and the temperature would rise.

"There was a terrific bang and a rush of air," said passenger David Duncan, when his heart stopped pounding later in the terminal. "The cockpit door was blown off its hinges and I saw the near-naked pilot hanging out the window covered in blood."

Atchinson, with the true grit of a seasoned airline pilot, calmly landed the 1-11 at Southampton, seventy miles southwest of London. It may not have been a typical day's work, but it was "something I had to do," he later said.

Valor has no territorial bounds when it comes to pilots.

"The crew was magnificent, and without them I wouldn't be here," said Lancaster the following day from his hospital bed, where he was recovering from frostbite to one hand and fractures of his elbow, wrist, and thumb. "I remember the buffeting of the wind," he says, "and I tried to shout back at the crew, but I'm sure they didn't hear me.

"I'll have to admit, the thought of death did cross my mind."

No one doubts the statement.

An anonymous British Airways employee said that the three-by-two-and-one-half-foot windshield was found intact on a farm near Wallingford, fifty-five miles west of London. "It's unusual for a windshield to blow out," he said, "but accidents of this type have happened before."

The Civil Aviation Authority and British Airways carried out investigations, but little more was said about the windshield, which had been installed only two days before.

Perhaps further statements were unnecessary. The British Airways incident points vividly to problems with maintenance, but what of incidents concerning the pilots themselves?

We all have heard accounts of pilots cavorting with flight attendants on the night before flights. And we have also heard, with anxiety, the tales of their drinking exploits. After all, a little amour is better than a rip-roaring hangover, particularly if your life hangs in the balance of the pilots' reaction times.

That is precisely why so many were concerned at the report of a Northwest Airlines jet taking off from Fargo, North Dakota, with a legally drunk cockpit crew. To make matters worse, an inexperienced FAA inspector at Fargo, who had been tipped off that the trio had been drinking heavily the night before, decided that they didn't appear intoxicated and he couldn't smell anything on their breath, so he called his boss rather than just ground them.

The Boeing 707, with ninety-one passengers on board, left while the inspector was frantically trying to reach his supervisor on the telephone. FAA regulations require a blood alcohol test when such matters arise, so the three-man crew was arrested upon arrival at Minneapolis–St. Paul. When tests showed more than the 0.04-percent alcohol level in their blood, their licenses were immediately revoked.

U.S. Transportation Secretary Samuel K. Skinner was enraged. "They had every opportunity not to fly that airplane," he said, "and they chose to disregard the safety of their passengers in doing so."

Predictably, a Northwest spokesman said there had been no irregularities during the flight, despite the fact that FAA regulations prohibit drinking within eight hours of flying a plane. Northwest has an even stricter "bottle-to-throttle" rule.

On March 17, 1990, just nine days after the incident, Northwest fired the crew. The airline learned that the trio had engaged in a rather riotous evening at a Fargo bar on the night before the 6:25 A.M. Flight 630. A cocktail waitress at the Speak Easy Bar had testified that the three spent the evening in the bar. The waitress said they showed up a few minutes before the 4 P.M. happy hour and "stayed several hours."

One bar patron reported, "Hell, it got *my* attention when I saw how those guys were putting the sauce away. I mean, they told everybody they were pilots and had a flight at six the next morning. I haven't even gotten on an airplane in ten years," he said. "And it'll probably be ten more now."

Such happenings as the Northwest incident are highly unusual in the overall picture of pilot behavior. For each sensationalistic newspaper account of pilot misconduct that is reported, scores of acts beyond the call of duty go *un*reported. But once in a while, reports of pilot valor make the front pages of our newspapers.

Take the case of Captain Robert Wilbur, Jr. "Routine" is the way Bob Wilbur describes his flying career from the time he joined Eastern Airlines in 1959 until 1970. But on a regular shuttle flight between Newark Airport and Boston's Logan Airport on March 17, 1970, all of that changed.

Flight 1340—a DC-9—left Newark on time at 7:30 in the evening, and was as routine as most shuttle flights. But when they were about five minutes from Boston, it became anything but routine.

Flight attendant Christine Peterson was moving from row to row, collecting fares, which was the custom on the commuter flights. As she stopped at the side of one passenger, she said in her usual friendly voice, "Your fare, please." She couldn't understand his reply, but he handed her eighteen dollars. The fare was twenty-one dollars. "It's not enough, sir," she said, still smiling. "You need three dollars more."

With that the man reached into a small black bag on the floor and pulled out a gun. This time she understood what he said: "I want to see the captain."

Peterson quietly asked the man to put the gun under his shirt so the "rest of the passengers won't see it," and the two walked forward.

"The first knowledge I had of any problem," reports Wilbur, "was when the flight attendant called the cockpit and said there was a passenger who wanted to talk with the captain.

"We weren't allowed to have passengers up during flight, so I said 'Tell the gentleman I'll be glad to talk to him after we taxi up to the gate.' 'You don't understand, Captain,' the voice said. 'He has a gun.'

"At that time our instructions were to comply with any would-be hijacker, so I told her to bring him up. To say that I was uneasy would be an understatement. Terrified would have been an overstatement, but it was somewhere in between. The truth of the matter—in spite of how 'composed' *The New York Times* said I was—is that I was scared shitless.

"I thought she was calling from the back," he says. "But it turns out that she was on the phone right on the other side of the cockpit door, so before I could even begin to think what I was going to do, the door burst open and there he was. There wasn't much light in the cockpit but the moonlight was shining in brightly and I could see the gun as if there was a spotlight on it. It looked like a .38 revolver. I also noticed a silver chain around his neck, with a skull and crossbones hanging from it.

"The first words he said were, 'Where are we going?' 'Boston,' I said, as calmly as I could. 'I don't want to go to Boston,' he answered. I remember thinking, then why the hell is he on this flight?

"I told him, 'This airplane doesn't carry a whole lot of fuel,' so he answered. 'Okay, then fly east, and let me know when we're about five minutes from running out of fuel.' I don't know if the gravity of the situation hadn't sunk in yet or what, but I said, 'Okay,' figuring to humor him."

Wilbur kept glancing at his copilot, Jim Hartley, who appeared to be calm. But when the two pilots' eyes finally met, even in the semidarkness, they could tell that they both had the same grave concern.

Flight 1340 was already on a downwind for Runway 27, which basically pointed them eastward, so when Boston approach control gave them a turn for the base leg, which is basically a three hundred and sixty degree heading, Wilbur didn't comply. It was a mistake to have the speakers on in the cockpit, because the hijacker heard the command.

"I don't remember if the speakers were on because it was procedure or not, but if it *was* procedure, it was a piss-poor one," Wilbur remarks. "I couldn't talk with Air Traffic Control without the guy hearing both sides of the conversation. And I sure as hell couldn't turn off the speakers. I decided to give the 3300 code, which meant hijacking.

" 'This is Flight 1340, requesting repeat on base leg,' I said. And then I said, '3300.' The guy didn't even pick up on it but repeated the base leg. 'Roger, ATC,' I said, '3300.' Nothing.

"That was the code then—it's a 7500 now—but I had never used it, and obviously the ATC guy had never heard it. Finally, after several messages which must have sounded pretty stupid to him, he said, 'Are you in some kind of trouble?' I said, 'Roger.' 'Continue on your downwind leg,' the guy said, so we continued flying eastward.

"When we got to within twenty miles of Boston control, I reminded the guy with the gun that we didn't have much fuel. 'Okay,' he said. 'Go to Boston.' At this point I didn't have the foggiest idea what he wanted.

"I had the airplane on autopilot and was trying to make very smooth maneuvers. I didn't want to alarm this guy any more than he already was. He was wearing dark sunglasses and a dark suit coat with an open shirt. He was perspiring heavily. So was I.

"I made a nice gentle turn back to the base leg and the final heading, and the guy asked when I was about three-fourths through the turn, 'Are we on our way in yet?' I told him we were, and then I turned to look out the left-side window because I didn't know a damn thing about the air traffic. I didn't know if we were having traffic vectored away from us because of the problem I had acknowledged to ATC or what.

"I was looking out the window when I heard what sounded like a cap pistol, right there on the flight deck. I felt a stinging numbness in my right arm. I whirled around and already Jim Hartley was grappling with the guy for the gun.

"Jim had gotten out of the seat and had a death grip around the guy's throat and his right arm trying to wrest the gun away. There were two more shots. Again I felt a burning sensation, this time in my left arm.

"I don't know how he did it, but Jim took the gun away from the guy. Then Jim shot him twice at point-blank range. The guy fell forward between the two seats and as he went down, I clearly heard him say, 'I can't even die.' I looked at Jim to tell him what a job he had done, but he was back in his seat, passed out. I took the gun from his hand and laid it on the shelf in front of the nose-wheel steering control.

"The first thing I did after that was get on the horn to Boston to tell them the situation. 'We've got a wounded hijacker on board and the copilot has been seriously shot. We need a doctor and ambulance and we need the police.' And then I glanced down to my right arm. The entire white shirtsleeve was red, from the shoulder down. So was the left. In all of the bedlam, I had forgotten the two stinging sensations following gunshots. I had been hit in both arms. When I sat back to study the situation, my arms began to throb. I called the tower again: 'We need immediate clearance for landing.' And then I added, 'Better get *two* ambulances.' "

Wilbur could feel the warmth of the blood as it trickled down his arms, and when he reached for the radio or any of the controls, he could feel it flow more. He wasn't sure how long he was going to last, so he was anxious to get the airplane on the ground as quickly as he could.

Suddenly the hijacker started to get up. Wilbur grabbed the gun, placed his right index finger on the trigger and pointed it at the injured man. But he didn't pull the trigger, fearing another shot might cause damage to the airplane. He turned the gun around and struck the man solidly on the head. The hijacker fell back to the floor. This time when he fell, his foot hit the bi-fold door and pushed one side of it open a few inches.

"I remember looking back through the crack in the door and seeing the passengers," says Wilbur. "They were all leaning forward in their seats. A flight attendant came up and asked through the crack if there was anything she could do. I told her just to take care of the passengers. 'Tell them everything's all right,' I said.

"It certainly wasn't one of the landings I looked forward to," he says. "I didn't pay attention to any restrictions, I just wanted to get it on the runway and into a slot, because I was beginning to get weak."

Wilbur looked over to see if Hartley had come to. He hadn't. "I couldn't figure out where he had been hit because there was no trace of blood anywhere. His shirt was as clean as it had been when we left Newark."

They found out later that the bullet had entered his left shoulder-blade area and had exited under his right armpit. It also had severed his aorta, and the reason no blood was showing was that he was bleeding internally. He was pronounced dead on arrival.

The paramedics quickly loaded Wilbur into an emergency vehicle and rushed him to the hospital. He was in pain but coherent. It was then that he learned of Hartley's death. Also by then the FBI had found out something about the hijacker. His name was John J. Divivo. He, too, was on his way to the hospital, badly wounded. He had been struck twice in the abdominal area by Hartley's shots.

Divivo had attempted suicide twice in recent years, so Flight 1340 was to be his third attempt. "I remembered what he said about not being able to die," recalls Wilbur. "And even though I'm no psychologist, it didn't take much to figure that this guy was definitely suicidal."

On the following Halloween night he was successful. Divivo hanged himself in his jail cell.

"I don't think any of it was a matter of maintaining composure," says the man who landed the DC-9 with bullets in both arms. "I think it was more reactive than anything. I can't attribute it to a thing. Maybe it was self-preservation. But I do know I kept thinking about the people in the back. That and getting that damn crate on the ground.

"I was a lot more concerned about Jim Hartley at that point than I was myself, because he was the one who had saved us all. He deserves the credit.

"There never was much pain from my gunshot wounds," he says, "but there was the throbbing and the numbness. Also the loss of blood concerned me a lot. But, you know, that landing was one of the best I ever made. The DC-9 isn't one of the easiest planes to land smoothly, anyway, because of the little rock-hard tires, but I guess I got lucky.

"After the landing, they told me to taxi to Gate 12, which was close. There they had paramedics and an ambulance. The Massachusetts Highway Patrol followed the ambulance that took Divivo away. They took Jim away and then I got up and walked down the air stairs. I sat down at the bottom and waited for the guys with the gurney."

Wilbur flew again the following June. He had no nightmares the night before the flight—or any night, for that matter. His first flight back in the air was routine.

Former astronaut Jon McBride began his NASA career by flying what is known as the chase plane for the first shuttle flight. He learned precision flying in his sixty-four missions in Vietnam, but he found out more about precise flying in the chase flights than in all of his combat missions.

"Next to flying the shuttle itself, it was the most exciting thing that happened in my NASA career," he feels. "I had cameras mounted on my T-38, and I flew around the shuttle after reentry to see if there was any damage to the orbiter before it landed. I was there to check on hydraulics and tiles and anything else that might look the worse for wear. Also I was there to give Bob Crippen and John Young a cross-check between their altitude and airspeed and mine."

McBride was to make sure everything had worked on the orbiter's first trip to outer space. He was to fly at precisely 285 knots, which was about top speed for the T-38. He practiced time and time again to be at a certain point, because he knew that if the orbiter got too far ahead of him, he would never be able to catch it.

"When the time came, it was tough," he admits. "The shuttle is built like a rock, but the T-38 is a very efficient machine, so I had to have it all dirtied up—flaps down, gear down, speed brakes on, everything I could do to simulate the descent of the shuttle. It was a challenge."

Perhaps it was even more of a challenge to fly the T-38 beside the shuttle than it was to fly "the rock" itself, but McBride got his big chance in August of 1983.

"Bob Crippen was the commander of the *Challenger* and I was the pilot," says McBride. "I knew from all of the simulator flights what it was going to feel like, but there really isn't any way to describe the feeling you have when you sit there and await the blast-off.

"When it happened, I was sitting there, working the controls and feeling some of the anxieties of such an important mission; I was doing something only a handful of people in the world had ever done. But the momentary daydreams went away because, as in any takeoff, whether it be from a runway or a launching pad, there are a lot of things to do.

"The shuttle is comparable in aerodynamics and versatility to a high-performance jet. If you wanted to make it roll or do a loop you probably could do it. Although it would cause a lot of coronaries back at mission control. I mean, damn, would that get their attention! I chuckled out loud when the thought crossed my mind.

"The biggest difference between flying the orbiter and a conventional aircraft is that you fly it with feel and thought rather than actual movement of a yoke or stick. If you want to compare it with something most kids can relate to, it's regulated with a hand controller much like the ones used on today's video games.

"To get the roll, pitch, and yaw," McBride explains, "you're limited to about an inch and a half of movement in any direction, so if you want to roll it left, it's almost like *thinking* left. You just think it and I'll swear you're not even aware that you're moving the control at all, but you do because the ship rolls left or right or it pitches up or pitches down.

"It's a very exacting machine and we were trained to fly right on the edge of its capabilities. It would be very easy to fly right past the juncture of that limit and get into a catastrophic situation, so that in itself keeps you on your toes.

"Aside from its being very precise and very responsive, you have to keep one other thing in mind: Unlike other aircraft, you only get one whack at landing it; you can't go and pull around. So you practice, practice, practice."

The night before shuttle pilots go into space, they must fly a Grumman Gulfstream, which is as close to the space shuttle as any off-the-shelf plane around. They are required to make about a dozen approaches and landings.

"That night it was like magic," says a satisfied McBride. "My twelve approaches were letter-perfect. It couldn't have come at a better time because John Young was standing there watching, and he was chief of the astronaut's office. I mean, damn, these were the best approaches and landings I had ever done in my life; I've never seen anything like it."

The success of the approaches is measured by the touchdown. It is how other pilots judge the quality of the landings. The rate of descent is measured in terms of one foot per second, which is so gentle a passenger wouldn't even spill a full cup of coffee. Each one of McBride's touchdowns were less than one foot per second and two of them were so close to zero, they couldn't even be measured. Passengers would not have been aware that the plane had touched down.

"I knew I was ready to fly into space," McBride states. "I guess this is one of the threads you asked about that runs between many pilots: A pilot rises to the occasion. It's not that any of my other landings had been less than perfect, it's just that when the chips are down, you make sure they *are* perfect. You do what you have to do."

The relative handful of Drug Enforcement Administration pilots have their work cut out for them as much as any group of pilots in the world. "For one thing, there are far more bad guys than good guys. We're greatly outnumbered," says Dave Ashton, special agent for the DEA.

Ashton was one of the first flying agents, starting fresh out of college when the agency was called the Bureau of Narcotics and Dangerous Drugs. "The BNDD didn't have a flying program at the time," he says. "But I kept putting out feelers and suggestions that one be started, because I had a commercial license and I wanted to do something with it. Besides, I thought there was a need for some flying agents.

"When they did get it started, I was the first agent they sent overseas," Ashton recalls. "And I'll tell you, we had our hands full. We flew reconnaissance, undercover work, marine surveillance, overwater work. You name it. We became heavily involved in helping support operations in South America by locating clandestine labs and then inserting troops to destroy them."

After the troops moved in, Ashton and the few other initial pilots supplied logistical support, intelligence, and photo reconnaissance. The whole ball of wax. But they got very little help at first from the Colombian government.

"I suppose the reason we didn't get much support was because they viewed us as very little threat to the drug trafficking," says Ashton. "I couldn't even fly to the north coast of Colombia, which is curious because that's where most of the drug activities were. But that section was controlled by the military. 'We'll take care of that,' they said. 'We don't need you guys over there.'

"They took care of it, all right," he says. "They were rotating generals on a six-months rotation, trying to get as many of them rich as possible by the payoffs from the traffickers. Then, suddenly, the responsibility of drug enforcement was shifted from the military to the national police, so we gained access to where we needed to be."

The biggest problem facing the DEA was still the lack of pilots. "Nobody wanted to go down there," remembers Ashton, "and the ones who did had little experience, and almost none in mountain flying.

"But I proved one day that even an experienced pilot can screw up," Ashton says. "I was flying out of Aruba, and we had moved over to Cartagena and were covering that portion of the coast. We had been flying a Piper Navajo about three hours when we spotted a small coastal freighter off the coast of Turbo.

"I had seen the boat before, but my copilot wanted to take some pictures, so we circled around and came in for a low pass. This particular day the water was very calm, like a mirror. If you've ever flown over water that looks like that, you know how you lose all depth perception because it *is* a mirror. With the sun glaring off it just right, you can't tell how high off the water you are.

"Being an experienced aviator, I *knew* this, so I was keeping an eye on the altimeter, so I could keep the airplane out of the water," he says. "I had no intention of making a real low pass, like we would normally do on a vessel, so that we could read the name on it and get other identification. We normally went down to about twenty-five feet and came right alongside, which is kind of exciting for us and for the folks on the boat."

On this one Ashton never intended to get below one hundred feet, but the copilot was having trouble getting the camera plugged into the cigarette lighter. It diverted Ashton's attention momentarily. "Bad mistake," he points out. "The next thing I know, my copilot looks up and gasps. I look up and gasp. We're right on the water. Wing level.

"I pulled back like mad and the airplane kissed right off the water," he says. "It skipped across the water like a flat rock. I managed to get it up a hundred feet but I could tell the power was greatly reduced.

"What a show it must have been for the people on board the freighter. I'm sure they went into port and said, 'You're not going to *believe* what we saw today.' "

Ashton limped into Turbo and landed, but when he tried to taxi back to the shack on the gravel strip, he couldn't get the airplane to move. When they got out and looked at the three-bladed props, they couldn't believe what they saw. All of the blades were bent back so far that only about one foot of the surface was working to propel the airplane.

"We had to spend the night in Turbo," states Ashton. "But the National Police came down there the next morning and hustled us right out, because the day before there had been three of the police murdered right there by traffickers. It was a primitive area, right on the edge of the jungle. I didn't worry much about the Navajo at that point—I just wanted out of there."

Leroy Altman was one of the people the DEA pilots were after. Altman was a pilot for a charter air taxi service in North Myrtle Beach, South Carolina, for a while; later he was a pilot for a company which flew round trips between Myrtle Beach and El Salvador. He enjoyed the long flights over water to Central America. Through an association with two contractor friends he began flying to Colombia to bring back marijuana.

"These guys contacted me when I was down in Houston flying for a drilling company from Texas to Mexico, and they asked me to meet them in Fort Lauderdale," says Altman. "I knew what they wanted, but I went anyway. They made it sound pretty attractive, so I said, 'What the hell, I'll try it.' "

They went to look at a couple of airplanes. The first one was a Cessna 337, an old push-pull job, and Altman turned that down, so then they found an old Beech 18 up in Savannah.

"It was like a small DC-3," he says. "I made about twenty-five takeoffs and landings and decided the old plane was all right. They had originally asked me to fly to Jamaica, so I agreed. Then they started trying to talk me into going to Colombia instead. 'Hell, no,' I told them. 'We'll give you seventy-five grand for each trip, and the airplane is yours,' they said. I said, 'Hell, yes.' "

Altman took off the next morning from Savannah before daylight, IFR [Instrument Flight Reference], and got as far as Orlando before the weather went sour. Orlando control put him in a holding pattern, but he didn't have enough fuel to do that and fly to Colombia, so he found a hole in the weather and went down near the beach. He landed at Fort Myers, where he planned to refuel and head out toward the Yucatan Cut, and then go down to San Andreas and straight into Colombia.

He was carrying two hundred gallons of fuel in a military fuel tank that was securely chained down, but he hit more bad weather out of Naples, so he decided to go in there, knowing they didn't have a tower and he wouldn't have to talk to anybody.

It was blowing and raining, and when he got the ship on the ground he almost did a ground loop. It was close. The landing was so rough that one of the fuel tanks had broken loose. He left the plane there and went on back to Houston.

The men called Altman a couple of days later and told him they had the airplane fixed and everything was all go again. He told them he thought the plane was a death trap and that he had a bad feeling about it, so they agreed to look at something else.

They bought a Cessna 402 for $250,000—a plane that Altman

eventually could keep—and they installed an auxiliary eighty-five-gallon fuel tank behind the seat. "I hauled ten five-gallon cans of fuel with me. But later, we carpeted it just like the rest of the plane," he explains. "Then it looked like it was supposed to be in there. We needed the extra fuel so I could fly down to Colombia, take on almost a ton of pot, refuel, and then fly straight back to Myrtle Beach."

With the modifications, the airplane met the arbitrary drug-smuggler's standard: It could fly 2,100 miles, haul 2,100 pounds, and land on an airstrip 2,100 feet long.

On that flight, Altman left Opa-locka Airport about 11:30 P.M., flew all night, and was on the ground in Colombia at about seven in the morning. After about forty-five minutes, he was off again, headed for the Carolina coast.

The first flight Altman made was to the desert in the eastern part of Colombia, where he was to find that the contacts were not as hospitable as he had expected.

He located the landing strip and sat down, and by the time he shut off the engines, four trucks had appeared out of nowhere. They were loaded with bags of pot and fifty-five-gallon drums of fuel.

Every man on the truck had a machine gun plus two or three more weapons. It was right from a TV screen somewhere. They boarded the airplane, took Altman's cooler, his food, his survival supplies, and everything that wasn't fastened down. "What the hell was I going to do?" he asks. "I mean, these bastards looked meaner than hell, and I sure wasn't going to argue with all that artillery over some sandwiches and Cokes."

The men methodically loaded on the pot and started rolling the fifty-five-gallon drums under the wings. They stuck a pump in one at a time and pumped it in, some of the fuel dirtier than Altman would have accepted anywhere else. "They wanted me gone," he says. "Hell, there was gasoline spilling everywhere and sparks flying. I got the hell out of there because I was sure they were going to blow that son of a bitch up."

The flight back to South Carolina was successful. And uneventful, although Altman changed his strategy. He landed in the Bahamas on a deserted island called Big William to add the fuel that he had brought from Colombia in the five-gallon cans. There were signs that others had been there—and for the same reason. He saw the wreckage of three airplanes—a Navajo, an Aztec, and a DC-3. There was nothing else there but sand.

When he had seen the sandy landing strip, Altman knew it wasn't going to be a simple landing. The three crashed planes were testimonials to that. "It's not easy to keep from bogging down and crashing in sand," he asserts. "What you have to do is keep the speed up to keep the airplane up on its tiptoes. You have to keep the power on until you get where you need to be, and then get it turned around before you stop.

"To take off you have to over-boost the engines to get the plane moving and you have to keep the power on. I always took a 'kicker' along. He's a guy who kicks the bags out of the airplane if we run into trouble aloft. This guy's eyes were as big as saucers by the time we got off the island.

"I looked at him and said, 'We gotta go for it,' so when I got up enough speed, I pulled back on the wheel and the minute it lifted off, I popped the landing gear up and took it up until it almost stalled before I pulled the nose back down. The plane sank down near the water and we were on our way. The guy said his first word since the takeoff began: 'Jesus.' "

As Altman neared the coast of Florida, he did a 360 to make sure nobody was around, and then he made a low-level flight right up the coast. As he got near Vero Beach, where there were a lot of flight schools, he took it up to about three thousand feet and became part of the air traffic. Unnoticed, he headed north to Socastee, near Myrtle Beach, and landed in broad daylight.

The next drug run was to a tiny clearing near the Panamanian border, where a new strip had been cut out of the jungle. He was advised not to go until it hadn't rained for four or five days, so he sat around the hotel in Fort Lauderdale, cavorting with friends and waiting for the report on Colombian weather. Finally it came.

Colombians and Cubans in Miami were making the arrangements at the other end. They phoned and told Altman everything was fine. They told him there was a single sideband radio on the landing strip and that if everything wasn't right, all he had to do was call Miami and they would make it right. It sounded like the perfect plan.

Altman and his kicker headed for Colombia again. They had trouble finding the strip because it was deep in the jungle—so far that it was a two-and-a-half-day horseback ride from the nearest dirt road. When we did find it, it was a long way from being what they had been promised. It was short and full of holes, so he told his kicker to "hold on," and he went in.

"I walked the runway while they were loading the pot, just so I could locate the worst holes and try to avoid them when we took off," he says. "When I got back, they had loaded about a ton of marijuana on. I knew I would never clear the trees at the end of the little strip with that much of a payload, so I made them take about five hundred pounds off.

"I fired it up and started down the runway. Now, keep in mind, this strip was so narrow that I only had about ten feet clearance on each wingtip, so I had to keep it straight. And I had to get it off real quick, because this sucker was short.

"It was a real hot morning, so I knew I wasn't going to have much lift. It was going to be a challenge," he says. "What I did on short strips like that was try to get the plane up to about a hundred-ten or a hundred-fifteen miles an hour. Just as soon as I got the nose up and was off the ground, I retracted the landing gear and brought the nose back down slightly to try and build up more airspeed quick. At that point, I was flying five or ten feet off the ground. Then I would put the flaps back up and pull out.

"But the runway was rough. Hell, they didn't even have vehicles so they had to cut this thing out by hand and level it the best they could. I got it going pretty good but then the right wheel hit a hole and dropped the wingtip down. It almost hit the ground. Then the left wheel hit another hole and it bounced the other way. The plane was ricocheting all over the runway, and I was still pouring the coal to it because I knew if I backed off it was over.

"The plane took a big hop and bounced back to the ground, and when it did, one wheel sank in the sand and pulled the wings around to the left. I pulled back on the wheel as hard as I could, trying to get it back up, but the wingtip caught in the vines and pulled the plane around completely sideways. Shit, I was flying wide-open right into the jungle. All I could see was green.

"I looked like a buzzsaw going through the underbrush. And all I could think about was that eighty-five gallons of avgas right behind me. The airplane must have gone a quarter of a mile before it came to a stop, and when it did, I threw open the emergency hatch and my kicker and I crawled out. I wanted to get away from it as quick as I could in case it caught fire and exploded."

Altman sat down in the jungle and watched the plane for about half an hour, until he was relatively sure it wasn't going to catch fire.

There wasn't much left of the plane. Both wings were ripped off and there wasn't a straight body panel on it. But eventually he worked his way back and reboarded it, very carefully unhooking the batteries first because there still were fuel vapors permeating the air. The slightest spark could have blown the airplane sky high.

The natives brought back the fifty-five-gallon drums, drained all of the fuel out of the plane, and unloaded the marijuana. Then they hacked away at what was left of the underbrush so they could get the wreckage out of there, fearing that the Colombian air force, which made regular checks of the area, would land if they saw the plane.

"You wouldn't believe how they got the plane out," Altman said. "They got a bunch of natives—I mean, a *bunch*—under the airplane and they literally walked it out of the jungle, all the way back to the strip. They had another little clearing where they had built a fence around it out of tree limbs, and they had some pigs they kept in there.

"They took part of the fence down, herded the pigs into another corral they threw together, and then they put the airplane in where the pigs had been. I went to the shack where the single sideband was and found out exactly what I had expected. The goddamn thing hadn't worked in months. I wondered how the hell I was ever going to get out of there."

One of the natives who spoke English said that a plane would be in from Barranquilla in about a week and that the two Americans could fly out on it.

By the time Altman got back to the airplane, they had already started stripping it. "They didn't have tools or anything, but they got the radio out. I didn't even want to watch, so I went back to the shack where they had some rum, and had a couple of stout ones."

That night one of the natives came to get him. He had a burning torch and Altman had a fleeting thought that they might be preparing him for human sacrifice. The landscape was bathed in moonlight; Altman could clearly see the trench they had dug around the airplane. The plane was propped up on poles and the whole thing was covered by branches and dry grass.

When they got to within about three hundred yards of the area, the guy threw the torch to the ground. They had poured gasoline all around the plane and down to where Altman and the man were standing. A line of fire raced toward the plane and as it reached it, there was an explosion, lighting up the entire sky. Altman's heart sank as he watched "his" plane being reduced to a pile of molten aluminum.

By the next morning, they had covered up what was left of the airplane, the fence had been built back, and the pigs were rooting around again, right where they had been the day before. There was no trace of the quarter-million dollar airplane. Altman wondered if any of it really had happened.

He found out later that two pilots had already been killed flying in or out of there, so there were at least three aircraft and two pilots buried there.

The next morning they took the two gringos by horseback up into the mountains to where the marijuana was grown. It was Wednesday. There were several huts where the family lived—the father, the grandfather, and sons and daughters. "There must have been fifteen of them," he recalls, "but they fed us well; that is, if you like chicken every meal."

They slept in hammocks, with chickens running around under them, clucking all the while. It was as far from sanitary as one could imagine. "I didn't even have a toothbrush, and after about a week, I felt like grass was growing on my teeth," says Altman.

On the following Sunday, they brought the horses out and motioned for the Americans to get on them. The old man stretched his arms out and made big, swooping gestures as he ran around the clearing. This was the day the airplane was coming. It was the day they would get out of there.

"We were an hour from the landing strip when I heard the airplane," Altman maintains, so he kicked his horse in the ribs and it upped its gait from slow to semi-slow. They knew that it would take a while to get the plane loaded but, still, the rest of the trip seemed like an eternity to the two men.

"We were less than half a mile away when I heard the engines start on the plane," says Altman. "I thought, oh, shit, and I kicked the hell out of my horse. But it was too late. I heard the engines rev up, and I knew he was getting ready for takeoff. I pulled back on the reins of my horse and sat there on its bare back and watched what was probably a perfect takeoff."

They turned the horses around and plodded back through the jungle to the tiny village for another regular diet of chicken, rice, and beans. And roots. For an undetermined time.

They sat there day after day in the tiny jungle commune, listening and looking skyward. "There was no noise at all," explains Altman, "except the animals and occasionally the talk between the natives. But they didn't speak much, so we sat there all day and all night, mostly in silence."

Twice they heard the sound of an airplane. And twice they got there too late. "Finally, I said, 'Fuck this, I'm going down to the airstrip and wait,' " Altman says. "I figured, shit, we might as well be going crazy down there as up here. The kicker agreed, so off we went."

They took along some rice and beans and chicken and headed for the airstrip, where they waited the two days. "And, sure enough, on the third day, we heard a plane," he says. "I decided right then, I don't know who's on that plane, but I'm going back.

"But it turned out not to be too easy, because the people on the plane were Cuban, and they obviously didn't want a damn thing to do with us, let alone take us out of there.

"The guy who was in charge had a butcher knife stuck in his belt, and I could tell he had taken an immediate dislike to me, so I figured I might as well confront him head-on. In broken Spanish, I said, 'All right, you motherfucker, we're in the same business as you are, so you're taking us out of here.'

"My Spanish was lousy then, but I was speaking a sort of universal language; you know, the one where you've got him by the collar and you're speaking right into his nostrils. People tend to listen. And the thing is, that's not really me, but I had been there for forty days and I didn't intend to stay one day longer. Even if I had to *eliminate* him."

Altman and his kicker left with the Cubans for Barranquilla, where they stayed another two and a half weeks before they could get a flight out of there. "But at least there was something to do there," says Altman. "We were out of the jungle and a little closer to civilization. Having 'something to do' didn't help much; we were told not to go out in the street because we would be taken hostage as sure as hell. It was still like being in jail.

"I had heard of cases where they would snatch an American pilot right off the street and send his head back in a bale of marijuana," he says with a grimace. "It made staying in the room a little easier."

Altman finally got a commercial flight from Barranquilla to Panama, where he had to wait two more days before getting a flight to Miami. As far as he was concerned, drug-smuggling was in the past. He retired.

Four years passed from October 1980 when Altman had settled back into a life of flying charter. But his past caught up with him. The South Carolina developers had also been dealing with a man who owned three restaurants and three or four shrimp boats. He was bringing in marijuana by boat, then storing it in three huge freezers in one of his restaurants. Somebody who was cleaning up the kitchen saw it and blew the whistle.

They arrested the guy, and he—in an effort to lighten his own sentence—sang like a bird. He told names and gave dates. The dates went back to 1980. The names included Altman's.

"The guy called me and told me he had squealed," says Altman, "but it was a year after that before they came after us." Finally Altman and the developers were indicted for possession of marijuana and conspiracy to import and distribute marijuana in 1985. They pleaded guilty, and the developers were sentenced to five years. Altman got four years.

He served thirty-two and a half months of his four-year sentence. He looks back on the whole affair with no remorse. "I don't think what I did was any worse than some of these savings and loans deals we're reading about today. All through the trial they kept calling it 'greed,' and I guess it was, but I just looked at it as a way to make some big bucks. Besides, if I hadn't done it, somebody else would," he said blithely.

Altman has gotten back his private pilot's license, which the FAA revoked when he was convicted. Soon he plans to begin taking the tests and check rides necessary to get back his multi-engine and commercial license. "It won't be tough," he proclaims. "They can take away your license, but they can't take away your knowledge.

"I *will* fly again," he says with determination. "But I won't fly any pot. I guaran-damn-tee you."

Chapter Eight

When the wingtip dug in, the DC-10 cartwheeled
in a ball of fire.

— Captain Al Haynes, United Airlines Flight 232

L owell Genzlinger typifies an immense band of aviators who refuse to "fly a desk" when that fateful day of retirement from active flying eventually comes—a day which assuredly is one of the occupational hazards most feared by pilots.

But Genzlinger is one of the more fortunate ones, because when his day *did* come, he had another form of flying to which he could turn. Many have no choice but to fly desks; they take jobs regulating young pilots or working for the FAA or at the local airport, or one of several positions where they find their wings clipped.

For some it is a physical problem that grounds them, for others it is legislated for them in the form of mandatory retirement age. But there are almost none who *choose* to quit flying. Feisty Edna Gardner White, who at eighty-eight still plans to take on the FAA in her quest for reinstatement of her pilot's license, is a perfect example. A cardiac bypass might seem an appropriate reason to the FAA to suspend the license of an octogenarian flyer, but it damn well isn't for Ms. White.

She is the rule, rather than the exception.

There are many more who feel exactly the same. Captain Jack Young, a former Eastern pilot who was "kicked out of the cockpit" at the mandatory age of sixty, has founded an organization called the Gray Eagles. At sixty-nine, he feels he is as capable—and maybe more so—of flying an airliner as he was at, say, forty-nine. But the FAA regulation, in effect for some thirty years, forced Young to step from the cockpit after thirty-five years of service.

Ironically, Dr. Herbert Karp, professor of medicine and neurology at Emory University, says there is a "great variability in the occurrence of physiological changes that occur as we get older." He feels strongly that there is very little justification of sixty as the cutoff point. "We can't say, but it might be as much as a decade too soon," he says.

Dr. Robert N. Blair, professor of geriatrics at Mount Sinai Medical Center in New York City, tends to agree: "We really think of problems emerging at seventy-five and above," he explains. "There is increased evidence of cardiovascular disease in the late fifties and sixties, but there's no sort of arbitrary jump at the magical age called sixty."

Perhaps the FAA has overlooked a significant point: In a jetliner there's at least one other crew member to fly the plane if the pilot suffers a heart attack.

The age sixty rule applies only to airline pilots; there is nothing to stop a one-hundred-year-old from flying a private plane anywhere, so long as he passes his physicals. All of this, of course, is music to the ears of Young and his Gray Eagles, who represent as many as one thousand veteran pilots who aren't quite ready for the front porch rocking chair. And surely aren't prepared to take a part-time job around airplanes.

To fully appreciate what it is that makes most pilots so determined to continue chasing clouds, it is important to understand the fierce desire they displayed in getting in the air in the first place. Seldom did I talk with a pilot who simply had his opportunity handed to him. More often than not they had to fight all sorts of pitfalls and jump all sorts of obstacles to get there—mostly financial, but, just as often, their relatives' and friends' fear of them entering this "dangerous" pastime.

Lowell Genzlinger could be the poster boy for this throng of pilots who face retirement from their infatuation with the sky. His beginning was like most:

"I grew up on a farm in South Dakota," Genzlinger points out, "but it was a tractor instead of an airplane that started the whole thing for me. And I guess it was my father's interest in flying that gave me the determination."

Genzlinger was too young to drive the tractor, so he had to stay back at the farm and take care of the mundane chores while his dad plowed the fields. But he always kept one ear cocked to the sky for the sound of the Aeronca Chief which belonged to a pilot in his hometown. It was the most beloved sound of his youth; it meant a flying lesson for his father and a ride for himself. The man came out to the farm each week and landed in the pasture next to the barn. The minute the airplane's wheels stopped rolling on the grass, the panting youth was at its side, reaching for the door handle.

"The guy always took me for a ride," says Genzlinger. "We'd fly out to the fields and buzz my dad on the tractor, and that was the signal for him to come back to the pasture and take his lesson. Of course, the guy could have buzzed him without stopping to get me, but he never did; he knew how badly I wanted to take that ride every week and he never let me down."

That was enough to launch Genzlinger into one of the most exciting careers a pilot could have. With his college diploma in one hand and his pilot's license in the other, he went looking for a job that would satiate his desire for adventure. The National Oceanic and Atmospheric Administration was just the ticket.

After flying into the eyes of 256 hurricanes over a span of two decades, Genzlinger retired from NOAA. But he didn't sit behind the dreaded desk or swing in the proverbial hammock; he went to work for the National Center for Atmospheric Research, flying weather reconnaissance.

"Even before I started flying hurricane watch with NOAA, I did fascinating things," he says. "We observed monsoons in India and Malaysia, and snow and ice storms in the Arctic. Sure, I probably could have flown for one of the airlines; they get big bucks, but there's also big boredom."

Stimulation is the key word for Genzlinger and a lot of other pilots.

"I just finished a job flying a Super King Air in the Caribbean Islands for NASA, where we had been out there flying all day at a hundred feet, dodging seagulls. This is *interesting* stuff," he exclaims. But there obviously are far more interesting tales for him to tell. For instance, flying into the eye of Hurricane Hugo, the most devastating storm ever to hit the mainland of the United States.

And, as if flying in there in the first place wasn't enough to get the adrenaline pumping, they lost an engine as they entered the eye.

Genzlinger and pilot Jerry McKim were at the controls of the Lockheed P-3 Orion, a four-engined plane that originally had been designed for Navy antisubmarine use. They were near Barbados and their job was to fly at a low level—about fifteen hundred feet—directly through the menacing winds and into the calm of the eye, from where they could study the storm. A second P-3 was to analyze it from the outside at a much higher level. Together they could supply the needed data to warn coastal areas from the Caribbean to the Carolinas.

"We didn't know much about the storm," says Genzlinger. "In fact, we didn't expect to find winds of much more than a hundred and twenty miles per hour. But as we got to the edge, the radar screen was red. That's a bad sign. We knew it was no ordinary storm, that's for sure."

The winds were becoming so fierce that they were forced to crab into the storm at about a forty-five–degree angle. What they discovered as they neared the eye was that it was an alarmingly fierce storm, one of the most powerful Caribbean hurricanes ever penetrated; strong enough, in fact, to snap the wings off the airplane like those on a balsa wood model, if not approached just right.

"As we got well into the storm, the winds approached two hundred miles an hour. This one was serious." Genzlinger speaks with candor.

The Orion bucked and was pitched about so violently that equipment began to tear loose from its mooring. Debris was flying everywhere inside the plane. Computer paper was flying around and it looked like a ticker-tape parade inside the Orion. The galley came apart; so did the tool chest. There were Coke cans and oil cans and salt and pepper shakers bouncing everywhere, and there wasn't a single drawer in all of the cabinets that hadn't lost its contents.

There was a sudden jolt—possibly a waterspout—and a two-hundred-pound life raft tore loose, damaging a strut on the ceiling of the airplane. Another jolt tore one of the computers loose and punched a hole in the ceiling. At one point the pilots couldn't even read the instruments because the vibration was so bad. But the last reading Genzlinger saw on the gauge that measures G-force was *six*. Six Gs is enough to rip this thing apart, he thought. But he kept the thought to himself.

"It was a tense moment," he says, "but it wasn't anything we all hadn't been through many times before. This one was just a little more awe-inspiring."

Awe-inspiring indeed.

"I wasn't all that concerned until I saw the burst of flame from the number three engine, the one nearest the cockpit. Flight engineer Steve Wade also saw the flame, so he immediately hit the kill switch. We had just reached the eye of the storm and within a period of a couple of seconds, the wind velocity dropped off to about forty miles per hour.

"At exactly the same time, we were hit with an updraft of about fifty miles an hour and then an immediate twenty-mile-per-hour downdraft. The plane lurched to the right, rolled severely, and dove for the water."

Losing an engine at a critical time like that probably is the worst thing that can happen in a low-level flight. Certainly when in the middle of one of the worst storms in history. In the characteristic nonchalance of a hurricane-chaser, Genzlinger said, "It got kinda rough in there for a while."

There was no tranquillity on the flight deck. Both pilots were wrestling to straighten out the airplane. But underpowered by the loss of the engine, the downdraft was sucking it straight toward the ferocious ocean. The waves, some of them fifty feet high, seemed as ominous as anything they had ever seen. But, at the same time, they had a beauty to them, much like a Winslow Homer watercolor. At eight hundred feet the command to dump fuel was given. As it got lighter, the airplane slowly began what would be an hour-long, demanding climb from the predicament they had been facing since they lost the engine.

In the meantime, the other Orion and the Air Force plane that was high above the storm had no radio contact with the airplane. When fuel is dumped all electrical equipment must be shut down. The crews on the other planes feared the worst, because the last transmission they had was: "We've lost number three engine and we're losing altitude." But there was no "Mayday." It's uncharacteristic of the type of men who fly such missions to give up. Or to even admit to trouble.

"One of the problems we had," muses Genzlinger, "is that the eye of Hugo was comparatively small—only eight miles in diameter—so there wasn't a whole lot of room for maneuvering. We had to fly tight circles, slowly spiraling upwards and dumping fuel."

The remaining three engines began overheating because they were working hard. Very hard. The upward spirals had to be in the direction of the bad engine, so it made the climb even more trying. That's why it took them the hour to become untrapped from their windy tomb.

"Just about the time I thought we were home free," says Genzlinger, "I looked out and saw what I thought was a prop boot coming apart. My first thought was that if it did come lose and the engine ingested it, we would be flying with two engines. I knew that would be the end.

"But after about ten more minutes it was gone. I found out later that it wasn't a prop boot at all, it was a piece of rubber that had been glued on to sort of smooth out the installation, and it just blew away."

By the time they got the Orion to ten thousand feet, they began to think seriously of getting out of the eye. "It was high time, we all knew that. We noticed that the northeast side of the storm looked a little less severe," he recalls. "There were fewer echoes on the radar, so we switched the radio back on and communicated with the Air Force plane. They said it wasn't too bad up where they were so we decided to give it a try.

"We flew straight out, as quick as we could, and I'll have to admit, I was glad to get back on land," says Genzlinger, in one of the rare times he or other hurricane-hunters ever admit to any "concern." They, of course, never refer to the situation as danger. And they most certainly never *speak* of fear.

What is it like inside the eye? "Almost none of them are ever the same," he says. "It's usually eerily calm. But they change. Sometimes the eye is not completely formed and there are spots where you can look out, but those spots slowly close in and it becomes like a big bowl. It's like being in the Rose Bowl.

"Hugo never did have zero winds in the eye, because the eye was so small. It was so wrapped up that the entire sea was boiling below us. It looked like a giant cauldron. And there was no ceiling above us because there was very little rain with this one."

When *asked* about fear, he looks with wonderment, as if anyone could possibly think any of them were afraid. If they were inclined to be *afraid*, they could always sell used cars. Or life insurance.

"Oh, there have been a couple of times when I asked myself if I was really in the right profession." As he speaks, a wry smile emerges. "Those thoughts go away real quick. I know I'm in the *only* profession that would ever suit me."

Others agree. Dave Turner, who at sixty-five has made more flights into hurricane eyes than any man alive—more than four hundred—says, "There's no occasion for me to quantify the job. It's just an interesting thing to do, and when it comes right down to it, I guess it's just the aeronautical challenge. It's maintaining control of the aircraft in that wild turbulence, with sort of seat-of-the-pants techniques, linked, of course, with experience tactics that seem to suggest to me what I ought to do *while* I'm doing it.

"If anything, it's easier now. We've got more scientists and more sophisticated equipment on board now. Early on we didn't have much of an edge over the storm itself. We just went out there and studied the wind field. But knowing something of how a storm circulates, we could keep the wing just forward of our port beam, and if we kept the wing there we would eventually spiral into the center of the storm. We never knew how bad it was going to be until we got there."

It seems somehow *over*simplified and *under*dramatized.

"We used to use all sorts of planes," says Turner, "such as the DC-6, but it was underpowered and there were times when it was simply out of control for a measurable period of time. But the P-3 is so much more powerful that I can pull myself out of almost any situation with ease.

"We use prop jets because the combination of the jet engine and the prop gives us instant response over the power of the airplane. A pure jet takes time to spool up, but our engines run at max RPM all the time, so all we have to do is control the prop."

Turner provides yet another answer to why pilots do wondrous things such as flying straight into the hubs of hell: "You've got to *enjoy* flying," he says. "Sometimes, in a perverse sort of way, you've got to enjoy the unpleasant challenge of the thing, even at its worst.

"I enjoy not being totally certain of what I'm going to run into. But I'm always confident that I'm going to be able to deal with it. So I suppose it's the satisfaction of meeting the challenge and doing a good job. I've got about forty years of experience now, and I'm sure that makes up for any slipping reflexes I might have," he says.

It is an interesting observation, and one that was made by several pilots—not to mention a few race car drivers. Perhaps the reflexes of people like Turner and Chuck Yeager and Edna Gardner White were so superior in the beginning that even after age has dimmed them somewhat, they are still as good as the average twenty-year-old.

"I don't need the same reflexes as a fighter jock," says Turner. "Mine is a job of realizing what I am getting into, and looking just ahead is more important than being able to strike like a snake."

Sometimes making the *right* decision is more important than making the faster one.

Race driver Richard Petty once said much the same thing when asked what the differences were between his twenty-five years of experience and perhaps the same amount of time for slipping reflexes when compared to the reflexes of his twenty-one-year-old son, Kyle, who had just started racing cars. "Well," Richard said, "when we're goin' two hundred miles an hour and something happens down in, say, turn one—you know, a bad wreck where there are race cars spinnin' and crashin' all over the track—Kyle runs down there and sees what's happening. Me, I see what's happening and *then* I run down there."

Once more the parallel between outstanding pilot and outstanding race driver is made.

"I'll never fly a desk," says Turner. "If the day comes when I can't fly, I'll just leave it all behind. Air racers don't want to sit in the grandstands. Neither do I."

On February 24, 1989, Captain David Cronin landed United Flight 811 in Honolulu. It was no ordinary landing; the eighteen-year-old 747 had a gaping hole in its fuselage, through which nine passengers had been snatched to their deaths. In addition, both right-side engines were inoperable, and the flaps would extend only ten degrees. Despite jettisoning as much fuel as they could in the short time they had to get back on the ground, the airplane was overweight for *any* landing, particularly this one at 195 miles per hour.

Was this the heroic action of a bright-eyed, hell-for-leather young pilot? Hardly. David Cronin was one flight from mandatory retirement. His feat was appropriately headlined in the *Wall Street Journal:* UNITED'S FLIGHT 811 SHOWED HOW VITAL CAPABLE PILOTS CAN BE.

It adds yet another argument to the question, "Why are pilots of such outstanding caliber grounded at age sixty?" Specifically it is the FAA regulation, Section 121.383 (c), which states "No person may serve as a pilot on an airplane engaged in operations under this part if that person has reached his sixtieth birthday."

It hasn't always been that way. In fact, not until President Eisenhower appointed ex-Air Force General Elwood Quesada to head the FAA was the regulation introduced. Quesada did not have a fondness for airline pilots, claiming that they were responsible for most aviation safety problems. So he vowed to bring commercial flying "up to military standards."

Grounding all airline pilots at age sixty seemed a perfect place to start.

The rule was implemented in 1960 without a public hearing. To make matters worse, a suggestion that the pilots at least become eligible for Social Security benefits immediately upon retirement was ignored. Therefore many pilots were faced with the loss of five highly productive years.

Other suggestions over the years have been disregarded by the FAA, even one urging that selected volunteers be allowed to continue flying past sixty under strict supervision and testing. The FAA steadfastly maintains that older pilots are more likely to be involved in accidents. It would be interesting to try to convince David Cronin or Chuck Yeager of this. Or any of the 345 passengers and crew who survived United's Flight 811.

There doesn't seem to be a single medical study that has been made that substantiates the FAA's fear of flying past sixty. Still, their comment when asked if Cronin's capability was truly outstanding was "What the pilot of UAL Flight 811 did would be expected of any captain," adding that it "cannot base its decision on isolated commendable acts."

Not even an "Atta boy, Dave."

What makes their stand even more ludicrous is their inconsistency in other matters relating to regulating pilots. They appear to be willing to recertify younger pilots with serious problems, such as histories of alcoholism, myocardial infarction, bypass surgery, monocular vision, personality disorders, strokes, and dysrhythmia. Many having "recovered" from such disorders have been returned to flight situations. It means they can resume flying. *If* they are under sixty years of age.

Len Morgan in *Flying* magazine suggests that the FAA would be much better served if it worried less about the pilots it certifies and more about the airliners it approves. "The recent rash of safety problems was caused by older airplanes bearing the FAA's stamp of approval, not by older pilots," he writes.

"One Braniff pilot," reports Morgan, "says 'The Feds say I became a poor risk at age sixty. How could they be sure I was safe at fifty-nine? ' This pilot flew for thirty-five years without taking a day's sick leave and is still healthy fourteen years later."

But let's take a closer look at David Cronin and Flight 811.

"I knew the aircraft was so badly damaged that I would have to land on the first attempt," says Cronin.

Experience told him that.

As they turned to go back to Honolulu, Cronin struggled to keep the aircraft stable, while copilot Al Slader radioed air-traffic controllers that they needed a straight-on approach, with no turns, to Honolulu's longest runway.

They only had to backtrack seventy miles, because as they climbed through twenty thousand feet Captain Cronin knew from experience that there was a problem with the inboard engine on the right side. It was losing power. Eight minutes later they radioed Honolulu that they also were losing power with the right outboard engine and that they were going to have to shut both of them down. The fact that Cronin immediately understood the immensity of the problem undoubtedly saved the ship.

He ordered fuel to be dumped, but the jet was fully loaded for the nine-hour flight to Auckland, New Zealand, and there wasn't enough time to bring the jet down to its proper landing weight of approximately 564,000 pounds. Cronin calculated that the weight was about 600,000 pounds as they brought the plane in heavy and hot.

Cronin had just completed 30,000 hours of flight time. The aircraft had flown 58,800 hours and had made 15,000 cycles (the term used to describe the combination of takeoffs and landings).

As they learned later, the forward cargo hatch apparently had come off, taking with it a large section of the fuselage, leaving a jagged ten- by twenty-foot hole. Inside the cabin, the noise was deafening as the wind ripped through the huge expanse of passenger compartment. There was chaos. Just before the side ripped out, the cabin attendants had rolled out the beverage carts; bottles and ice cubes and articles of clothing were flying through the air. Through the huge hole in the fuselage passengers could see the clouds and stars. The loss of engine power undoubtedly was caused by the engines on that side ingesting debris. Even more gruesome, human remains were later found in the engines.

It wasn't until they were on final approach that Cronin discovered that the flap controls also had been damaged. Instead of the usual twenty-degree flap, all he had was ten degrees. It took him no time at all to assess the situation: He had only one shot at landing the plane, despite the speed and other problems that plagued them as they approached the runway.

Jack Kennedy, of Melbourne, Australia, said his first thought was, "This is it. I'm going down." And then he reflected, "This is a great way to end up a skiing holiday, isn't it? A couple days in Honolulu and two weeks in Aspen down the tubes."

Kennedy's son, sitting next to him in the third row from the rear, looked at him and said, "It looks as though this is it, Dad."

Passengers reported that a few became hysterical but that most methodically put on their oxygen masks and life vests and awaited their fate. Their fate was in the hands of a pilot on his final flight before retirement. It was to be his last airliner landing. And, in spite of the odds, it was as routine as any he had ever made. The cabin was filled with cheers and tears.

David Cronin is now retired and lives near Lake Tahoe, but there are 354 people who will never forget his swan song for United Airlines. And 354 who would take strong opposition to the FAA's mandatory retirement age of sixty.

Immediate and accurate decision-making and the ability of flight crews to converse during such trying times is no longer left to chance. Thanks to an extensive pioneering program developed by United in 1979, crews are trained to operate calmly and reliably under the most stressful conditions. The Cockpit Resource Management program was begun following the crash of United Flight 173 in Portland, Oregon.

It was a perfect example on which to build a seminar: Everything seemed normal on the final approach. There was excellent visibility, no rain, no traffic, and the flight was on time, so there was no pressure to get on the ground quickly. It was the sort of flight pilots wish for. Until the landing gear was lowered. One of the three square green lights that indicate the gear is down and locked failed to illuminate. Captain Malburn McBroom, a veteran commercial aviator, took the controls from First Officer Roderick Beebe, who had been handling the routine landing. He increased the power and pulled out of the landing pattern, settling into a loose oval path as he circled the city.

He made circle after circle, but all efforts to determine whether it was actually a gear that was not locked into place or a faulty indicator light failed to resolve anything. His flight engineer, Forrest Mendenhall, gave him fuel readings. McBroom was not alarmed at the consumption.

After nearly an hour, McBroom asked to have the fuel figured for another fifteen minutes before landing. "Not enough for fifteen minutes," the flight engineer replied. In the next loop, all four engines on the DC-8 quit simultaneously. The powerless aircraft dropped like a rock.

There was nothing to do but look for a big, open space and try to take the ship in. There was one to the south so McBroom headed for it. Just before it struck the ground, it plowed through a series of high-tension wires, which probably slowed the airplane's forward speed considerably. Still, as it tore through a stand of trees, its wings were ripped off and the forward section of the airplane was crushed. Mendenhall, a flight attendant, and eight passengers were killed.

The National Transportation Safety Board cited evidence that the pilot was so preoccupied with the landing gear that he failed to fully consider the effect of the prolonged holding pattern upon his fuel consumption. The NTSB concluded, "[We] believe that this accident exemplifies a recurring problem—a breakdown in cockpit management and teamwork during a situation involving malfunctions of aircraft systems in flight."

That was enough for United. The Cockpit Resource Management (CRM) program was born. It is, in essence, the application of managerial techniques to the field of aviation. But, beyond that, it gives even seasoned pilots another dimension of experience, one that surely will assist them in the avoidance of accidents caused by mechanical failures.

At first even the most steadfast advocates of the program were not sure that it would work. "After all," one said, "every pilot for every airline is drilled endlessly on how to handle a landing gear problem." It was a point well taken. That is not an unusual problem, so how could three competent professionals allow such a situation to deteriorate into a disaster?

The United task force that had been assigned to develop the training program quickly recognized a parallel between the snare that the crew of Flight 173 had fallen prey to and that which they, as corporate officers, had been taught to avoid in managerial seminars. The flight crew had not been done in by insufficient training *or* by the mechanical failure. They had been undone by an inability to communicate.

What it meant was that the age-old solution all airlines use to solve problems—adding a checklist—would not work in this situation. It also suggested that the traditional airline stance that the captain is always right and junior crew members are supposed to be "seen and not heard" wasn't the correct approach either.

NASA got into the act, determining that of the fifty most recent crashes, thirty might have been avoided if the crew had communicated more. Suddenly there were people flying desks in all directions. But they were flying them in the proper direction.

If CEOs could be taught to work closely with their subordinates, so, too, could the four-stripers in the cockpits. But it didn't stop there; some of the second and third officers would have to undergo personality transplants as well.

One United official, who wishes to remain anonymous, says, "After about three years in the copilot's seat, most guys start to get numb above the shoulders. It takes a rare type of captain to push the thinking chores over to the right side of the airplane."

They found that many of the so-called "junior" pilots were actually highly experienced. For example, one veteran captain added, "I've flown with a former two-star general current in an F-16; a retired bird colonel; a former fighter pilot in the Indian Air Force, who was MiG-qualified; and a whole bunch of reserve and National Guard types current in just about any type of aircraft you can imagine. They're not really 'junior pilots,' it's just how United rates them in terms of airline service."

Suddenly there was sufficient fuel to the supposition that more cooperation, as well as conversation, was needed up there on the flight deck. For one thing, it might slow down some of the grousing usually done by many second and third officers about the arrogance of some captains.

The airlines discovered that it worked best to put teams of people together who are most likely to disagree on some matters. "Say we have one person who says he doesn't want to be on a team with people who smoke," states Ed Soliday, a United captain who serves as seminar administrator. "Guess where he goes? We make sure he is on a team of smokers, because we want to see how the issue is handled by the team. We will not say, 'Okay, there's not going to be any smoking.' If someone on the team wants no smoking, he's going to have to work it out with everyone else."

They quickly found that a cockpit is no different than a business office and that the better the crew was able to work out problems, the better prepared they were to work out *real* problems—the emergencies that arise from time to time.

In the final part of the seminar, the pilots have an opportunity to put their theories to work: They participate as a team in a reenactment of Flight 173. By taking the transcript of the conversation among the three-man crew, and between the crew and the tower, they turned it into a video that reenacts the occurrence. United has highlighted seventy points in the video where the crew of 173 could have reacted more effectively.

"What we're after in the seminar," says Soliday, "is to show how the captain will make his decisions based upon the maximum amount of information available in the time available. What we're saying is that the captain has to learn to respect other people's decisions and then make his decisions based on the objective evaluation of data. In no way are we taking the authority out of the captain's hands. All we're saying is, 'You're still going to have to make the decisions, but we want you to have so much respect for this other person's opinion that he knows you're going to listen."

Most refer to the seminars as "charm school," but apparently they work. Since starting its program, United's accident rate has dropped from one per one million operations to one per 4.8 million.

No better example of the effect of the Cockpit Resource Management program is Captain Al Haynes's handling of a DC-10 on United's Flight 232 on July 19, 1989.

Not only is it a model of faultless cockpit management, it is an outstanding paragon of pilot excellence—perhaps *the* single most outstanding example in the annals of airline flight. Few times in the history of U.S. aviation has a pilot performed more flawlessly than Haynes as he and his superbly competent crew manhandled a 168-ton flying brick into an Iowa cornfield. Assuredly it will carry over well into the next century as a case history for future pilots to study.

Haynes was less than two years from retirement at the time.

Without Haynes and his crew, Flight 232 was destined for disaster from the very moment the number two engine exploded, sending a torrent of razor-sharp parts throughout the tail section of the DC-10.

As it turned out, the crash near Sioux City was spectacular, but because of the crew's uncanny ability both to control an uncontrollable airship and to work together as a single entity, there were 186 survivors.

It is a tragic yet courageous story. In the air, there was a valiant effort to save the ill-fated airliner; on the ground, a massive team of seven hundred emergency workers watched in horror at the giant ball of fire as the huge airliner cartwheeled across the cornfield, sending debris for hundreds of yards. Not one among them expected anyone aboard to survive, let alone nearly two-thirds of the passengers and crew.

The jetliner broke up into huge sections upon impact, but even larger segments remained intact. In one—the forward portion of the coach-class section—passengers sat strapped in their seats, upside down and in smoky darkness. But, seemingly inspired by the calmness of the crew, there was little panic; they carefully unstrapped themselves and crawled around in the crumpled portion of fuselage, desperate but orderly as they tried to escape their murky tomb and find the bright Iowa sunshine on the outside.

It is hard to imagine a captain whose plane has just crashed as being dubbed a hero, but the mere fact that he came within yards of landing safely was a miracle in itself. Haynes and his crew fought valiantly for forty-two minutes to save the plane, even though the entire hydraulic system—a system that controls the whole ship—had been eliminated by the explosion of the engine. As the crew grappled with the plane through the Iowa skies, the gigantic team of workers below prepared themselves for the worst.

The DC-10 came roaring toward Sioux Gateway Airport's runway 22. Although it was coming in very fast, it looked to all as if it was going to make it; nobody in the control tower or on the ground could understand *how* it was being accomplished. It was close. At the last second, a wingtip dipped to the ground, dug in, and sent the mighty aircraft tumbling and then skidding across one mile of airport and fields.

"It was unbelievable," remarks Dr. David Greco, who hovered above in a helicopter. "We expected everyone to be dead, and then when we landed, we saw all those people walking toward us from out of the cornfield. I thought it was a miracle, and then I saw all those other people with heads squashed like pumpkins." He was referring, of course, to some of the 110 who died in the crash.

Mike Simons, one of the first of the emergency crew who got to the crash site, still gets emotional when he speaks of the accident: "I jumped out of my truck and ran toward where the one big section of the fuselage lay in the cornfield. It was smoking, and it was crumpled like aluminum foil. There were bodies strewn everywhere. I kept running and then I saw people coming through the tall rows of corn. They were like zombies in one of those horror movies you see. I couldn't believe there were survivors. I just sat down in the dirt and cried."

Much of the reason for the orderliness of the passengers presumably was that they either didn't understand the danger when the engine exploded, or they had no idea of the drama that was going on in the cockpit. There was no way anybody could realize how much effort was going into even keeping the airplane in the air, let alone trying to land it.

The engine that disintegrated and sprayed the blades of its fan through the tail section had done more damage than anybody realized—on the ground, in the cockpit, or at any of the many emergency locations that had become deeply involved in the drama.

Here's what contributed to the immensity of the problem: An

aircraft's hydraulic system provides the "power steering" that enables the pilot to maneuver a craft as large as a DC-10. Complete hydraulic failure means that the ship is virtually impossible to control. It failed.

In layman's terms, it means that none of the vital functions of the airplane's control system work—the flaps and slats, which change the shape of the wing so that the craft can fly at lower speeds for takeoff and landing, which significantly increases the plane's landing speed and rate of descent; the rudder, which turns the plane; the elevators, used for controlling the pitch (nose up or nose down); and the ailerons, which regulate the airplane's ability to roll to the right or left. With hydraulic failure, nothing is functioning, not even the brakes, which come in handy at landing speeds, particularly that of Flight 232.

Investigators later found out the reason for the severe damage: The plane was equipped with three General Electric CF6-6D turbo fan engines. It was discovered that the entire fan stage, a ring of blades which measures about six feet in diameter and provides thrust to the engine, was missing from the jet's tail-mounted number two engine. Parts of the fan obviously severed not only the primary hydraulic system, but the two backup systems as well.

"We had no warning whatsoever," exclaims Haynes. "We were at cruise, the autopilot was on, and the copilot, Bill Records, was flying the ship. We were just sitting there, enjoying the scenery, when, with no warning at all, we heard what sounded like an explosion. Before that there had been no drop in oil pressure and no vibration.

"There was a tremendous shaking of the airplane following the explosion and then the vibration which followed that. We began going through the regular procedures for an engine failure because we thought that's all it was. I had never lost an engine in the air, only in the simulations in our seminars," he says.

"My first thought was that we had an explosion decompression; I mean, it was that loud throughout the cockpit, but there was no rush of air, no dirt flying around the cockpit like we had been told in CRM would happen in such a case.

"The standard procedure at United is that the pilot who is flying the airplane takes control, so I let Bill go right on flying it. I saw the two red lights come on that indicated that the autopilot was off, but I didn't know if he had taken them off or they had been kicked off."

The airplane started down but Haynes figured that was good,

because he knew they certainly couldn't fly the airplane at thirty-seven thousand feet with only two engines. Past experience had taught him that planes with reduced power are easier to fly at lower altitudes.

Haynes and Dudley Dvorak, the second officer, began the process of shutting the engine down. The first thing encountered was that the number two throttle was frozen. It wouldn't budge. And then they had trouble getting the fuel shut off to the faulty engine, so Haynes pulled the fire handle to knock off all the fuel to number two.

The business of flying this particular plane was not going to be an easy task. Nor a routine one.

At that point Records turned to Haynes and said, "I can't control the airplane." His tone was calm but firm enough for Haynes to realize the problem was beginning to worsen.

"I glanced at the yoke," Haynes relates, "and I saw that he had full left aileron deflection and full elevator deflection, and it was still making a descending right turn. I looked back over my shoulder and saw that the hydraulic pressure read zero.

"I'm not sure how long all this took because we lost the first part of the cockpit voice tape; it's a thirty-minute tape and then it rewinds, so since the whole thing took forty-two minutes, it means we lost the first twelve minutes or so," he says. "I've tried to recall exactly what happened and it's hard to reconstruct. We've *all* tried and we can't be sure. I don't think we want to remember."

Is this something Haynes learned, or was it instinctive? "I don't know," he ponders. "I took control of the airplane and I couldn't get any response out of it either. By this time we were almost up to a forty-degree bank, so we immediately closed the number one throttle and fireballed the number three. Where we got that idea, I don't know; it had come from somewhere—training, experience, I can't say where, but it was an immediate reaction."

"But it brought the wing up. In fact, it acted like it had corrected the problem. We fought that on and off for a long time and then we began to try other things. We went to max throttle on each side to try to keep the wings up until we could try to get the thing settled down.

"Now that I think about it, I think it must have been instinctive, because I don't ever remember anything like that in training," Haynes says with a distant, still puzzled look in his eyes. "Finally, I said to

Dudley, 'Get on the radio and try to get hold of San Francisco Air Maintenance and see if there's anything they can tell us about this.' I knew there were certain things we could do if the electric lines to the autopilot failed—if we had problems with the bottom lines, we could hook up the top lines. I *knew* we could get the autopilot hooked up. But what I really wasn't aware of was that we didn't have any hydraulic fluid at all."

Haynes and Records were still trying to fly the airplane, while Dvorak was trying to work with San Francisco on the radio. He was going through the book to see if there was anything that could be done. The pilots were making clumsy circles in the sky to lose altitude and hopefully scrub off some speed. They were steering the plane in an unorthodox and highly imprecise manner, by using the thrust of first one engine and then another.

"You see, most of our procedures are irregular ones. We have very few emergency procedures, maybe two or three immediate actions, and then we have to go by the book."

Dvorak was going through the book under hydraulic failure, trying to see if there was anything that would help. After about twelve minutes, Haynes remembered that there was a training check instructor in the back, so he asked one of the flight attendants to go get him to see if he could help. He thought that since the guy taught about the airplane, perhaps there might be things about the airplane that they didn't know.

"I knew it was a long shot, but I thought maybe something that had happened on a training flight or something he had dug up in the book to try to catch his students might work," says Haynes.

Dennis Fitch, the instructor, went forward, sat down, and studied the situation. He couldn't believe a thing he saw, so he went back to look at the wings to see if anything was moving back there. Nothing was moving.

"He asked what we needed him to do," Haynes says, "so I told him we were having to manipulate the throttles so much—moving from one to the other—that it might help if he could take hold of both of the working ones and try to coordinate the throttle control better than we could.

"We didn't know if we were doing any good or not with the yokes. We thought we were, but now we know that the response was coming from the throttle movement. After working for five or six minutes, with a throttle in each hand, Dennis began little by little to figure out what we needed to keep the wingtips level. He was trying to coordinate the throttles with what we were doing with the yokes.

"It was an absolute team effort; all of us were making input," Haynes emphasizes. "And, you know, it was a prime example of what the United seminars on cockpit management had done for all of us. We were in a situation none of us knew anything about, but we were working as a team to correct it. And it wasn't just the cabin crew, it was the crew in the back and all the people on the ground. Everybody."

There was a total of 107 years of experience in the cockpit.

One of the true miracles of the entire ordeal is that everybody melded together so well—air controllers, the emergency crews, San Francisco's operation, and United's Flight Center. But perhaps it was because few, if any, really knew the severity of the situation. Even on the day after crash, after listening to tapes of cabin conversation, experts said 'They *had* to have some kind of control, otherwise the airplane wouldn't fly.'

"All the guys thought they were misunderstanding Dudley," says Haynes. "They thought he said one system was gone and he would correct them: 'No, they're all three gone.' And then they said, 'Oh, you don't have number three?' It was very difficult, even for us, to understand the situation we were in."

With the belief that it was impossible to lose *all* the hydraulic fluid, they continued to fly the yokes, even though all three gauges read "zero."

What went through their minds? "I don't know," Haynes wonders. "We were so busy that we didn't have time to pause and think about anything. When I listened to the cockpit voice recorder, I heard things I didn't realize I had said; you know, what we're going to do and what we're not going to do.

"All four of us were talking at the same time, advising one another."

The team effort was nothing short of miraculous. Everything seemed lined up perfectly for the landing, but then at the last second, the right wing dipped and the picture quickly changed.

"I don't know why it dipped," he says. "The airplane had been doing that all day. It was constantly trying to turn to the right. The minute you upped the throttles, it would begin the turn, so we had to play with the throttles a lot even then, otherwise it would roll to the right.

"We had a quartering tail wind to add to the problem when we were landing, so we can't even be real sure if the right wing dipped or the left one came up at the last minute."

It all appeared as if it was going to work. Until the wing dip.

But what did the pilots think? "In all honesty, I didn't think we had much of a chance," Haynes comments. "At times the thought of getting it on the runway wasn't important. I didn't think we were going to even *make* the airport most of the time.

"We expected to crash-land somewhere, and if we could possibly make the airport, that would be wonderful," he says. "We knew that there would be all sorts of emergency equipment there, and if there was a chance at saving anyone, the airport was the best bet. Maybe the *only* bet."

But what was happening to further concern the crew was the rapid rate of descent. It was picking up to 2,500 feet per minute, and Haynes began to think, "Man, if I don't stop this, we're not going to get anywhere but straight into the ground."

When the plane got into the heavier air at lower altitudes, they were able to modulate the throttles a little better, so the plane's response was improved somewhat.

"We certainly weren't controlling it," says Haynes, "but we had modulated the oscillation so it wasn't quite as severe. It was very inconsistent. We learned that from the voice box recording. First we would be down a thousand feet and then up fifteen-hundred. But by the time we got to within ten minutes of the airport, I had begun to think we might make it.

"I never really thought we would make the runway, but I figured we could set it down in a cornfield nearby. And if the rate of descent happened to decrease as we got lower, there was even a chance of getting to the runway."

Haynes knew deep inside that the chances were slim. Instead of the normal 140-mile-per-hour landing, the DC-10 was doing 250 miles per hour. In spite of it all, the huge airliner was heading straight for runway 22, fast but at a good rate of descent.

It continued straight. The descent was perfect. The speed was still very fast. The airplane was a few feet over the runway, three seconds from touchdown.

"I wasn't even aware the wing had dipped," relates Haynes. "I knew we were going to hit the ground hard. I expected that. But I was surprised later when I saw the videotape—first at the wingtip digging in and then at the cartwheeling and the huge ball of fire the aircraft had become."

Haynes's voice is calm, his mannerisms not animated, but he has sunk down in his sofa a little as if expecting a sudden jolt. "The only thing I remember feeling when we hit was a sudden loss of air, probably from my chest being compressed against the shoulder harness, sort of like the burst of air if you pulled the plug on an air mattress and jumped on it. That sound and a very large thump is all I remember. Either I was unconscious briefly or my mind doesn't want to remember it."

Dvorak was in and out of semiconsciousness and remembers very little. Records recalls the most, that he was thinking the long slide down the runway at such a high speed was going to end up in a terrible crash into something. He remembers debris flying all around the cockpit, hitting him in the head. He didn't know it at the time, but the airplane was beginning to disintegrate. Haynes doesn't remember anything after the tremendous impact until he awoke in the hospital.

Al Haynes flew again three months later. "It was a very routine flight," he says. "But I had a little concern about it, so I asked for a check pilot to go with me. I had no idea how I was going to react and I surely didn't want to get close to the ground on the landing and freeze up."

It was much the same as having a pair of hands to put one's foot into when getting back on the horse.

Haynes had been in a flight simulator several times since the crash, going through emergency procedures, but he had not made an actual landing. "As it turned out," he comments, "there was no problem at all [with the first landing after the crash.] As I taxied to the gate, I remember thinking what a beautiful day it was."

But what of the other survivors of Flight 232? How have they fared emotionally? Do they tussle with questions that can't be answered—about life and death? Do they suffer from nightmares or strain in relationships with loved ones?

One woman simply couldn't concentrate on her work for six months; another hasn't "had a good night's sleep since." Many are more nervous and high-strung since the accident, and one man shakes every time he hears an automobile backfire or even the report of a child's cap pistol.

They have become a fraternity. One group meets together regularly, to evoke stability from each other. "On the plane, as we were going down, it didn't matter how rich or how poor you were, what color you were, or what your religion was, or where you came from," says survivor Gary Priest of Denver. "We were all in it together and we drew strength from each other. We were all special at that time."

"I have a fear of things falling and things happening that are out of my control," declares Rod Vetter, who is a former Navy pilot who had flown more than a quarter million miles with United before the crash. "I have fears about things like interstate bridges collapsing when I am driving under them," he says. "A lot of weird things like that."

Vetter says he thinks of that day in the Iowa cornfield frequently. "Things like black smoke or loud noises or screeching brakes key in the thought of the crash. And especially the smell of burning plastic."

Perhaps it will take much longer than one year to get the thoughts of the crash neatly stored in the portion of the brain that can handle them properly.

Paul Oliver is quick to talk about Flight 232; perhaps that is part of the reason he can get back on an airplane, even though he has a decided dread. Before the crash, "The girl next to me talked about how everything was going to be all right. We talked about how we would exit and I told her that if the plane filled up with smoke she should grab onto my belt."

Oliver was thrown from the DC-10. The girl died.

Oliver broke his collarbone, right knee, right foot, and several ribs in the crash, as well as suffering a crushed vertebrae, and severe burns, but he has flown more than 100,000 miles since he healed. None of them, however, on a DC-10.

On one trip after the crash, the terrible afternoon seemed to return to Oliver. For no reason. As the plane prepared to land, he gasped for breath. "I did everything I could to get a gulp of air," he says with some visible emotion, "but I just couldn't breathe. That's the worst it's been."

Still, as well-adjusted as he appears, he admits that he has to force himself to get on an airplane. But he has had success; he has flown ten round trips to Hong Kong.

William Robertson has decided that it is high time for him to begin accomplishing all of the things in life he has dreamed of doing. So he has prepared a list and is methodically doing and checking off. One of the items was hot-air ballooning, and that already is on the "accomplished" side of the ledger.

"I give more time to my family and friends now," he says softly, "and I'm a lot more particular about those with whom I choose to spend my time."

Another survivor, Lori Michaelson, whose one-year-old daughter was rescued from the burning plane as passenger Jerry Schemmel ran back in to get her, has taken the crash as her own personal "cause." She is actively lobbying for mandatory infant seats on planes.

In addition to that, she is making herself more aware of what is going on around her. "I try to constantly focus on each day and realize how out of control your life can be—how quickly things can change. You think you're creating your own destiny and you're not," she says.

Gary Priest has overcome a crisis of faith. "I kept thinking, Why am I more special than that eight-year-old boy I saw dead on the runway? I thought, If that's the Lord, if that's the way he works, then I don't want any part of it."

But a Catholic priest counseled him and helped restore his faith. When he threatened to quit his job, his boss talked him out of it. He has received even more consolation from the thirty survivors who meet monthly to discuss their anxieties and accomplishments, in sort of impromptu group-therapy sessions.

Priest's family is having some trouble understanding why he seems not to be totally recovered. "I *am* getting better," he claims. "They just can't see it. My family lost this person they knew before. I can never be that person again. But I can care now, and I can make a difference."

Ronald Rohde has a very positive attitude toward life, perhaps the most positive he has ever had. "I should have been dead, I know that," he says. "Now it's a lot easier to find the silver lining in things. The irritations of life are a lot easier to shrug off now. I mean, how can I get worked up, when I could be upside down in a burning plane?

"Every time the sun comes up I think how lucky I am to be able to see it. I will say one thing," he adds. "Every time I fly now, I look at the stewardesses and the pilots, and I wonder if it came crunch time would they be able to perform as well as the captain and crew of Flight 232."

With more than one year past, Haynes is philosophical about the crash: "There's no substitute for experience," he says. When asked if some pilots *are* better than others, he unassumingly replies, "You know, it's like anything else; anybody can develop their skills. I suppose anyone who wanted to could pick up a paintbrush and with enough practice could be a painter. But maybe not a good one.

"I think there has to be an ingrained or inborn talent for anything that you're going to excel in. I've seen this with pilots one time after another. It's just something that's part of your makeup; you can learn it to a degree, but not to the degree you're talking about when you ask, 'What makes a great pilot?'

"It's the same with the talent of a great musician or someone like that. Anybody can do almost anything if they really work at it. They may not be the best, but they can do it. Then there are others who become the best. Take someone like Jessica Tandy, who won the Academy Award for *Driving Miss Daisy;* that lady just has to have a natural-born talent for acting, otherwise she wouldn't be as great."

Epilogue

Our crop-duster friend Dusty McTavish has told us that most good pilots he has trained have been good athletes, and that they have come from farms, where they drove tractors and did mechanical things. Perhaps it is an oversimplification. Perhaps not. Farm boys are, for the most part, loners. So are pilots. Athletes have better-than-average coordination. So, too, do pilots.

Generals Robin Olds and Chuck Yeager say that one is *born* with "the right stuff." They claim that you can teach almost anyone to fly, but for someone to be a *great* pilot, it has to be ingrained. This may seem a gross generalization but, after all, they have spent a lifetime dealing with pilots who daily put their lives on the line. And they have done it themselves.

Somewhere in between the farm boy and the "natural" lies the average pilot. But is there a thread that runs between all pilots? It turns out, after all this research, that there are *several* threads, some of them common only to combat pilots and some peculiar to private pilots. A few are common to all:

Pilots *are* highly confident, individualistic, aggressive, and fun-loving, from the private aviator to the fly-for-your-life airplane driver.

The one thread that runs between them all is that they respect danger, be they piloting Cessna 150s or Tomcats. Obviously the fighter pilot or the guys who fly into the eyes of hurricanes have a substantial confidence and aggressive thread, while, on the other hand, the "guy down the street" has a strong fun-loving and individualistic one. Still, they are not an unassuming group. Not a single one of them.

Many of the threads were put there by their environments. That's why the farm boys usually become fighter pilots. They were used to being alone. And it's why a lot of the city boys opted for the commercial route; admittedly, they weren't too wild about being up there "alone." They were *used* to a lot of people around them.

General Olds put it well: "Chuck Yeager and I could fly a 747, and do it well. But we wouldn't like it a damn bit."

To Olds and Yeager, being up there alone, taking deadly aim on an enemy, was what they needed. But don't think for one minute that only fighter pilots have the survival instinct. Al Haynes surely has it, otherwise he wouldn't have tried so valiantly to save the lives of the passengers on Flight 232. Cale Yarborough had it that night in the terrible storm in his Bonanza when the one thing that kept him from giving up was saving the lives of his wife and tiny daughter.

I said it before, but it bears repeating: Pilots *are* slightly bigger than life.

Another thing all good pilots have in common—and in most cases we've spoken with *good* pilots—is quick response. Most fly almost by intuition, be they man or woman, black or white, young or old. There are no gender, color, or age barriers.

Some factors have changed over the years, as the airplane itself has changed. In the 1920s when Dorothy Stenzel began flying, she was considered good because she "flew like a boy." Freely translated, it meant that she could "manhandle" the airplane.

Today, student pilot Erin Slaney says that women have a *lighter* touch, so therefore they make better pilots. As the airplane has improved, so too has a female's chances. It decidedly is no longer necessary to muscle an airplane around. Maybe it isn't even desirable.

Often, overcoming fear has been the major obstacle with pilots. You will remember that World War II bomber pilot Jack Moore admitted there was a great sense of exhilaration to his first flight. He also confessed that there was a certain amount of fear. The way he put it was: "My subconscious kept pounding, telling me I was out of my element. 'You're in the air. You shouldn't be here. You're a land animal. You're going to get killed.' "

That same apprehension is what has spurred many pilots on to greatness. Astronaut Jon McBride readily admits that there is fear before a mission, but quickly adds that it goes away. He says, "The fear turns into confidence. You learn to channel this fear into accomplishing even more. Fear and anxiety actually turn into aggression. In combat you always feel that this is the day I'm going to go out there and get five MiGs.

"You've schooled yourself and you've thought about it, and you know you can do it: 'Put me in, coach.' "

And more than one combat pilot—most, in fact—are absolutely sure that they *will* return. They know it's a highly dangerous pastime, but they, without exception, feel, "It will never happen to me." They have no choice: If they don't feel that way, then they need to get out of the business.

Hurricane-chaser Dave Turner observes, "You've got to *enjoy*, sometimes in a perverse sort of way, the unpleasant challenge of the thing, even at its worst . . . of not being totally certain of what I'm going to run into."

Aha! Perhaps there *is* a single thread after all.

Pilots *do* fly directly into the eye of the challenge. They know that it is safe up there, so long as they properly maintain their aircraft, carefully study the weather, and pay strict attention to what they have learned and what their experience tells them—from Jimmy Doolittle to the corner druggist who flies for fun. The ones who don't follow these rules either give up flying or they become a statistic.

Confidence, along with the exhilaration of flight, keeps them flying toward the "eye." But the thrill of the unknown also spurs them on. The uncertainty. "The only thing a good pilot worries about is finding a suitable parking space if the engine quits," was the way Charlie Brown so aptly put it.

I know one thing: There is little doubt in *my* mind that pilots are a very special breed.

I still don't know who said it, but if I did, he or she certainly would get credit: they "have shaken the surly bonds of Earth and are reaching for the skies."

INDEX